THE HONOUR RICHMOND

A HISTORY OF THE LORDS, EARLS AND DUKES OF RICHMOND

by

David Morris

William Sessions Limited
York, England

ISBN Hard 1 85072 240 4
ISBN Card 1 85072 241 2

By the same author:
The Dalesmen of the Mississippi River
The Swale: A History of the Holy River of St Paulinus

Printed in 11 on 14 point
New Century Schoolbook Typeface
from Author's Disk
by Sessions of York
The Ebor Press
York, England

Contents

* References and other information at the conclusion of each
chapter of Part 2.

Introduction

HISTORY IS SHAPED by individual events and William the Conqueror's decision to reward his favoured henchman Alan le Roux with a great estate of lands, mainly in eastern England, marked the beginning of ten eventful centuries of Richmond history. Alan's estate became known as the Honour of Richmond, a name originating from the formidable castle he built high above the River Swale in Yorkshire. It was a castle built mainly to emphasise his presence in the area and it also acted for a time as the administrative headquarters of the Honour.

In the centuries which followed, successive Kings of England came to value the Honour as a means to ensure loyalty and support and it was a prize sought particularly by Breton barons to finance their warlike lifestyles. Possession of the Honour usually carried with it the Earldom of Richmond but during the long periods of war in France, few of these barons devoted their time to administering their estates in England and ultimately there was little left of the Honour except Richmond Castle.

To do justice to the lives of these men who held the Honour of Richmond and to provide an adequate but concise historical record of the subsequent earls and dukes of Richmond, has provided a challenge. In some cases, information has been scarce though the lives of others have been quite intriguing and deserving of further research. The history of the Hundred Years War has certainly tempted wider coverage but I have been concerned only with the Richmonds who participated in that extended conflict. There has been much geographical interest in preparing this book for, far from being insular, the activities of the Richmonds have taken them to Ireland, Brittany and France, as well as

Spain, Italy, Holland, Belgium and other European countries. To Canadians, the story of the 4th Duke of Richmond provides a fascinating episode in the history of their country.

Since the 16th century, the fortunes and experiences of the Richmonds have been enhanced by their links with the Lennox and Gordon clans as well as by the creation of the Richmond Shilling but, throughout these last ten centuries, and into the present time, those carrying the Richmond name have most certainly contributed much to our history. and it is my hope that this book provides an adequate record of their experiences and achievements.

D.M.

Acknowledgements

IN WRITING THIS book, I have received valued help and support from many sources and I must acknowledge with gratitude the information and advice provided by His Grace, the 10th Duke of Richmond and Gordon. I must also record my thanks for the considerable help I have received from:

> Rosemary Andreae, Curator of Goodwood House.
> Timothy J. McCann, Assistant County Archivist, and the West Sussex Record Office.
> Pat Mussett, formerly Senior Assistant Keeper in Archives and Special Collections, University of Durham,
> and my wife Grizel, without whose assistance the preparation of this book would not have been possible.

Others who have provided much valued information and assistance are:

> Derek Dutton M.A.
> The late Madam Kincaid of Kincaid.
> Dr George Lindsay of Ottawa, Canada.
> Ralph W. Waggett.

Chapter Index

PART 1
THE LORDS AND EARLS

PART 2
THE DUKES OF RICHMOND

Pictures, Lineage and Illustrations

Back Cover: Charles Gordon Lennox, 10th Duke of Richmond
Examples of the various Insignia, i.e. the Seals and Coats of Arms etc., are taken from the *Registrum Honoris de Richmond.*

Abbreviations

C.P.E. The Complete Peerage of England, Scotland, Ireland, Great Britain and the United Kingdom by G.E.C. (6 volumes) (Volume 4 to which reference is frequently made in the biography section of this book was edited by Geoffrey H. White, first published 1945 (Alan Sutton)).

C.P.R. Calendar of Patent Rolls.

D.N.B. Dictionary of National Biography, edited by Sidney Lee (21 volumes) (Smith Elder & Co 1909).

E.Y.C. Early Yorkshire Charters based on the manuscripts of William Farrer and edited by C.T. Clay (Y.A.S. Record Series) (12 volumes; volumes IV and V refer to the Honour of Richmond).

P.R.O. Public Record Office.

V.C.H. Victoria History of the Counties of England; North Riding, edited by William Page (2 volumes) (Constable 1914).

Y.A.S. Yorkshire Archaeological Society publications (approx. 70 volumes), issued to members only, published by John Whitehead.

The Lords of the Honour – The Earls and Dukes of Richmond

THE LORDS AND EARLS

ALAN RUFUS (d.1089)

ALAN THE BLACK (THE FIRST) (suc.1089 d.1093)

STEPHEN (suc.1093 d.1135)

ALAN THE BLACK (THE SECOND) (suc.1136 d.1146)

CONAN (suc.1146 d.1171)

GEOFFREY (b.1158 d.1186) AND CONSTANCE (b.1160 d.1201)

RANULPH DE BLUNDEVILLE (Earl of Chester) (d.1232)

ARTHUR (b.1187 d.1203)

PETER DE BRAINE AND DREUX (b.1187/90 d.1250)

PETER DE SAVOY (b.1203 d.1268)

JOHN DE BRETAGNE (b.1217 d.1286)

JOHN DE BRETAGNE (b.1239 d.1305)

JOHN DE BRETAGNE (b.1266* d.1334)

JOHN DE BRETAGNE (b. 1286 d.1341)

JOHN DE MONTFORT (b.1293 d.1345)

JOHN OF GAUNT (b.1340 d.1399)

JOHN DE MONTFORT (b.1339 d.1399)

JOHN OF LANCASTER (b.1389 d.1435)

EDMUND TUDOR (b.1430 d.1456) AND MARGARET BEAUFORT (b.1443 d.1509)

HENRY TUDOR (b.1457 d.1509)

THE EARLY DUKES

HENRY FITZROY (b.1519 d.1536)

LUDOVIC STUART (b.1574 d.1624) (Titles extended to include the Dukedom of Lennox)

JAMES STUART (b.1612 d.1655)

ESME STUART (b. 1649 d.1660)

CHARLES STUART (b.1639 d.1672)

THE PRESENT LINE OF DUKES

1. CHARLES (b.1672 d.1723)
2. CHARLES (b.1701 d.1750)
3. CHARLES (b.1735 d.1806)
4. CHARLES (b.1764 d.1819)
5. CHARLES (b.1791 d.1860) (Titles extended to include the Dukedom of Gordon)
6. CHARLES HENRY (b.1818 d.1903)
7. CHARLES HENRY (b.1845 d.1928)
8. CHARLES HENRY (b.1870 d.1935)
9. FREDERICK CHARLES (b.1904 d.1989)
10. CHARLES HENRY (b.1929)

TITLES

THE DUKEDOMS OF RICHMOND AND LENNOX, D'AUBIGNY, AND GORDON.
THE EARLDOMS OF MARCH, DARNLEY AND KINRARA, AND THE BARONY OF SETTRINGTON AND TORBOLTON.

* The accuracy of this and some other early period dates listed have been found impossible to verify.

PART 1

THE LORDS OF THE HONOUR AND THE EARLS OF RICHMOND

CHAPTER 1

William the Conqueror and the Honour of Richmond

WILLIAM LE ROUX, named the Conqueror, had a tough childhood. Born of a romantic affair between a Duke of Normandy and the daughter of a tanner, he became known as William the Bastard. He was always embittered by his upbringing and grew up a hard and ruthless campaigner. Yet he was his father's only son and, though he was illegitimate, the Duke persuaded the Norman barons to accept him as his heir. He was only aged eight when his father died leaving him the title of Duke of Normandy. In those harsh times a minor's hold upon his inheritance was precarious. He was too young to govern and, without a ruler, Normandy began a ten year period of revolt and disorder. William's cousins clearly wanted him removed and it was only because of protection given to him by King Henry of France that he survived a boyhood of considerable violence and intrigue. By the 1040's he was old enough to take on the responsibility of governing but he found himself continuously at war either with Norman rebels or neighbouring princes. In time however he consolidated his ducal position and, against the wishes of the Pope, he decided to marry Matilda, the daughter of a distant relative. Despite the Pope's displeasure, his marriage was successful and he fathered at least nine children.

William was a distant cousin of Edward the Confessor who, at a time when he needed Norman support, dangled before William the prospect of succession to the English throne. Yet on his deathbed the King nominated Harold, son of Earl Godwin, as his heir. William felt he had been cheated and insisted that Edward had promised him the throne. Such was his anger that he began straight away to prepare for the invasion of England with the intention of claiming the throne. To William, it was to be a personal venture which he proceeded to plan as a business enterprise. When he prevailed upon Pope Alexander for his support to the invasion, the Pope responded by sending him a consecrated banner. This was important for it secured the influence of the clergy. At first the barons of Normandy he approached gave him little official support, but the prospect of laying hands on some of the wealth of England persuaded them to provide their quota of ships and men. Yet William was well aware that the limited resources provided from Normandy would be unequal to the task ahead and the invasion would never have succeeded without the support of a large contingent from Brittany and some mercenaries from elsewhere.[1]

The role played by the Bretons in the invasion was of particular interest. Brittany had for long considered itself different from the rest of France and direct contact between the rulers of Brittany and the Kingdom of France had virtually ceased by the end of the 10th century. Relations between Normandy and Brittany were not much better a century later when William began recruiting men for his invasion force, but Brittany was itself weakened by internal strife and many Breton Lords were attracted into William's service, particularly from the north-east part of the Duchy. Links had been established between Brittany and England as well as Wales when there was emigration to Brittany from across the Channel to escape the Anglo-Saxon intrusions. Families also left for Brittany at the time of the Pictish and Scottish raids on England's western seaboard. There was also some migration in reverse and, before 1066, there was never a period in which movement across the channel in either direction ceased entirely.[2]

By August 1066, William's invasion force was ready and, if it had sailed at that time, there is little doubt that it would have met the full force of Harold's army. As it was, the invasion was delayed by six weeks bad weather and the ultimate landing in Pevensey Bay was made without difficulty. By then Harold was engaged in fighting off a Viking intrusion in the north and had to rush back to engage William's forces which had soon become well established. The Battle of Hastings and Harold's defeat and death provide their own story and with no English leader capable of organising further resistance, William was crowned King on Christmas Day, 1066. It soon became apparent that William's victory made him master only of the south-east of England and gained little acceptance in the north or for that matter in the south-west or Wales. Northumbria in particular was unwilling to recognise William's authority and claimed that Edgar Atheling, their "Royal Prince", should be King.[3] York became the centre of an uprising and, to counter this opposition, William marched an army to the north-east and forced the rebels to yield and disband their troops. Twelve months later, there was a further uprising however and Robert of Comines, sent by William to take control of the area was attacked and burnt alive, many of his supporting troops being massacred. This so angered the King that he moved further troops to the north and again routed the rebels at York, killing many of those who could not escape.

Yet this was certainly not the end of the uprising for in the autumn of 1069 a major rebellion developed with support from the Scots. The Danes sailed up the Humber to help and the rebels proceeded to overwhelm the stronghold the King had established in York, many of his soldiers being slain in the onslaught. William at that time was busy quelling a revolt in the south-west but when word of the new major rebellion reached him he vowed to re-take York and ravage Northumbria. He is said to have bribed the Danes to quit but, whether or not this occurred they sailed back down the Humber leaving the rebels to fend for themselves.

William then moved north in considerable force and laid siege to York which was eventually forced to yield though only when famine compelled the English garrison to do so. There followed the savage massacre and ruthless devastation of the land and people of Northumbria. It was an appalling act of vengeance for which William was responsible and, on his deathbed, he is said to have acknowledged his guilt and sought forgiveness.[4]

Though he was a harsh but efficient leader it was to his credit that he rewarded those who served him well in battle and he adopted a policy of feudalism under which his chosen followers were granted land in return for pledges of service and loyalty. The Breton leader Alan Rufus had given outstanding service both at Hastings and during the turbulent years which followed, reaching a climax with the siege of York and the rout of Northumbria. Aware perhaps that, unlike other barons and nobles amongst his followers, Alan possessed no estates in France, William granted to him extensive lands in eastern England, a considerable estate which later became known as the Honour of Richmond.[5]

The areas comprising the Honour extended from the borders of Durham down to the vicinity of London, a huge estate with lands in eleven counties including Yorkshire, Nottinghamshire, Lincolnshire, Cambridgeshire, Dorset, Hertfordshire, Norfolk and Suffolk, a total in excess of 400 manors occupied by over a thousand tenants-in-chief. In view of his many holdings in the Eastern Counties, particularly Lincolnshire and Suffolk, Alan became known as the magnate of East Anglia. The Honour was the third richest of all such estates in England and included much of the land formerly held by Earl Edwin of Mercia and forfeited because of his rebellion against William in 1068. In the north of England, only the Honour of Lancaster eventually ranked above the lands granted to Alan Rufus in wealth and size. Without doubt William's award to Alan Rufus included areas of England of considerable strategic, military and political significance. There were many castles and monastic houses which became established within the huge estate and the majority remain as historic monuments today. The foundation of the Abbey of St Mary in York and the great Abbey of Bury St Edmunds depended much on the support of Count Alan Rufus as well as that of his younger brother Alan the Black.[6]

Alan Rufus was not the only member of William's family to give service in the Conquest, for Alan the Black and his younger brothers as well as their cousin Alan Fergent were all William's followers. Apart from the lands granted to Alan Rufus, rewards for particular service were made to Alan the Black and also to Alan Fergent, the reigning Duke of Brittany, who had married Constance, William the Conqueror's daughter. They shared lands in Lincolnshire, Cambridgeshire, Norfolk, Essex, Hertfordshire, Northamptonshire and Dorset. Alan Fergent was also granted areas previously held by the Northumbrian Earl Morcar and by Earl Edwin of Yorkshire. Brian, a younger brother of Alan Rufus, had land assigned to him in Cornwall but he married Inogena, heiress of the Château Brient and returned to live in France.

Alanus Fergent Dux Britanniæ.
A.D. 1119.

It is significant that, following William's Conquest, the Bretons established themselves prolifically in England at the level of baronial and knightly society though their number amongst the highest aristocracy was limited. Many lesser Bretons were allowed to settle, particularly as agricultural tenants, on the lands of Count Alan in the Honour of Richmond and honorial tenants with names like Alured, Gurwant, Guihomar, Harscouet, Herve, Hoël, Roald, and Rualent testify to their Breton ethnic roots. Bretons also settled in other areas of

5

eastern England and there was a particular concentration in the Welsh border counties, as well as Devon and Cornwall. By 1086, as much as 20% of England was in Breton hands. They were a people very aware of their origins and history and a pattern of inter-marriages developed in England between families of known Breton stock whilst close links were maintained with relatives back in Brittany even after Henry II's accession. In time, a number of these Bretons are believed to have returned to their homeland.

After the days of Alan Rufus, possession of the Honour of Richmond was much sought after by the French knights, the more so when the Lords of the Honour were granted the Earldom of Richmond. As the Duchy of Brittany became intimately connected with the Honour of Richmond, the lands Alan Rufus had acquired were frequently referred to as being part of the Honour of Brittany. This connection was given emphasis by the fact that charters relating to the Honour of Richmond were issued in Brittany with others relating to France. However, the situation between England and France which developed into the Hundred Years War had a very divisive effect on both titles and possessions. The Breton baron holders of the Richmond Honour were placed in a difficult position for, though the Dukes of Brittany were subjects of the King of France, the Lords of the Honour of Richmond were the English King's subjects. Whenever the two kings were at war, it could become impossible to hold both English and French titles and estates. Naturally the choice depended on which side the holder was fighting.[8] The size of the estates included in the Honour of Richmond changed in some measure with each holder and there were periods when both titles and the Honour reverted to the Crown. The holder of the estates became heir to a well defined series of local courts in individual lordships of the Honour. These were administered by local bailiffs and provosts chosen by the community under the supervision of seigneurial stewards. The lordships each had a Receiver who paid over monies to the Receiver General.

Despite these administrative arrangements, it is clear that the French aristocrats who held the Richmond Honour were prone to give preference to managing their estates and affairs in France and, all too frequently, the mainly Breton tenants of land within the Honour had to contend with absentee landlords. It was probably inevitable that, in the course of time, there would result a gradual break-up of the great estates and comitatus* of the Honour. Indeed, the frequent absences of the Breton Earls from their English estates meant that, by the 14th century, the Honour was in an alarming state of decay. The absence of control resulted in poor administration and lack of any adequate link between the scattered manors and lordships of the Honour. By the year 1300 the Honour held estates in only seven counties.

It was not until the end of the 14th century that the French connections were broken. However, the importance given to the Earldom and Honour of Richmond was such that even after the Duchy of Brittany was separated from Richmond in 1399, the Dukes of Brittany prolonged an ineffective claim by still styling themselves as Earls of Richmond. There had been a long succession of lords and earls of Richmond before Henry VIII decided to break the sequence by creating a dukedom for his illegitimate son Henry Fitzroy. The new Duke however was to die of consumption in 1536 and the title was not created again until 1623 when it was granted by James I to Ludovic (Stuart) Duke of Lennox. Four further dukedoms were created before the present

---

* In this context, the word "comitatus" is taken to mean the retinue of nobles and administrators of the estates comprising the Honour. By the time of Edward IV and Henry VI, the Honour had largely lapsed to the Crown though it was granted to the Duke of Clarence during his life and held in part by the Duke of Gloucester. Richard III appears to have made possession by the Crown more secure and, though the First Duke of Richmond, Henry Fitzroy, was granted the Honour by Henry VIII, the King recovered possession and, though clearly depleted in value, it continued to remain in the hands of the Crown. This did not apply to Richmond Castle however, the ownership of which has been retained by subsequent Dukes of Richmond. (Refer the Victorian History of England, North Riding Vol.1, p.10).

line began by the granting of the title to Charles Lennox, natural son of Charles II and ancestor of the present 10th Duke, Charles Henry Gordon Lennox.

Though the Honour of Richmond now exists largely in name only, Richmond Castle together with the Sussex seat and home of the Richmonds at "glorious Goodwood" serve as a reminder of the important part the Lords, Earls and Dukes of Richmond have played in the history of England and the Duchy of Brittany.

Reproduced from the Registrum Honoris de Richmond *(London MDCCXXII)*
depicting Alan le Roux kneeling before King William and receiving what appears
to be a document of title to Earl Edwin's lands.

9

CHAPTER 2

The Story of Alan Rufus and the First Alan the Black

T OWARDS THE END of the 10th century, a wedding took place between Geoffrey, Duke of Brittany and Hawise (or Havoise), a daughter of the Duke of Normandy. It was an important occasion for not only did it link together two important aristocratic families, it helped to harmonise relations between Normandy and the more independent Bretons. There were three children of the marriage, two sons named Alan and Eudo and a daughter Adela. Geoffrey, their father, died in 1008 having gone on a pilgrimage to Rome from which he never returned. He left his sons under the protection of Duke Richard II of Normandy and, while their mother was alive, they seemed to have acted amicably as joint rulers of Brittany, Adela having become an abbess of St Georges in Rennes. However, when Hawise died, dissension broke out between the two brothers and this was only settled when it was agreed that Eudo should have a territory corresponding roughly to the dioceses of Dol, St Malo, St Brieuc and Tréguier while Alan retained the rest of Brittany.

On the death of his father, Alan the elder son took the title of Duke of Brittany. He married Bertha, daughter of the Count of Chartres and they had a son they named Conan. When Alan died in 1040 his brother Eudo proceeded to take over the government of the whole of Brittany to the exclusion of Conan, his nephew. It took seventeen years before Conan eventually became Duke of Brittany and recovered what had been his father's territory.

Eudo had also married and he and his wife are recorded as having no less than eight male children; moreover Eudo seems to have fathered four illegitimate sons. Three of the four sons born within the marriage did not survive childhood and another died before his father. This left only four surviving descendant sons, Geoffrey Boterel (or Botterill), Alan Rufus, Alan the Black and Stephen. When Eudo died, Geoffrey Boterel, his eldest son, succeeded to all the family's Breton estates and continued to live in Brittany. It was his younger brother Alan Rufus who was destined to come to England and become one of William the Conqueror's most trusted followers. Not only was he one of William's chief advisers during the preparation for the invasion, he commanded the rearguard at the Battle of Hastings. For his services, Alan Rufus became the first of a line of Lords of the Honour of Richmond, a sequence broken only during some periods when the Honour reverted to the Crown.[9]

There is some evidence that, when Alan Rufus was given the Honour of Richmond, he was granted an earldom for his services, though this is not generally accepted. The Complete Peerage of England describes him and his immediate descendants as "comes Britanniae", Lords of Richmond and, on the evidence of the Domesday Survey, Alan described himself only as "Count Alan". In the years following the Conquest, the French speaking aristocrats who ruled England styled themselves indifferently as Dukes or Counts. The English Chancery preferred the style "Count" and this came into common use.[10]

Having been granted the Honour of Richmond, Count Alan took steps to administer his great estates. As it was in the north of England that King William had encountered fierce unrest and opposition, his concern was to ensure that, in the future, this northerly part of his territory was properly defended. Though it was fairly late in his life, he decided to build a castle, probably for prestigious purposes but also with the intention of subduing further local unrest and providing a fortress against any invaders. There was a continuing threat of Scottish incursions and indeed, it was not until the reign of Edward II that England diverted its

THE HONOUR OF RICHMOND

The origins of Count Alan Rufus and the lineage of those who subsequently had possession of the Honour during the 11th and 12th centuries.

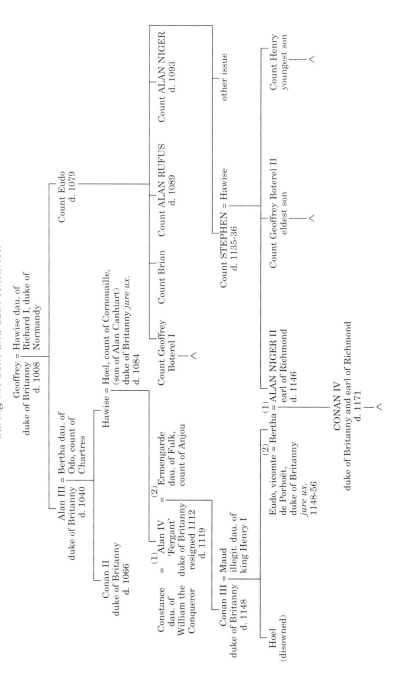

attention from fighting the Scots and concentrated on achieving its ambitions in France.

Alan chose a site for his castle by the River Swale near the site of the old Roman stronghold of Cataractonium, later known as Catterick. He had concluded that the site of the former centre at Gilling, used by the Earl of Mercia and called by Bede "Ingetlingum", would not provide protection against any attacks from the Scots, Danes or Anglians. The site he chose held a commanding position above the River Swale, and it was appropriately given the name Riche Monte, meaning strong hill. Alan's castle was unique in that it was built in stone rather than using the motte and bailey method common at the time. It was begun in 1071 and, a century later, a great defensive keep was added by Alan's great-nephew Earl Conan. This keep is regarded today as a magnificent example of early twelfth century military architecture. The formidable stone built castle became not only a stronghold for Count Alan and his successors but also the "caput", or administrative centre, of the whole Honour of Richmond. The tenants of the Honour had to furnish the guard at the Castle; approximately thirty knights were assigned for each period of two months throughout the year. In time, the name of Richmond gained much favour and was widely used not only in England but also in the former colonial countries of America, South Africa and Australia. There are many Richmonds in the world today and the origin of their name can only be found on the site of Count Alan's castle in North Yorkshire.[11]

For much of his life Alan Rufus was involved in warfare both in France and, during his service with William, in England. Yet in his later years he not only established a priory in Cambridgeshire, he is known to have inspired the foundation of the Abbey of St Mary at York. There is no doubt that the foundation or endowment of a monastery was one of the acts expected of someone in his position and indeed many French barons of that time donated some of the lands they acquired to religious houses. This put them in a position of social prestige as well as ensuring that the monks would pray for their souls in the world to come and might provide "insurance" against misdeeds committed on earth. The foundation of St Mary's Abbey received full support from King William, probably to atone for the devastation which he had caused when York was under siege, and Alan Rufus, who had given land for the Abbey to be built, formally gave up the patronage to the King. In his later years, Alan was believed to be a suitor for the hand of Maud, the daughter of Malcolm, King of Scotland, but she married Henry I. Alan died unmarried in 1089, only two years after William the Conqueror, and he was buried within the Abbey Church at Bury St Edmunds in Suffolk to which he had been a recognised benefactor.

An extract from the Annals of Bury written in Latin by a monk (MSS Bodl 297 No.VIII A.D.1093) can be translated as:

About that year after the birth of the Lord, Alan Count of Brittany and builder of the noble Abbey of St Mary outside the City of York, died but it was in St Edmunds, to which Church he has shown himself to be a great benefactor, that he was buried by the Abbot Baldwin firstly next to the southern door of the Church but at a later date he was entombed beneath.

and some lines which follow are given as:

The star of the Kingdom is destroyed, the flesh of
  Count Alan is in decay
England is to confusion turned: flower of the satrapies
  to ashes burned
Once Brito, flower of kings, now decay in order of things
Teacher of laws, he gleams, risen from the blood of kings
Highest Duke he grew to be second to the King in
  rubicundity
When you see this I beg you say "May he rest in peace
  Lord when we pray"
Of noble Bretons he was born, a shining light amongst
  them all.

In 1086 AD, three years prior to Count Alan's death, one of the most important statistical surveys in English history had been completed. The Domesday Book provided an extraordinarily detailed account of land ownership, population and productive resources in England at that particular time and the material collected was arranged to present clearly the way in which the land was divided amongst the various barons. Whether the Domesday Book proved to be of any value to William the Conqueror is doubtful, but the information gathered must have been appreciated by his successors and has been of immense importance in the historical records of this country. All of Count Alan's extensive holdings of land were included as were tenancies held by three of his four bastard brethren - his father Eudo's illegitimate sons. Bodin, the eldest, was shown to be one of his more important tenants in Yorkshire being listed as having the manors of Great Langton (Thorfin), where there was a hall, Rokeby, Romaldkirk, Broughton, Newsome, and Bedale. He was Lord of Ravensworth and held land at Reeth, Grinton, Melsonby and Scorton as well as in other village areas. In his old age, he decided to split his lands as between his brother Bardulf and Scolland, who was Lord of Bedale.[12] Bardulf was another of the bastard sons and is known to have succeeded to the Church at Ravensworth and given it to the Abbey of St Mary, in York where, in his old age, he took refuge as a monk. As already mentioned, many Breton tenants had holdings in other parts of the Honour and Ribald, another of these sons, was a tenant not only at Middleham, Spennithorne and Hauxwell in Yorkshire but also in Norfolk and Lincolnshire. The remaining son of the four was Ernald but it is seems unlikely that he held any tenancies.

The natural successor to Alan Rufus was his blood brother Alan the Black who had already been granted some lands by William the Conqueror for his service during the invasion. Though Alan the Black succeeded to the Lordship and all the lands of the Honour on his brother's death, it was for only a short period, as he died four years later. Little is recorded in history about him and his life was overshadowed by that of his brother Rufus. However, he is known to have been a benefactor not only of St Mary's Abbey in York but also of the Abbey at Bury St

The entrance to the Abbey of Bury St Edmunds.

16

Edmunds to which he granted an area at Saffron Walden in Essex. He gave Cranfield to the monastery at Ramsey and persuaded William Rufus to assemble a High Court of Parliament in York in the year 1089.

An element of scandal arose concerning the two brothers Rufus and Alan the Black for it became known that both enjoyed the favours of an unnamed nun at Wilton who was subsequently disciplined by her Superior. The scandal which this caused became more piquant when the nun was identified as Gunhild, the daughter of King Harold. When Alan the Black died he was buried at the south door of the great Abbey at Bury St Edmunds, his brother Rufus having been buried inside the Abbey.[13] The choice of Bury St Edmunds as a resting place for the brothers is explained by their apparent liking for this Suffolk area where Alan Rufus in particular was held in high regard and where the Domesday Book lists a considerable number of holdings in his name. For administrative purposes the County of Suffolk was divided into sections known as "hundreds", each having its own judiciary courts. There appear to have been twenty-four "hundreds" or "half hundreds" in fourteen of which the Honour had holdings.

CHAPTER 3

Stephen (suc.1093 - d.1135), the Second Alan the Black (suc.1136 - d.1146), Lords of the Honour and Conan IV (suc. 1146 - d.1171) Earl of Richmond

STEPHEN LIVED LONGER than them all. He was ninety years old when he died and, being the youngest son in Eudo's family, he had to wait until he was approaching fifty before succeeding to the Honour of Richmond. Four years after the death of Alan Rufus, his brother Alan the Black had died and, in the same year Geoffrey Boterel, the eldest of the brothers, was killed in France. This resulted in all the Boterel estates in Brittany passing to Stephen and in addition, he inherited the title of Count of Penthièvre. In this way Stephen succeeded not only to the Honour of Richmond, but to all the remaining possessions of his family.[14] He soon found that administration of the considerable Boterel estates entailed spending much of his time in Brittany and this so displeased the English King William II that Stephen was made to forfeit the Richmond Honour for two years; but when Henry I came to the throne in 1100 he was regarded with more favour and regained the Honour. He later acted as surety for the new King for observance of an alliance with Robert, Count of Flanders.

Stephanus Dux Britannie

Stephen had married a lady referred to as Avicia of Guincamp and they had four sons and two daughters. His eldest son died during his father's lifetime but the second son, known as Alan the Black remained in England and helped considerably by looking after the estates of the Honour. He married Bertha, the only daughter and heiress of Conan, Duke of Brittany and, with this marriage, Stephen had high hopes that not only the Honour of Richmond but also the Dukedom of Brittany would pass to his family.

During his long life, Stephen was a great benefactor, giving some of his largest and richest possessions to St Mary's Abbey in York which his brother Alan Rufus had founded. He gave to that house churches, tithes and lands in Yorkshire, Lincolnshire, Cambridgeshire and Norfolk which formed part of the Honour of Richmond. He also enriched monasteries at Swineshead in Lincoln, as well as Swavesey in Cambridgeshire and founded a Benedictine house at Romburgh in Suffolk, whilst in Brittany he is known to have given a bell to the Abbey of St Sergius and Bacchus in Anjou.

He died in April, probably in the year 1135, the same year as King Henry I, and he was buried at Bégard in Brittany at a Cistercian monastery which he had founded. He ordered that his heart be taken to the Abbey of St Mary in York where, on the twentieth of April in every year, funeral obsequies were performed for him and his wife, with great splendour. His eldest son

Geoffrey Boterel II took over his father's Breton title and estates and, as Stephen anticipated, his son Alan the Black succeeded to the estates of the Honour of Richmond. Maud, one of Stephen's daughters, married Walter de Gaunt who was owner of the extensive manor of Healaugh and founder of Bridlington Priory. The death of King Henry I brought to an end a thirty year period of peace and order. It was to be followed by years of unrest and disorder in which Stephen's son, the second Alan the Black, was to play an active part.[15]

As he had looked after the properties in England when he father was alive, succession to the estates of the Honour convinced Alan the Black that his future was in England. He appears to have styled himself as Count of Brittany and England, Earl of Richmond as well as, for a time, Earl of Cornwall[16] and it was his lot to become much involved in the troubled period of unrest, rebellion and anarchy which followed the death of King Henry I.

As he had no surviving son, King Henry I had made a plan that, on his death, his daughter Matilda, known as Maud, should become Queen.[17] She had been married to the German Emperor Henry V and spent over ten years in Germany as his Empress. When her husband died she reluctantly returned to England at her father's behest and married Geoffrey of Anjou. Though they had three children, it was never really a happy marriage. Despite King Henry's plan for his daughter, he had built up an affection for Stephen, the son of William the Conqueror's daughter Adela. Her husband had been killed in the Holy Land and King Henry had made himself responsible for Stephen's upbringing. A situation was created in which both Maud and Stephen were to claim the throne of England.

When Henry died in 1135, Maud was in Anjou with her husband. Stephen, who had married Matilda, heiress and granddaughter of Margaret of Scotland, took advantage of the situation successfully to claim the throne. However, it soon became apparent that he did not possess the ability to provide effective government or indeed to gain the confidence of his barons or the majority of his people.

After a short period of relative peace, there followed six years of anarchy which, though it did not cover the whole country, created considerable suffering amongst the population. In September 1139 Maud, now Countess of Anjou, came to England to challenge the new King Stephen and she gained support from the Earls of Gloucester and Chester and from the Angevins. Alan the Black however made clear his support for the King and, in recognition, Stephen granted him the County of Cornwall. Maud gained a substantial following in the western shires, particularly around Gloucester and Bristol where much of the fighting between the opposing factions took place. By 1140, a state of civil war had developed over a wide area of southern England resulting in considerable bloodshed and devastation. Earl Ranulph of Chester and his half brother, the Earl of Lincoln, deserted the King and seized and occupied Lincoln's Castle. Though Stephen at first condoned the occupation, the citizens complained of harsh treatment and the King returned and besieged the Earl of Lincoln in the castle with a force which included Alan the Black.

The Earl of Chester then called in reinforcements and asked for support from Earl Robert of Gloucester, one of Stephen's most determined opponents. He returned to Lincoln not only with his own retainers but also with a strong body of Earl Robert's men. Although his own army was much smaller, the King marched out to meet them but his fighting strength was much depleted and he was unable to withstand a charge by his opponents. Earl Alan and other earls who comprised the leading cavalry division on the King's right, turned and fled in disorder and, though King Stephen remained and fought with great tenacity, his remaining forces were overcome and he was taken to Bristol where he was imprisoned in chains. Despite his failure to remain and support the King at the Battle of Lincoln, Alan made plans to avenge Stephen's capture by laying an ambush for the Earl of Chester. However, he was himself captured, imprisoned and compelled by torture to give up the County of Cornwall which the King had earlier put in his charge.[18]

The Battle of Lincoln might well have ended the tragic reign of King Stephen for ever but the fact that it was not decisive was largely due to Empress Maud herself.[19] In the hour of her triumph, she conducted herself with such arrogance and lack of tact that she not only failed to gain public confidence, she antagonised the people of London who expelled her from their gates and then proceeded to welcome the arrival of King Stephen's Queen Matilda. Maud's main supporter, the Earl of Gloucester, was taken prisoner and, after the death of the Earl of Hereford, one of her staunchest allies, she had to accept failure in her efforts to gain the throne of England. After being besieged by Stephen at her headquarters in Oxford, she escaped capture and in 1148 returned to France. In the final years of his troubled reign, King Stephen tried unsuccessfully to secure the throne for his eldest son Eustace but the future was to rest with the Plantagenet Henry II who was crowned King on Stephen's death in 1154.

The historical records of the second Alan the Black in the troubled period of Stephen's reign indicate that he was himself a man of cruel temperament. He is known to have attacked and seized a castle at Galelint, thought to be near Rushden in Northants, and occupied by William d'Aubigny, but he was forced to relinquish this after his capture at the Battle of Lincoln. He also seized a castle at Hutton Conyers and plundered the stores and barns of the Archbishop William Fitzherbert, then using the barns as a base from which to attack and ravage Ripon. Later, he entered the Church in Ripon with his soldiers and assaulted the Archbishop at the shrine of St Wilfred. He was in York when the City was visited by King Stephen and the Queen, and the King found it necessary to stop a tournament involving a duel between Alan and Earl Williamson.[20]

Despite his cruel nature, Alan made a number of gifts during his lifetime, including donations to Fountains Abbey and the monks of Durham. In about 1145, he granted to Richmond its first known charter though the town was already established as a borough and may have derived its liberties from the days of Count Alan Rufus.[21] He also issued two charters of confirmation for the Abbey of Jervaulx, adding a gift of common pasture. In the same year he crossed to Brittany never to return and he died in 1146.

Alan had married Bertha, the daughter and heiress of his second cousin Conan III, Duke of Brittany, and they had three children, two daughters and a son, who was given the name Conan after his grandfather. Alan is also known to have had three illegitimate sons. When he died, Bertha remarried, and her new husband Eudo, Viscount of Porhoët and Duke of Brittany, became stepfather to Conan IV.

The young Conan was next in line for the Earldom of Richmond but he was a man with a problem: he was too small. From an early age he became known as "le petit" and he had to live with it the rest of his days. He had still not come of age when his father died leaving him not only the Lordship of the Honour of Richmond but also his estates in France. His mother's death was soon to follow and her powerful second husband Eudo, Viscount of Porhoët, proceeded to claim control of the Duchy, which led to considerable unrest and made it difficult for Conan to take over his father's estates. For some years the Duchy was effectively partitioned between the acting Duke Eudo and Hoël, who was also related to Conan.

Perhaps because of his size, Conan was thought to be lacking in courage but, supported no doubt by the Angevin King Henry II who had confirmed Conan's succession as Earl of Richmond,

23

he belied such criticism by crossing over to Brittany, taking Rennes by force, and putting Eudo to flight. Soon afterwards, Eudo was taken prisoner and Conan became recognised by the Bretons as their new Duke of Brittany. King Henry's younger brother Geoffrey had established himself at Nantes but met an early death in 1158 and Henry made plans to seize Nantes for himself. His plans were forestalled by Conan who was now ruler of a nominally united Duchy and he quickly took possession. Yet he was a man without the strength of character to avoid becoming a slave to the will of the King and this weakness became apparent when he agreed to acknowledge Henry's overlordship. This he did in Avranches at Michaelmas 1158 and he was destined never to escape his vassalage to the Angevin King.

During the next few years, Conan was a familiar figure at the Angevin court and his interests in Richmond brought him across the channel on a number of occasions. In 1160, he married Margaret, sister of Malcolm IV of Scotland and daughter of Henry Earl of Huntingdon, an alliance which has sometimes been seen as a token of defiance, though it is unlikely to have been entered into without the King's approval. If it was an attempt to break free of the Angevin yoke, it was short-lived for, when a daughter Constance was born from the union, the King quickly arranged for her to marry his fourth son Geoffrey, though she was still only an infant. Conan's position as Duke of Brittany was continually under threat and he was frequently troubled by quarrels with the nobility. In the end, he agreed to a form of escheat which meant handing over the administration of most of Brittany to King Henry for Geoffrey's future use and he retained only the lordship of Guingamp which had been in possession of his paternal grandfather Count Stephen.

Conan was the first Lord of the Honour to adopt the title of Earl of Richmond in his charters and, in the annals of Richmond, he holds a prominent place for being responsible for building the town's magnificent Castle Keep. On his visits to England, he gave support to a number of religious houses including St Mary's Abbey in York. He also gave aid to Denny Abbey in

Cambridgeshire, the monks of Durham and Fors Abbey, which became Jervaulx Abbey at East Witton. On one of his visits in 1158, he issued several charters including the restoration of Roald as Constable of Richmond, but his last visit was in 1164 and he died in France six years later leaving his daughter Constance aged about nine as his sole heir. For twelve years, King Henry acted as guardian to Constance whilst at the same time keeping the Honour of Richmond in his hands. He gave recognition to Conan's widow Margaret of Scotland by granting her the dower of the Honour of Richmond in Moulton and Forcett as well as wapentakes in Lincolnshire and Suffolk.[22]

CHAPTER 4

Geoffrey (b.1158 - d.1186), Constance (b.1160 - d.1201) and Ranulf de Blundeville (d.1232)

THE MARRIAGE OF Henry II's son Geoffrey to Conan's daughter Constance did not take place until 1181 when she had reached the age of twenty-one.[23] When she was only nine she became the sole heir to her father's estates and adopted the titles of Duchess of Brittany and Countess of Richmond. After the marriage, Geoffrey became Duke of Brittany and Earl of Richmond. Though the King relinquished the Honour of Richmond in favour of his son, he is thought to have retained Richmond Castle and, even when the couple went to live in Brittany, he continued to keep a close watch on his son's actions. However, there were constant quarrels within the Angevin family, often involving open warfare between the King and his sons and this allowed Geoffrey a freedom which he was not slow to exploit. Despite their quarrels, there is no doubt that the Angevins succeeded in bringing a degree of governmental organisation to Brittany and this was of enduring significance. For the first time, many Bretons experienced the results of firm central control though it was not always to their liking.

Geoffrey and Constance remained in France for much of their time and they are known to have issued a great number of Breton charters. Geoffrey's visits to England were infrequent though he came in 1184 for a family reconciliation. There were two children of the marriage; the eldest was a son named Arthur, who was

Geoffrey

destined to succeed to the family titles, and there was a daughter called Eleanor. The name of Arthur seems to have been given to their son at the expressed wish of Duchess Constance and it had particular significance to the Bretons who compared the present Angevin control with the independence and military success they had enjoyed in the days of King Arthur. Apparently, there was little love lost between Constance and her Angevin relatives. The successes of the Angevins however were probably matched by those of the French Crown and even Henry II had to acknowledge the influence the French King had over the affairs of Brittany. It became politically important that, during the quarrels of the Angevins, Geoffrey built up a close friendship with Philip Augustus, heir to the French throne, and this naturally involved political considerations as well as personal emotions. However, in 1186, after only five years of his marriage, Geoffrey was thrown from his horse and killed at a tournament in Paris.[24] When the news reached Philip Augustus he was so upset that he had to be prevented from throwing himself into Geoffrey's open grave. He then proceeded to claim the wardship of Geoffrey's daughter Eleanor but Henry proved to be too shrewd to allow her to escape from his clutches.

Only a year later, Constance was apparently directed by King Henry into a second marriage, this time with Ranulf de Blundeville, the Earl of Chester, who also took the Richmond Earldom. It proved to be a disastrous match. King Henry II died and Richard I, Coeur-de-Lion came to the throne; in 1196, at his instigation and under the influence of jealousy, Ranulf kept Constance in prison for a year. Moreover, King Richard is believed to have used this as a pretext to take control of the Honour of Richmond. It was a case of Richard exercising his powers of escheat over the Lordship of the Honour. When Constance was released after appeals to the King by her son Arthur, she proceeded to repudiate her marriage to Ranulf de Blundeville and later the same year married Guy de Thouars. This seems to have been a happier match and there were two children, daughters named Alice and Catherine.

RANULPH of Chester.
Azure three garbs or.

The English King Richard died in 1199 from wounds he received in a minor encounter at Chalus in the Limousin and the history of the Honour of Richmond between the death of Geoffrey, Constance's first husband, and the crowning of King Henry III in 1216 is somewhat obscure. Yet it is clear that the harsh rule of the two Kings, Henry II and Richard I, with the continued control over Constance and her son, caused mounting resentment. It seems however that, although Constance did not have all the lands which belonged to her father and, though Richard I seized the Honour for a time on a very slender pretext, she was able to retain undisturbed possession of most of her estates during her lifetime. After her death, there followed a period when the Honour was divided and the Richmondshire portion was granted, with some reservation, firstly to Robert Earl of Leicester, and then to

Ranulf de Blundeville. The southern portion of the Honour seems to have been partitioned off and divided between the Crown and Peter de Braine, who was to become Alice's husband. However, Peter was eventually given possession of the whole Honour. Constance died in the year 1201 at Nantes and her young daughters, Alice and Catherine, were placed in the custody of the French King. Though their father, Guy de Thouars, was recognised for a short time as tenant of the Honour, this was terminated two years later. He never succeeded to the Earldom of Richmond but he was a Count of Brittany and his daughter Alice was recognised by Breton churchmen and barons as the rightful heiress of the Duchy. When she was about 12 years of age, and despite opposition from other local aspirants, King Philip II arranged for Alice to be married to Peter de Braine, the 25 year old son of the Count de Dreux. He was granted some of the southern estates of the Honour of Richmond before taking possession of the whole Honour.

On his mother's death Arthur, the only son of Geoffrey and Constance, succeeded to the Dukedom of Brittany and the Earldom and Honour of Richmond but it was only a brief succession for, as will be described, he was murdered in France at the beginning of 1203, and ownership of the Honour then passed to the Crown. Geoffrey's sister Eleanor was the heir presumptive but she was married to Leopold, son of the King of Austria. When Leopold died, King John imprisoned her for the sole reason that he feared she would marry again and provide an heir to the English throne. The unfortunate Eleanor died in 1241.[25]

THE EARLS OF RICHMOND

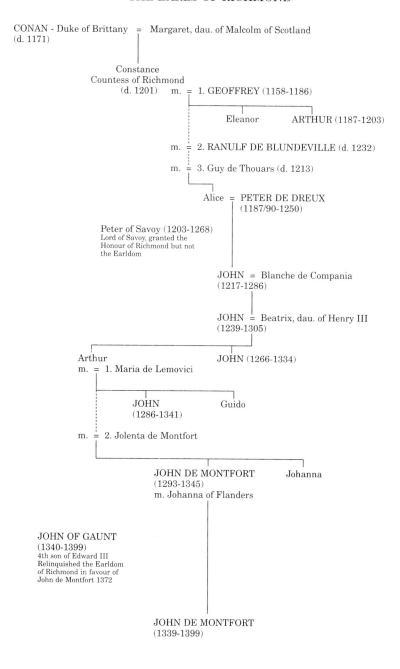

CONAN - Duke of Brittany = Margaret, dau. of Malcolm of Scotland
(d. 1171)

Constance
Countess of Richmond
(d. 1201)   m. = 1. GEOFFREY (1158-1186)

Eleanor   ARTHUR (1187-1203)

m. = 2. RANULF DE BLUNDEVILLE (d. 1232)

m. = 3. Guy de Thouars (d. 1213)

Alice = PETER DE DREUX
(1187/90-1250)

Peter of Savoy (1203-1268)
Lord of Savoy, granted the
Honour of Richmond but not
the Earldom

JOHN = Blanche de Compania
(1217-1286)

JOHN = Beatrix, dau. of Henry III
(1239-1305)

Arthur   JOHN (1266-1334)
m. = 1. Maria de Lemovici

JOHN   Guido
(1286-1341)

m. = 2. Jolenta de Montfort

JOHN DE MONTFORT   Johanna
(1293-1345)
m. Johanna of Flanders

JOHN OF GAUNT
(1340-1399)
4th son of Edward III
Relinquished the Earldom
of Richmond in favour of
John de Montfort 1372

JOHN DE MONTFORT
(1339-1399)

30

CHAPTER 5

Arthur of Britanny.
Ermine.

Arthur – Earl of Richmond (b.1187 - d.1203)

TO THE BRETONS, Arthur had been the name given to their national hero, a name which took their minds back to a remote golden age, and conjured up new hopes of independence which at that time was threatened by both the Kings of France and England. Arthur, the son of Geoffrey and Constance, was born in the year 1187 and succeeded to the Dukedom of Brittany as well as the Earldom and Honour of Richmond. There being no love lost between Constance and her Angevin relatives, it is very likely that she made the choice of name as a deliberate appeal to Breton sentiment, yet the birth of this son named Arthur served to emphasise the growing unease between the powers of Brittany, France and England.

The death of his grandfather, Henry II of England, in 1189 gave Arthur a momentous political status as heir presumptive of his Uncle King Richard to the exclusion of John, Henry's fourth son. Despite the strength of Arthur's hereditary claim to the English throne however, it became evident that John intended to supplant King Richard and viewed the young Arthur as his most dangerous enemy.

When Arthur was only three and living in France, King Richard I arranged a marriage for him with a daughter of Tancred, King of Sicily, and claimed his wardship. The Breton nobles objected however and handed him over to King Philip of France who, with Constance's agreement, proceeded to have him educated with his own son Louis in Paris.[26] In 1198 when Arthur was eleven, Richard contrived to reverse the situation and persuaded Arthur to agree that he should follow his uncle's guidance in his relations with France. Only eight months later Richard died and Arthur was left to face up to John who was firmly resolved to succeed his brother in both England and France.

In England, both the Archbishop of Canterbury and Queen Eleanor gave their support to John who was then accepted without demur and crowned King of England on 27th May, 1199. Though he was declared Lord of Normandy, John was not acceptable to the nobles of Anjou, Touraine and Maine who chose the twelve-year-old Arthur as their Lord. Under Philip's guardianship Arthur was knighted, confirmed as Duke of Brittany as well as Count of Anjou and he adopted the style of Earl of Richmond. He was also installed as lay canon of St Martin's in Tours.

The new English King John was the last of the children of Henry II and Eleanor of Aquitaine. After a difficult upbringing, he was said to possess the ruthlessness of a hardened warrior and the craft of a Machiavellian. In France, Arthur became upset by King Philip who apparently paid little regard to his rights as Duke of Brittany and he decided to cross to England in an effort to make peace with King John. John had always disliked Arthur but received him warmly. It was soon apparent however that, if he stayed in England, Arthur would be imprisoned and he promptly returned to France where he renewed his support for Philip.

King John's strength in France was limited to Aquitaine and Normandy and the growing popularity of Arthur could only exacerbate the situation. In 1202, Philip issued a summons against John in respect of charges made by the barons of Poitou the outcome of which deprived John of all the lands which he held in France and, on the strength of this, Philip proceeded to invade Normandy, capturing many towns without resistance. Arthur, Earl of Richmond, was then sixteen and Philip contracted him in marriage to his own infant daughter Mary. Word had reached Arthur that his grandmother, the hostile old Queen Eleanor, was at the castle of Mirabeau in Poitou. He gathered forces to besiege and capture Eleanor in her castle but in the nick of time she was able to warn John of the approaching attack. He was at Le Mans and immediately went with his troops to her defence. The result was disaster for Arthur, who was captured, and for his supporters who were overwhelmed. Arthur was imprisoned at Falaise and later at Rouen and those barons of Brittany who remained loyal to John asked that the Prince should be released but John clearly felt that he would never be safe while Arthur lived. No one knows what eventually happened to Arthur but there is little doubt that he was killed at John's direction in 1203. It was perhaps lucky for Constance that she did not live to hear of her son's fate as she had died two years earlier, but there is no doubt that the murder of Arthur confirmed the Breton hate for the Angevins and increased the pressure to expel John from his continental possessions.

In England, King John proceeded to divide up the estates of the Honour and ordered that one of the manors in Norfolk be granted to the Bishop of Norwich with the rest going to Robert, the 4th Earl of Leicester. However, the Earl died a few months later and his lands were again returned to the Crown. In 1204, the Richmondshire estates were granted to the Earl of Chester, former husband of Constance, and the other estates were divided by the Crown. In the French courts, John was held to be responsible for Arthur's murder and, it is said, condemned to the loss of his English Crown. Though this was never substantiated, the allegation was used by Louis, son of the French King, to justify his decision to cross the channel and give his support to the English barons in their opposition to King John.[27]

The very name of Arthur remains legendary in Brittany today and the young Duke's disappearance has gone into the Breton legend as a dastardly deed associated with the English. There are in fact as many associations with the Arthurian legends in "Bretagne" as there are in "Grande Bretagne", though the English and Welsh legends largely relate to the romantic Arthur of Nennius and the Saxons.

CHAPTER 6

Peter de Braine and Dreux
(b.1187/90 - d.1250)

WHEN THE FRENCH King Philip Augustus arranged for the Capetian Prince Peter de Braine to marry Alice, the elder of Constance's two daughters by her third marriage, the King clearly intended to extend the link between Brittany and the rest of France, but subsequent events can hardly have developed as he had planned. Peter was a junior member of Philip's own family, the second of three sons of the Count de Dreux, descendants of the French King Louis VI. When he was young, he was given the nickname of "Mauclerc", indicating his incompetence as a student, and he grew up to be arrogant, unreliable and a gambler, but he was ambitious and he, and later his son John le Roux, did much to improve Brittany's economy.

When he married Alice, he became Duke of Brittany and in 1215, by granting him the Honour of Richmond, King John tried to persuade him to come to England with horses and arms to support him against his rebellious barons. However, Peter decided to give his support to Philip of France and particularly to Louis, the King's son. It was the year in which the rebellious English leaders forced King John to seal the Magna Carta at Runnymede though subsequent attempts to implement the terms of the peace treaty only led to further quarrels. The fact that they had become at loggerheads with John decided the barons to ask the French King's son to come to England and be their leader against the royalists. It was a situation which appealed to the French, and Louis crossed the channel bringing with him an invasion force.

He soon gained support and made an unopposed entry into London as well as capturing much of south-eastern England and taking control of several royalist centres. However, King John died in the following year and, though he left a country which had been torn in two by civil war, his death weakened the cause of the anti-royalists. Despite the incursions made by Louis and the rebel forces, the royalists gained an important though bloodless victory at Lincoln and Louis was forced to return to London. The main concern of the royalists was then to get Louis out of the country and Peter de Braine is known to have helped to negotiate a "form of peace" which resulted in Louis being paid 10,000 marks to return to France and give no further support to the rebels.[28]

In Brittany, Peter proved to be one of the most ambitious of the Capetian princes, resentful of any criticism or control from above. He set out to increase the authority of the Dukedom but his assault on seigneurial privileges met with violent opposition. All too frequently he quarrelled with the Bishops and he was excommunicated several times. His dispute with the Bishop of Nantes in particular resulted in considerable mayhem. With apparent good reason however, he sought to limit some local customs like the unrestrained use of lagan or the right to shipwreck. As an example of this custom, there was the case of one thirteenth century lord who claimed that a single jagged rock was worth a huge sum of money to him each year because of the shipwrecks it caused. Despite the fact that Peter's efforts to enforce his authority throughout the Duchy met opposition from baronial coalitions, there is no doubt that he did much to improve the administrative network of Brittany. For his arrogance, he was widely disliked and his absences and intrigues both in Brittany, and in England with King Henry, always allowed his domestic enemies new opportunities to unseat him.

In 1216, the new English King Henry III came to the throne and soon made clear his intention to use Peter in the war against France.[29] However, Peter was by nature both a crusader and a turncoat who divided his allegiance between the Kings of France and England to suit his own ends. Having been granted the Earldom and Honour of Richmond he left to join a crusade against the Albigenses in Southern France. King Henry was clearly displeased at his continued absences and towards the end of 1224 he took over possession of the Honour until Peter's return. Though Peter did eventually come back to England, he went away again two years later to continue his crusading ventures.

Alice had died in 1221 and it was King Henry's intention to marry his daughter Yolande to Peter but arrangements broke down and, in 1227, the King again ordered that all Peter's lands should be seized though they were once again returned when Peter decided he would pay him homage.* A three year truce was negotiated by Peter between the English and French Kings but at the end of that period, Peter finally gave his support to the French King Louis which resulted in the loss of his English title and his lands of the Honour of Richmond, which reverted to the crown.

---

* During the period of the 100 years war, it was frequently the practice of French barons wishing to retain the favour and support of a French or English King, to "pay homage". In feudal law, the act of homage is interpreted as formal and public acknowledgement of allegiance wherein a tenant or vassal declared himself the man of the king and bound himself to his service (Refer Shorter Oxford Dictionary p.913).

Though Peter received support from Richard, Duke of Cornwall, opposition to him grew to such an extent that the French King had legitimate reason for intervention and, in 1231, Louis IX marched into Brittany. As many of Peter's more powerful subjects had already been won over by the King he was forced to sue for peace. A commission sent by Louis IX collected a long and revealing litany of complaint against Peter's arbitrary rule and it was clear that his possession of the Dukedom had to come to an end. However, the Breton Lords were prepared to allow Peter's son John to succeed him when he came of age and, in 1237, John was declared to be the new Duke of Brittany.

With his son John succeeding to the Duchy, Peter embarked on what some have referred to as a new career as an adventurer and crusader. In 1239, he led a French crusade to Palestine and then to the Nile Delta where he was wounded in the Battle of Mansurah. He was then taken prisoner by the Muslim forces and, on his release, is believed to have died at sea in the year 1250. Though he was the Earl and Lord of the Honour of Richmond for only short periods, he was without doubt one of the most colourful of all Breton holders of the title.[30]

CHAPTER 7

Scel de Pierre

Peter of Savoy (b.1203 - d.1268)

PETER OF SAVOY was different; he was not just another in
the sequence of French barons but a man born in Italy in
1203 whose father Thomas of Savoy intended him to become a
man of the church. In fact, that very nearly happened for he was
made a Canon of Valence and then Canon of Lausanne. His
younger brother Boniface was a Carthusian who became
Archbishop of Canterbury, but his election to the see was so
unpopular that he is said to have returned to Rome between
1250-2 in disgust though he retained the see until 1270 when he
died while accompanying Edward I on a crusade. Unlike his
brother, Peter decided the church was not for him and, though he
had become Provost of Aosta, he resigned from all his ecclesiastical commitments. In 1234, he proceeded to marry his cousin
Agnes, a lady known to be heiress to a considerable family estate.

When his father died, Peter had a major dispute with his
brother Amadeus about their inheritance, but this was eventually settled and his share of the estate included two castles in

39

south east France. Moreover, his marriage was to secure him a considerable additional estate. At heart, Peter was clearly something of a warrior and this was shown when he became involved in warfare with a certain Count of Geneva, though he was taken prisoner and only released after intervention by his brother Amadeus. In view of his break with the church, it was something of a surprise that he accepted the advocacy of a monastery of Payerne in Vaud after which he began referring to himself as the Count of Romont.

In England, the marriage of King Henry III to Eleanor of Provence brought into the country an increasing number of Eleanor's kinsfolk who came to London expecting to make their fortunes. The King was much criticised for surrounding himself with foreigners rather than making use of natural born English counsellors, but Peter of Savoy, who had evidently been brought to the notice of King Henry, was invited to come to England to provide added support in the face of the critical English barons. Henry lavished many favours on Peter, knighting him at Westminster Abbey and holding a feast in his honour. In 1240 the King granted him the greater part of the Honour of Richmond and though he became popularly known as the Earl of Richmond, there is in fact no evidence that he was ever given the title.

Early in 1242, Peter accompanied the King to Poitou in France and later to Bordeaux. Having returned to England, he began to fear the envy of the English nobles who were well aware of the favours being bestowed on him by Henry and he begged the King to let him return to France. At first Henry agreed but then changed his mind, recalling Peter and bestowing on him new favours, making him Sheriff of Kent and Warden of the Cinque Ports.

Nevertheless, during the succeeding years Peter spent many months in France where some of his lands had been attacked, and in 1263 he succeeded his nephew as Count of Savoy. He undertook to accompany the King to the Holy Land and, at Henry's direction, he acted as marriage broker between Richard of Cornwall and Sanchia of Provence. This was an experience that may have encouraged him to return to England bringing a bevy of foreign ladies to be married to English nobles, one of these being known to have married the Earl of Lincoln and another the son of Hubert de Burgh. Peter's role in "the marriage business" caused much indignation, the more so because he obtained the wardship of several young nobles including the sons of the Earls of Warenne and Derby as well as of John Gifford of Brimpsfield.

Despite the jealousy and criticism which seemed to follow his activities, Peter continued to receive favours from King Henry. He was allowed a lengthy visit to Italy and in 1253 he went with the King to Gascony and stayed there for a year. His role of marriage broker came to the fore again when he arranged the marriage between Henry's daughter Beatrice and John of Brittany, and as a mediator and negotiator, he did much to reconcile the King with his eldest son Edward as well as arranging negotiations with the French Court and the Pope in Italy. In 1264 a political struggle broke out between the King and Simon de Montfort, who had the support of his barons, and this led to the Battle of Lewes at which the King was captured. The royalists however gained more support and at the Battle of Evesham in the following year Simon de Montfort was killed and his forces defeated.

When these troubles began, Peter was advised to leave the country and he went to France and Italy. Though he always appreciated his role as an English landowner, his obligations in France and Italy prevented him from identifying himself more with his adopted country. His estates in the Honour of Richmond were confiscated by Simon de Montfort but returned to him in 1265 after the Battle of Evesham. It is said that King Henry offered to exchange some of the lands of the Honour for other properties but Peter seems to have retained his holdings until his death in 1268 when the Honour reverted to the Crown.

Peter was married twice, firstly to Alice of Brittany and then to Agnes, daughter of the Lord of Faucigny. He was described in the Chronicles of Savoy as a prudent and proud man who could be as terrible as a lion yet he was a loyal and perhaps the wisest of King Henry's personal friends.[31]

CHAPTER 8

The Earls John of Richmond

FOR OVER SEVENTY years following Peter of Savoy's death, there was a sequence of eight Lords of the Honour possessing the name of "John". Seven became Earls of Richmond and five were Dukes of Brittany. As the Hundred Years War developed, it is perhaps not surprising that the allegiance of those who were Breton barons came frequently into question as they were subjects of both the Kings of France and of England. Though the machinery for controlling their estates in England was well established, it was dependent on adequate supervision by these Lords of the Honour.

The sequence of "Johns" included the famed John of Gaunt and the Duke of Bedford as well as two members of the Montfort family but, before their time, there were four Breton barons whose history is recounted in the ensuing chapter. Only one of these lived most of his life in England, the others spent much of their time fighting battles in Brittany or elsewhere, crusading and looking after their Breton estates. When not fighting, they indulged in their second hobby of hunting which involved the use of a considerable entourage of estate workers and others. There was need for potbearers, basketmen, harecoursers, guardians of the hunting dogs and greyhounds, masons and blacksmiths.

Despite their absence from England and the lack of attention they gave to their Richmond estates, they still expected to receive the financial benefits which accrued to the holders of the Honour. Small wonder that, from time to time, the Honour was taken back by the Crown, though this did little to prevent the decay of the estates. As a result, by the fifteenth century, the expected level of income from the Honour could not be maintained.[32]

✳   ✳   ✳   ✳

JOHN (1) EARL OF RICHMOND AND DUKE OF BRITTANY (b.1217 - d.1286)

Johan. I. D. Brit.   Com. Richm.
b. A. D.   1286.

THE FIRST OF these four Breton barons who acquired the Honour of Richmond was the eldest son of Alice and Peter de Dreux and he appears to have been styled as "Le Roux", Duke of Brittany. Having received the Dukedom of Brittany from his father, he continued to increase his private estates and improve their administration. He established a mint in Vannes, which began to thrive as a seaport and trading centre. In the north, he purchased a fortress at Dinan which served as a vital ducal stronghold and mirrored Vannes as an important commercial centre. There was evidence of growth in a number of small northern Breton ports. It was at Saint-Gildas - now Port-Blanc, Côtes-d'Armor - in the Bay of St Brieuc, that Richard, Earl of Cornwall, landed in 1230 on his way to assist Pierre Mauclerc. St Malo, for a time known as the home of merchants, pirates and explorers, was destined to become one of the major ports of the Duchy with close cross-channel trading connections. It was a period in which Brittany's international trade gradually increased, particularly in cereals, textiles, parchment, leather, fish, bacon, grain and timber.

Perhaps to mark the independence of the Duchy from the rest of France, the walls on the south coast of Brittany were increased and reinforced and the fortifications of the Castle at Suscinio on the gulf of Morbihan were developed to make it the most important residence of the Dukes of Brittany. Despite his Duchy's growth in economic strength, John le Roux had little option but to recognise that, at that time in its history, the power of the French monarchy exceeded even that of the English, and Matthew Paris, a recognised chronicler of those times, put the position in focus when he proclaimed "The King of France is the King of all earthly Kings".

Though he eventually made peace with the clergy, John le Roux is remembered for his quarrels with the French Bishops, like his father before him, and this led to his excommunication for a time. There is ample evidence that, long before the more vehement and appalling actions of the German Reich, John le Roux was strongly anti-Jewish and not only did he expel all members of the Jewish faith from Brittany, his name was closely linked with the massacre of Jews in both Brittany and Poitou in 1236.

His marriages in France were firstly to Alice of Brittany and, when she died, to Blanche the daughter of Theobald, the King of Navarre. This second marriage brought with it a right of succession to the Kingdom of Navarre but, when the King married for the third time, he and his new wife had several sons, the eldest of whom was able to claim the succession. In the end, Alan le Roux agreed to surrender his rights after being provided by the King with a handsome annuity.

In England, Alan petitioned Henry III for restitution of the Earldom of Richmond and, in 1268. it was eventually granted. Having achieved this, he surrendered the title, as he had done in Navarre, to his eldest son, also named John, and in 1270 he went on a crusade taking part in the siege of Tunis with Louis IX. Though he appears to have survived the crusade, he is known to have died in 1286. In the Cathedral of St Gildas at the tip of the Rhuys peninsula are to be found the tombs of four children of his marriage to his second wife Blanche.[33]

JOHN(2) - EARL OF RICHMOND AND DUKE OF BRITTANY (b.1239 - d.1305)

FOLLOWING HIS FATHER'S surrender of the title, his son John became the second in this sequence of Breton barons to become Duke of Brittany and, in addition, King Henry III not only granted him the Earldom and lands of Richmond, he gave him the Honour and Rape of Hastings. This John was so keen to go on a crusade that he arranged to mortgage some of the lands of the Honour for 2,000 marks and he then accompanied his father to the siege of Tunis and on to Palestine. For a period he adhered to the French cause and took part in the invasion of Aragon in 1285. In consequence he was made to forfeit the lands of the Honour but, after he took part in arranging the truce at Tournay in 1297/8, they were restored to him for a period and this was subsequently confirmed.

John was present at Edward I's Coronation and he was one of the nobles who escorted Margaret, the French King's sister, to England where he was present at her wedding to Edward I in 1299. Six years later, he journeyed to Lyon to attend the Coronation of Pope Clement, but when he was leading the procession with the French King's brother, the weight of spectators caused an old wall to collapse. Though the Pope was knocked down, he survived, but John was mortally injured. On his death, King Edward proceeded to re-claim the Earldom and lands of of the Honour.

John had married Beatrice, the second daughter of Henry III King of Provence in 1260, but she had died in 1275 and was buried at Grey Friars, in London. It is recorded that when she died, John arranged with Egglestone Abbey that six canons should be perpetually resident and provided for in order to say masses for her soul and, after his death, for both their souls.[34]

* * * *

JOHN (3) EARL OF RICHMOND (b.1266 - d.1334).

UNLIKE HIS PREDECESSORS the third Richmond John passed most of his life in the service of the Kings of England. He had been appointed in 1294 as Lieutenant of Aquitaine and Captain of the English but, as a General, he was not a success and, though he remained in Saxony for a time, he was soon back in England. In 1306, he was granted the Earldom and Honour of Richmond by Edward I who regarded him as one of the most responsible of the French barons. The King died the following year and he was succeeded by Edward II, who proved to be weak, effeminate and an incapable successor whose reign was one long struggle with the barons of his time. When he was crowned King he gave the Earldom of Cornwall to Piers Gaveston who had previously been banished by Edward's father. Gaveston has been described as a handsome Gascon knight who had been a close companion of Edward since childhood. The favours and affection bestowed on him by the King soon roused the jealousy of many magnates of that time and they were further insulted when Edward went over to Boulogne to bring back his bride-to-be, Isabella of France, leaving Gaveston as Regent. After his marriage, the King soon made it clear that the delights of marriage were not going to cool his love for Gaveston and his behaviour and the arrogance of Gaveston built up a situation that could not be resolved peacefully. Eventually Gaveston was captured by his enemies and executed. John of Richmond, being a fervent loyalist and supporter of Edward II, remained neutral throughout this affair to his later advantage. There followed the conflict between the King and the Earl of Lancaster which ended in March 1322 when Lancaster was sentenced to death as a traitor before an assembly of seven earls which included John, Earl of Richmond.

It was the final wish of King Edward I that his son should pursue the war with Scotland to the bitter end but, though the need to protect the safety of the northern counties of England was accepted, his son considered the subjugation of Scotland to be of secondary importance. Seven years later however came the battle of Bannockburn where, because of what has been described as a display of incredible incompetence by the King and his military advisers, the English were totally defeated by the Scots. There followed a period during which the English people suffered acute distress and famine, particularly in the North. The Scots ravaged the countryside as far south as Richmond and, in September 1319, Myton on Swale was the scene of a massacre which has gone down in history as one of the worst cases of human slaughter in those troubled times.

Despite his father's wishes, Edward II then decided the time had come to end the English campaign against the Scots and a truce was called. John, Earl of Richmond, was appointed a Lieutenant, Keeper of the Peace and Guardian of Scotland. In support, Edward ordered the sheriffs to assist where necessary with horses, arms and the entire comitatus. John soon made known the King's wish to make peace with the Scots but subsequent events did nothing to encourage any improvement. In the summer of 1322, the truce expired and the Scots swarmed over the border, ravaging north west England down to Preston. Over in the east, word had reached them that the Queen was in York. Though she managed to escape by sea, the King was meeting John. Earl of Richmond at Byland Abbey. They were dining together when the Scots, under Robert the Bruce, penetrated towards York and went to Byland clearly intending to take the King prisoner. With John's help, Edward II managed to escape on horseback and reached Rievaulx but John was taken prisoner by the Scots. Having failed to obtain money from Parliament for his release, the King addressed a letter to the tenants of the Honour, asking them to contribute according to their holdings. The appeal seems to have been successful and, after payment of a large sum of money and with intervention by the Pope, John was eventually released after two years imprisonment.[35]

Any permanent peace with Scotland seemed impossible as Edward refused to recognise Bruce as King of the Scots but, eventually, a thirteen year truce was negotiated which brought the war to an end for the rest of Edward II's reign. His wife Isabella, who had been treated shabbily through several stages of their marriage, had nevertheless provided a son and heir as well as a second son and two daughters. With the agreement of Edward and the Despensers, Lords Marchers on whom he relied, she went on a supposed peace mission to improve relations with the French. Having crossed the channel she set up her own court and formed a relationship with Roger Mortimer who had earlier escaped from the Tower. They began a campaign against Edward and particularly his supporting Despensers. The heir to the throne, Edward's eldest son, then joined his mother.

There were rumours which did not materialise of an invasion of England by the King of France and the Queen of England with support from an influential group of exiles in Paris which by then included John, Earl of Richmond. However, despite the fact that Isabella's liaison with Mortimer was becoming a scandal and that King Edward had threatened Mortimer with death should he return, the Queen with her company eventually arrived in Suffolk where they went to Bury St Edmunds and from there to Cambridge, their purpose being to annihilate Edward's supporting Despensers and forcibly remove the King himself. When the arrival of the Queen was made known she was given much public support and her presence unleashed considerable violence against the King's followers. London was soon in tumult and mob rule began to develop. The Bishop of Exeter was dragged from his horse and murdered and the Bishop of Hereford suffered a similar fate. The Queen with a supporting army went to Hereford intent not only to capture Edward but to destroy the Despensers. The outcome was inevitable; there were executions and Edward was compelled to relinquish the Crown in favour of his son. His continued existence proved to be an embarrassment however, and Mortimer's solution was to have him secretly murdered in the dungeon of Berkeley Castle.

The part played by John, Earl of Richmond in these sordid events seems uncertain but his presence in Paris in company with Queen Isabella confirmed that he had lost patience with Edward II. After Bannockburn, Edward seemed to give up even the pretence of ruling and though John was a confirmed royalist he must have been well aware of the King's inadequacies and concluded that the future now rested with the Queen and the young heir to the throne. As the Earl of Richmond, he had given the King years of service as attendant and counsellor to the Prince of Wales, joint ambassador to the Pope and, for a while, ambassador plenipotentiary to the King of France, during which time he had accompanied the King and Queen to France.

John, Earl of Richmond died in Brittany in 1334. He had never married but, shortly before his death, he demised the castles, manors and towns of Richmond and Bowes to his niece Mary, Countess of Pembroke, for life. His successor was his nephew, yet another John. Edward III was crowned King in 1327 and Charles IV King of France died a year later. The new King of England was to do much to restore the shattered dignity of the monarchy and, after disposing of Mortimer, he began a reign of strength and toleration; yet war with France was becoming inevitable and was to occupy most of the next hundred years. It was a complex period of history in which succeeding Earls of Richmond were much involved.[36]

* * * *

JOHN (4) EARL OF RICHMOND AND DUKE OF BRITTANY (b.1286 - d.1341)

ON THE DEATH of his uncle, the fourth of the barons in this sequence of French aristocrats given the name "John" proceeded to claim possession of the Honour of Richmond. Born in 1286, he had already taken the titles of Duke of Brittany and Vicomte of Limoges and, in England, the King not only accepted his claim to be Lord of the Honour but in 1334/5 granted him the Earldom of Richmond. Spencer's Guide of 1898 reported that he was given a licence to wall the town of Richmond and, though houses were cleared away for it to be done, the work would have taken a considerable time to complete. An original wall of earth and wood, with gates to guard the entrances, was certainly not strong enough to keep out the Scots or other intruders. To pay for the new wall, the King allowed a grant of murage enabling the inhabitants to collect tolls over a period of five years on all goods exposed for sale in the Market Place. The amounts range between a farthing for a quarter of flour to two pence for a cartload of lead.

Possession of the Lordship and Earldom of Richmond did not bring John to England for any lengthy periods. Even in the early

1330's the seeds of a war between England and France were beginning to grow and, as the Duchy of Brittany was geographically situated between the two powers, its involvement in any major conflict could not be avoided. The origins of what became the Hundred Years War were complex but the most important was the disputed ownership of Gascony, with its very lucrative wine trade. Other causes of the conflict were the whole dynastic system which existed in France and the relationships each country had with Scotland, the Low Countries and the Rhineland.

Despite the abundant reasons for conflict with France, the English King Edward III was busy campaigning against the Scots and had no wish to fight Philip of France. Philip was less peacefully disposed but, in 1332, both Kings decided to go on a crusade together, perhaps in an effort to sort out their differences particularly about Gascony. Yet it was clear that sooner or later, war between them was inevitable. What delayed it was lack of money for both Kings, particularly Edward, who found great difficulty in persuading Parliament to provide the funds he needed. It was not until 1337 that Edward made his first, though expensive, incursion with his forces into the lands of the Count of Flanders, and the earlier stages of the War were conducted at sea. Both sides suffered casualties, but Edward had a considerable victory when he routed the French Fleet at Sluys in 1340.

John Duke of Brittany clearly had no wish to take sides in the dispute but, as the conflict developed, he made his decision to support the French. He gave up his interests in England and the lands of the Honour of Richmond were returned to the Crown. It was surprising that, despite his decision and the fact that he then served for a period with the French army, he remained on friendly terms with King Edward. He married three times, each of his wives being daughters of French aristocrats, but he had no legitimate children. His first wife Isobel was the sister of Philip VI of France and, after her death, he married Isobel of Castile. His third wife was Jeanne, daughter of a Count of Savoy.

In 1317 John decided to endow his younger brother Guy with estates in Penthièvre. Guy was later to marry Jeanne d'Avaugour, member of a ducal family with whose possessions he formed a huge apanage of Northern Brittany. It was their daughter, also given the name Jeanne, who was considered by most parties to be John's probable successor since precedent allowed female succession in Brittany and she was the Duke's closest descendant. However, her half-uncle John de Montfort was a rival for the succession and the major contest which followed indirectly affected the progress of the Civil War which was to follow. The Duke died at Caen in the spring of 1341 and there seems no record of him making any return visit to England.[37]

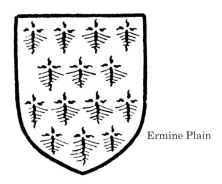

CHAPTER 9

Ermine Plain

John de Montfort – Lord of the Honour of Richmond and Duke of Brittany (b.1293 - d.1345)

THE DEATH OF John, Duke of Brittany and Earl of Richmond without an heir did indeed create problems in Brittany if not in England. As expected, the ducal succession was immediately disputed between Jeanne de Penthièvre, daughter of the late Duke's younger brother and John, Count of Montfort, the Duke's half brother. It was a dispute which led to a state of civil war in the Duchy which divided Brittany for almost a quarter of a century. Moreover, active intervention by the Kings of England and France to quell the dispute only led to a greater struggle between the two Kings themselves.

As precedent allowed female succession in Brittany, the French King Philip VI recognised Jeanne as the Duchess of Brittany. As might be expected, there were various suitors seeking her hand in marriage and one was Edward III of England.

Yet it was Charles, the younger son of the Count de Blois, who was to become her husband. Both John of Montfort and the Count de Blois had requested the French King to receive their homage but John had first visited the English King Edward at Windsor and, in return for recognition of Edward's title to the Crown of France, he was promised supporting military aid.

Though there is some doubt as to whether John de Montfort became entitled to the Earldom of Richmond, he was certainly given the Lordship of the Honour. His bargain with King Edward upset Philip of France and the French King's acceptance of Charles de Blois as Duke of Brittany was almost inevitable. Nevertheless, his decision was to have far-reaching consequences. It ensured Montfort's support for King Edward who, at that time, was casting around for another excuse to invade France. Moreover, though support for Montfort in Brittany seemed limited, the Bretons were not happy about the marriage between Jeanne and Charles de Blois for it symbolised a closer link with France, always a delicate issue. Indeed, though the greater lords gave their support to Charles de Blois, it was the Breton-speaking knights and ordinary folk who feared increasing French influences and began to favour Montfort's cause.

John de Montfort was the son of Arthur, Duke of Brittany, and his mother was Arthur's second wife Yolande, Countess of Montfort l'Amaury. John had married Jeanne, daughter of Louis, a Count of Flanders, and she was to prove a redoubtable lady who gave great support to her husband against Charles de Blois. Neither Montfort nor his mother Yolande ever accepted that they had been sufficiently well endowed by Duke Arthur, bearing in mind the great landed wealth of the Dukes of Brittany. In fact, Montfort became a life-long seeker after land, exploiting to the full whatever rights he possessed as a result of his marriage or through other family relationships. He engaged in a long dispute with his father-in-law over lands in Rethel and Nevers which he claimed on Jeanne's behalf and, on hearing of the death of his half brother, he was quick to claim his inheritance even, as one chronicler observed, to the extent of hurrying to the duchy and to Limoges to secure his half brother's property.

He is thought to have owned the County of Montfort (Seine-et-Oise) and, as he spent much of his time in Paris, his visits to Brittany had been few and far between; this was clearly about to change. In 1341 he was known to be in the Loire area and Philip VI of France decided to establish his rule in Brittany and give support to de Blois. He sent his son John Duke of Normandy to the Duchy with a large army. The Duke crossed the Breton frontier and reached Nantes just as a French naval force sailed up the Loire to join in the blockade of the Duchy's leading city where Montfort and his army made a stand. Montfort was able to resist the opposing forces for nearly three weeks but, in the end, the city capitulated and, when he was captured, he was taken to Paris and put in the Tower of the Louvre.

Yet the French forces and Charles de Blois had not reckoned with Jeanne de Montfort, described by the historian Froissart as having the heart of a lion and the courage of a man. With a small enthusiastic band of followers, she resisted further attacks until early in 1342 when help was provided by Edward III. In the following months however, the French de Blois forces consolidated their positions and slowly made some headway inland but Jeanne staunchly defended her husband's interests and, in May 1342, she is said to have confronted Charles de Blois at the siege of Hennebont where she set fire to the camp of the besiegers and was able to hold out until the arrival of an English relief force. Edward began sending increased military help and landed himself with 5,000 men at Brest in October to help restore the Montfort fortunes. Establishing their hold on Rennes and Vannes they brought a ring of coastal fortresses under Montfortist control.

Through the mediation of two cardinals, a general Anglo-French truce was arranged in Brittany and Edward returned to England taking with him Jeanne and her two children. Montfort had been a prisoner but he broke parole in 1341 and made his way back from Paris to England. He did homage to Edward and committed his infant son to the King's care. A short time later however, word reached him that de Blois had made an advance around Quimper and, together with the Earl of Northampton, he returned to Brittany to attack the opposing forces. Hardly had he set foot in the Duchy again when he died, the victim of an infected wound he had previously sustained.

His successor was his eldest son, the young John de Montfort. Jeanne, his widowed mother, decided to remain in England and is thought to have retired to Tickhill Castle, south-east of Richmond in North Yorkshire. In the aftermath of her husband's death, the confused and protracted civil war in Brittany was destined to continue and there was a succession of small hard-fought battles between the forces of Charles de Blois and the Anglo-Breton supporters of Montfort as a result of which the countryside was thrown into turmoil. In one encounter in 1347 Charles de Blois was captured and then sent as a prisoner to England. In his absence, his wife Jeanne de Penthièvre proved to be as indomitable in defence of her husband's cause as had Jeanne de Flandres, John de Montfort's wife.

During the period of the Black Death there was little active warfare between English and French forces though both countries were engaged in several theatres of war. The situation in Brittany was to change when Edward III came to an agreement with Charles de Bois allowing him to return in 1356 for a considerable ransom and an undertaking to take no further part in the war until the ransom had been paid. This release of de Bois was a surprising development especially in view of King Edward's role as guardian of the young John de Montfort. However, in 1362, after John de Montfort had accompanied the Duke of Lancaster at the siege of Rennes, one of the longest in the Hundred Years War, Edward allowed him to return permanently to Brittany.

Attempts at a settlement with de Blois had not succeeded and a climax to the situation in Brittany was reached in September 1364 when de Blois mustered a strong army to attack the English who were besieging Auray. Despite their numerical superiority the French were heavily defeated and Charles de Blois was killed.

It was a victory for John and for the Montfortists who gained the throne for which they had long contended. John de Montfort's victory was to lead to his acceptance as Duke of Brittany by the King of France and eventually to his being granted the title of Earl of Richmond, a title possessed for thirty years by the King's son, John of Gaunt.[38]

CHAPTER 10

JOHN of Gaunt. *The royal arms of EDWARD III with a label ermine.*

John of Gaunt (b.1340 - d.1399) Earl of Richmond (1342-1372)

WHEN HE WAS only fifteen, King Edward III married Philippa of Hainault and their fourth son, born in 1340 in the town of Ghent, became known as John of Gaunt. The title of Earl of Richmond, and all the lands of the Honour, were given to him when he was an infant, confirmed when he had reached the age of eleven, and held for over thirty years. To his later regret, he relinquished the Earldom as part of an Anglo-Breton alliance when he reached the age of thirty two. He lived during a particularly eventful period of our history and his name has probably been remembered more than that of many holders of the Richmond Earldom.

It was in 1342 that King Edward III decided to take a personal hand in the French campaign, intending not only to preserve the sea route round the Breton coast but to maintain an Anglo-Breton presence and give support to the Montforts. Before leaving with his army, he entrusted his wife Philippa with the guardianship of their children and, for their upkeep, he granted to her the benefits of the Honour of Richmond. Young Gaunt grew up under the tutelage of his elder brother the Black Prince whose part in the victory at the Battle of Crécy in 1346 and the capture at Poitiers of King John II of France had been widely acclaimed. These successes put the English into a strong position and when the French agreed to sign the Treaty of Bretagne-Calais in May 1360, it granted the English Crown the extensive Duchy of Aquitaine, as well as Ponthieu and the famous port and City of Calais. Moreover, John II, who had been imprisoned in the Tower, was to be released but only after payment of a considerable ransom of three million gold crowns. The Treaty was weighted in favour of the English though, for his part, Edward III agreed to renounce his claim to the French throne.

Gaunt was still very young when the Black Death entered the continent from the Crimea and in the course of twenty years destroyed at least one third of the entire European population. It ravaged the people of both Britain and France and, at its peak, brought the encounters of the Hundred Years War in France to a virtual standstill. As part of his upbringing, the young Gaunt had the excitement in 1350 of witnessing the Black Prince and his father in battle but his first real experience of war was at sea on board his father's ship in a clash with the Spaniards. A further experience of battle came when he accompanied his father to the borders to recover Berwick from the Scots. He was barely nineteen when he married his cousin Blanche, youngest daughter of the Duke of Lancaster and, by this marriage, he stood to inherit a large share of the huge estates of the Dukedom, regarded as the largest in England after the Crown. Only two years after the wedding, the Duke died of the plague in what became known as the second pandemic and, when his death was soon followed by that of his daughter Maud, Gaunt was destined to become an exceedingly rich man. Though he had only just come of age, he was given the heavy responsibility of administering the vast estates of the Dukedom. Division of the inheritance gave him a half of the estate to the north of the River Trent which included the Earldoms of Lancaster and Derby. His enhanced new style was then "John, son of the King of England, Earl of Lancaster, Richmond, Derby and Lincoln and High Steward of England". His wife Blanche became a favourite of King Edward but she died when aged only twenty-seven, having given birth to five children in nine years.

As Earl of Richmond, Gaunt became heir to a well-defined series of local courts in individual lordships of the Honour. As already mentioned, these were administered by local bailiffs and provosts chosen by the community under the supervision of seigneurial stewards. The lordships each had a receiver who paid over monies to a Receiver General. Without doubt, there had been a considerable decay in the property of the Honour and in 1355[39] it became the task of Gaunt's officials to remedy this. Yet it was the old and imposing Richmond Castle which provided the young Gaunt with his principal base and for which his father, Edward III, granted him money in 1358 for repairs.[40]

Gaunt developed a liking for hunting and the sport took him to many parts of the country. From Richmond Castle, excellent hunting was available to him in the extensive forests of the Gaunt family in the adjoining manor of Swaledale. The manor comprised an area of 52,000 acres granted early in the 12th century to Walter Gaunt on the occasion of his marriage to Count Stephen's daughter Maud. The Gaunt family were related to the early Flemish Earls and came to England at the time of the Norman Conquest. Walter founded Bridlington Priory and Maud granted to the Priory "the church of St Andrew of Swaledale" which included the right to the tithes from the whole manor of Healaugh.

In time, Gaunt's army and parliamentary life drew him towards London and, as Richmond was remote from the usual habitats of the royal court, the King agreed that he should have the use of Hertford Castle which later became one of his favoured residences. Within London, Gaunt also spent much of his time at The Savoy, a beautiful house near Charing Cross, but he owned and had to maintain a number of great houses and castles particularly in the Midlands and the North. He visited them as often as possible and his preferences were the castles of Lancaster, Leicester, Higham Ferrers, and Kenilworth but he had a particular attachment to Lincoln Cathedral and to the Abbey of St Mary in York. His enthusiasm for sport is reflected in the care he lavished on his forests and parks, described as the finest private collection of hunting preserves in England.

John of Gaunt developed considerable literary interests and both John Wycliffe and Geoffrey Chaucer received his patronage. In his verse "The Boke of the Duchesse" Chaucer clearly had in mind Gaunt's liking for hunting from his base in Richmond Castle, when he wrote:

> *Gan (quikly) homeward for to ryde*
> *Unto a place ther besyde,*
> *Which was from us but a lyte,*
> *A long castel with walles whyte,*
> *By seynt Johan on a riche hil (i.e. Richmond).*[41]

It was in 1366 that a civil war in Castile led to the first active interference by the English in Castilian affairs, and this was to have a great influence on the fortunes of John of Gaunt. A bitter struggle had developed between Castile's tyrannical leader, known as Pedro the Cruel, and his illegitimate half-brother Enrique of Trastamara. Both England and France were competing for an alliance with the Castilian kingdom which had a tradition of strong kingship, a warlike nobility and a powerful galley fleet which could operate in more northerly waters. The Black Prince had been able to restore Pedro to his throne in 1367 but it proved to be of no avail for, with French support, Enrique was reinstated and Pedro fled to Gascony.

An English expedition commanded by the Black Prince went to Castile to oppose the French involvement, but the first attack was beaten back and proved a failure. The Prince re-grouped his forces and won a fierce battle at Najera which enabled him to reinstate Pedro. Gaunt had been put in charge of the English vanguard in the battle and, though he was highly praised for his leadership in resisting a fierce attack by the French, his ability as a commander in sole charge of major army operations was soon to be questioned.

Gaunt had returned to England when Blanche died in September 1368 and the Black Prince was diverted from Spanish affairs by growing Anglo-French tensions. By 1370 the main French threat was on Aquitaine and, as the Black Prince was by then far from well, Gaunt agreed to take over command of the English forces there until the summer of the following year. This he did with some success and was able to resist French encroachment. Castile however again fell into French hands and they proceeded to assassinate King Pedro and make their former ally Enrique a prisoner though Pedro's daughter Constance and her sister Isabel were able to escape to Gascony.

After the death of Blanche, his first wife, Gaunt contemplated re-marriage and after being refused by Margaret, daughter of the Count of Flanders, he turned his attention to Pedro's daughter Constance. She was regarded as heir to the Castilian throne and, in September 1369, she and Gaunt were married at Roquefort, south of Bordeaux. The newly married couple are believed to have made their journey to England in a salt ship which Gaunt requisitioned, having obliged the master John Payn to discharge his cargo of Bay salt. They landed at Fowey but were so short of cash that Constance had to pawn a cloth of gold and a chalice to some Dartmouth men. When they eventually reached London, she was well received, particularly by the Black Prince, but on a personal level, the marriage was not to prove a whole-hearted success. Constance was full of hatred for those who killed her father and clearly found it difficult to reconcile herself to the climate and the people of London. A major rift which soon developed between her and Gaunt was her husband's affair with his mistress Catherine Swynford, who was Geoffrey Chaucer's sister. Gaunt's marriage to Constance brought them one daughter, a future Queen of Castile, but no male heir, whereas Catherine Swynford's relationship with Gaunt resulted in three illegitimate sons and a daughter. Gaunt arranged for these children to have

JOHN OF GAUNT

Ancestors and Descendants

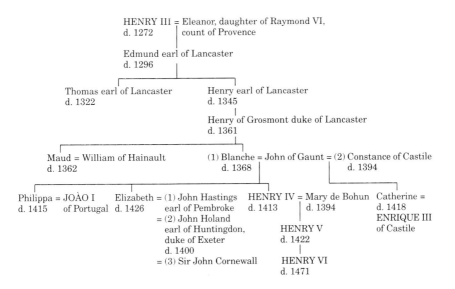

HENRY III = Eleanor, daughter of Raymond VI,
d. 1272   count of Provence

Edmund earl of Lancaster
d. 1296

Thomas earl of Lancaster
d. 1322

Henry earl of Lancaster
d. 1345

Henry of Grosmont duke of Lancaster
d. 1361

Maud = William of Hainault
d. 1362

(1) Blanche = John of Gaunt = (2) Constance of Castile
d. 1368   d. 1394

Philippa = JOÀO I   Elizabeth = (1) John Hastings
d. 1415   of Portugal   d. 1426   earl of Pembroke
                       = (2) John Holand
                       earl of Huntingdon,
                       duke of Exeter
                       d. 1400
                       = (3) Sir John Cornewall

HENRY IV = Mary de Bohun   Catherine =
d. 1413   d. 1394   d. 1418
                    ENRIQUE III
HENRY V   of Castile
d. 1422

HENRY VI
d. 1471

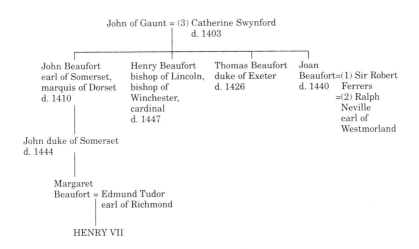

John of Gaunt = (3) Catherine Swynford
d. 1403

John Beaufort
earl of Somerset,
marquis of Dorset
d. 1410

Henry Beaufort
bishop of Lincoln,
bishop of
Winchester,
cardinal
d. 1447

Thomas Beaufort
duke of Exeter
d. 1426

Joan
Beaufort=(1) Sir Robert
d. 1440   Ferrers
         =(2) Ralph
         Neville
         earl of
         Westmorland

John duke of Somerset
d. 1444

Margaret
Beaufort = Edmund Tudor
         earl of Richmond

HENRY VII

the surname Beaufort, a name which became a familiar one in English history.

Gaunt's marriage to Constance gave him a link with the Castilian crown and he proceeded to have the name and arms of the Duke of Lancaster changed to describe himself as King of Castile and Leon. He took the arms of Spain, quarterly with a label, and for the next sixteen years he was in the unusual position of a son of a King of England who claimed to be a King of Spain as well as Duke of Lancaster and Earl of Richmond.

The year 1372 brought further English failures both at sea and on land and with the French taking over much of Aquitaine and extending their attacks on Brittany there was considerable public alarm. By then, the Black Prince was a sick man and much public criticism was building up against Gaunt. In 1373, he was put in command of a large expedition into France which historians subsequently regarded as a major failure and an example of Gaunt's lack of military ability. There was doubt about his objectives and the expedition suffered from lack of proper planning as well as Gaunt's failure to take the strongholds he assaulted. His army suffered heavy losses at the hands of the French and also through privations which were probably intensified when he took his weary men on a difficult passage through the Massif Central. By the time they reached Bordeaux in 1374 their numbers were greatly depleted and when Gaunt sailed for home it signalled the end of an expedition the results of which did little to appease his critics. Yet he had some good qualities as a commander and in the army he was thought to be at his best when conducting sieges. There were some successes resulting from this 1373 expedition for it relieved pressure on Duke John's supporters in Brittany and revived English allegiances in Limousin. In particular, it left a heavy toll of devastation which may well have influenced the French as well as the English in seeking peace. It was the Pope who initiated peace talks which ended in a truce being agreed to last until April 1377. Gaunt was certainly involved in these talks and the valuable part he played in the diplomatic affairs of his time should not be under-estimated.[42]

Gaunt relinquished the Earldom of Richmond in 1372. He had always been aware of the claim to the Earldom by John de Montfort, Duke of Brittany, who regarded Richmond as an apanage of the Breton Dukedom. Montfort had married Gaunt's sister Mary and Gaunt had a close personal relationship with the Duchy. However much he and Duke John had in common however they were both governed by a sense of self-interest and, when the Duke drove a hard diplomatic bargain with King Edward III as part of an Anglo-Breton alliance, Gaunt was persuaded to relinquish his Richmond title. As some compensation, he was granted the Lordships of Knaresborough and Tickhill. This arrangement to give up the Richmond Earldom was somewhat soured when a dispute arose between Gaunt and the Duke over payment of wages to troops and, at that time, an angry Gaunt clearly wished he had retained his Richmond title. Duke John's tenure of the Richmond title was not to be prolonged however for it was confiscated by Richard II in 1384. One of the last decisions Gaunt made as Earl was to grant the Franciscans of Richmond the right to take fuel from the forests, a decision perhaps indicating a caring aspect of his character.

The Black Prince's failing health and the death of Lionel, the King's second son, resulted in Gaunt becoming one of the principal figures in domestic politics during the closing years of Edward III's life. When Parliament assembled in April 1376, the King was too ill to preside and the Black Prince had to retire through sickness after the opening session. Gaunt had then to fulfil a role described by one of his contemporaries as "lieutenant of the King to hold Parliament". The clerical party had been driven out because of discontent with the war in France and the feudal party were voted in with John of Gaunt at its head. It was inevitable that he should be regarded as the foremost representative of the government and also the man responsible for its mistakes.

There was a general feeling of discontent and mistrust and a vast number of petitions to Parliament ranged over the whole field of administration and law. Complaints were made against the levels of taxation, the Church and the jurisdiction of the courts. Gaunt was placed in an unenviable but responsible position in Parliament and, though it led to him becoming even more unpopular, there is no doubt that he contributed a great deal to the political stability of England during a difficult period of its history. In the University of Oxford, which was the national centre of theological study and learning, there was criticism of Papal pretensions and power and the distinguished scholar Wycliffe voiced his indignation at the corruption of the Church and its failure to observe the true principles of Christianity. At a time when Wycliffe was accepted in government circles, he and Gaunt became strange bedfellows but, in the end, Wycliffe's attack on Church doctrine rather than Church privilege lost him Gaunt's support. Though Wycliffe took his case to the people he found they were more concerned with social revolution than Church reform and he gained little support. It is important however that, with the help of his students, he translated the Bible into English.

A man who crossed Gaunt's path and became a strong parliamentary adversary was Bishop Wykeham of Winchester. He is assumed to have been the source of a scandalous story concerning Gaunt which appeared in the St Albans Chronicle. It reported that Queen Philippa, when brought to bed at Ghent, had given birth to a girl whom she accidentally overlaid and, fearing the King's anger, she substituted the baby son of a Flemish woman. On her deathbed, the Queen confessed the secret to the Bishop of Winchester with the injunction that, if there became any prospect of Gaunt becoming King, the truth should be made known. Gaunt's anger at the publication of this story was to some extent matched by his resentment against Edmund Mortimer, Earl of March, whose son would have had a prior claim to the English throne.

In 1377 a further major expedition to France had been planned in which Gaunt was to have taken part and perhaps improved his popularity but it was cancelled when the death of the King was announced on 21st June. He had been in failing health for some time and, by general consent, the Black Prince's son Richard was immediately recognised as his successor. On the day his grandfather died, the Crown of England passed to a minor. John of Gaunt now became head of the Council of Regency and to all intents and purposes he ruled the land. He realised that this was a new situation above day-to-day politics and that he was liable to be blamed for any disasters which might occur. He decided not to remain too much in the public eye and sought permission to retire to his estates and spent some time in Northumberland before going to Edinburgh with the intention of improving Anglo-Scottish relationship but he was in Yorkshire when a major uprising developed in the spring of 1381.

It began when villagers in Essex refused to pay their taxes but the rising which followed was the culmination of long gathering discontent, the application of the poll tax being only one of the root causes. A judge was sent to Essex to quell the trouble but he was seized and the revolt spread to Kent and to London where Wat Tyler was at the centre of the troubles. The uprising then spread to Hampshire and north to Yorkshire but the worst outrages were in East Anglia. A number of leading people were killed including the Archbishop of Canterbury and the Chancellor, both of whom were beheaded in the Tower, and many properties were destroyed. Much of the anger was levelled at John of Gaunt, there were calls from the mob for him to be beheaded and his magnificent Savoy building in London was wrecked. The young King Richard tried to meet and parley with the angry mob without success but eventually, after Wat Tyler had been killed, the peasants' rebellion collapsed.

Gaunt was clearly shaken by the rebellion and the feeling which had developed against him. When the French sent troops to Scotland in May 1385 and an invasion from that quarter was expected, Gaunt went with the King and a large army to protect the borders. Yet it was clear that he was regarded by Richard II with some suspicion and a convenient pretext arose for Gaunt's removal from the country. It arose from a proposal to invade Castile again with the support of the King of Portugal and this provided a welcome opportunity for Gaunt to return to Spain and claim what he regarded as his Kingship of Castile. He went with his wife and daughter and a large army to Corunna but the proposed invasion was destined to fail because Gaunt and many of the troops fell ill with a climatic sickness. In the end, diplomacy and romance prevailed and the reigning King of Castile's son married Constance's daughter Catherine. A treaty was signed and Gaunt gave up any thoughts he had of becoming King of Castile in return for a substantial payment and the promise of an annuity for him and the Duchess.

When Gaunt returned to England he was given a welcome by the King and made Duke of Aquitaine for life, but the national feeling against him was to remain. Constance died in 1394, and Gaunt was soon to marry his mistress Catherine Swynford. He demonstrated his affection for the Beaufort children not only by arranging to secure their legitimation but also to advance their

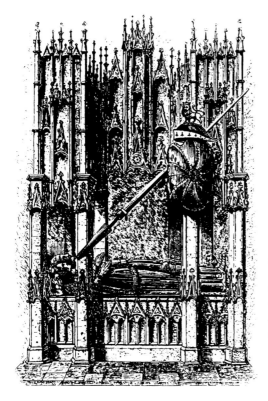

The tomb of John of Gaunt and Constance his wife. Sketched by Wenceslaus for Dugdale's 1658 History of St Pauls Cathedral. *J.B. Post writes "with the destruction of old St Pauls in the great fire of 1666, the last physical traces of the tomb were lost".*

fortunes as they approached adulthood. They were John who became Earl of Somerset, Henry who entered the Church and became a cardinal and bishop of Winchester, and Thomas, later Duke of Exeter. The daughter of the relationship was Joan, who became Duchess of Westmorland and whose effigy can be seen in Staindrop Church, County Durham. She was buried beside her mother in Lincoln Cathedral.[43]

Gaunt was a wealthy, ambitious and in many respects a remarkable man but his achievements seemed not to receive the recognition they deserved. He was not a popular figure partly because he lacked the prestige of a successful soldier. He lost public confidence because of government corruption and its failure to provide the social reform that the people demanded. His vast wealth made him the subject of envy and mistrust and he suffered from unsavoury rumours created by his opponents. Though he ultimately married his mistress, his earlier open lifestyle with Catherine Swynford provided ammunition for his critics. Yet he was the son, uncle and father of kings, a defender of royal authority and strong supporter of his father Edward III. When his father died he held the key position of Head of the Council of Regency during young Richard II's early years but he never developed a harmonious relationship with the new King. He spent his last days at Leicester Castle where he is believed to have been visited by the young King Richard and he died in February 1399. His tomb was in St Paul's Cathedral. It was Gaunt's son Bolingbroke who eventually overthrew Richard leaving Henry IV, Gaunt's son by first wife, to become the first King of the Lancastrian line.

CHAPTER 11

Iohan. IV. *ob.A.D. 1399*

John de Montfort (b.1339 - d.1399) Earl of Richmond

WHEN GAUNT RELINQUISHED the Earldom of Richmond in favour of John de Montfort, it was the first time a Montfort had held the Earldom, though John's father had possessed the Lordship of the Richmond Honour. It was 1372 and John was by then in his early thirties. He was born in France but when only three years old he was taken to England and spent his childhood very much under the watchful eye of Edward III. The King was his guardian under the arrangement made when John's father was killed in the early days of the civil war and his exiled mother came to England with her children. As a little boy, Montfort lived mostly in the household of Queen Philippa and, as he grew up, he spent much of his time with Henry Duke of Lancaster, accompanying him on a campaign in 1356-7 involving the siege of Rennes.

In these early years of his life, John de Montfort had some personal servants but, for income, he had to rely on hand-outs from King Edward. He had inherited his father's claim to the Dukedom of Brittany and to the County of Montfort l'Amaury and, though that Montfort area had been confiscated from his father in 1341, the French King had agreed that John could take possession. For twenty years, King Edward had his lieutenants maintaining an administration in Brittany but John had come of age by 1362 and, as there was then no legal justification for this arrangement to continue, he was allowed to return to the Duchy. In that year, John was married to the King's daughter Mary on the understanding that, should the marriage prove childless, the title would revert to the Crown. The wedding established a connection between the English Royal Family and the Montforts but, as might be expected, it did not please the French King. However, the marriage was to end only two months later with Mary's death.

After the death of his daughter, the King became reconciled to the need for John to return to the Duchy but he was not prepared to let him go without laying down a number of conditions. These covered several political, financial and legal matters and included agreement to a treaty of alliance, an acknowledgement of a debt of 64,000 nobles, and the handing over of two castles as surety for this sum. John had also to promise that he would not re-marry without Edward's consent but, taking into account the King's guardianship and the military support being provided, he was hardly in a position to protest against this or any of the other conditions.

He was returning to a Brittany divided by a major succession dispute. Although he laid claim to the Duchy as the late Duke's younger half-brother, another claimant was Jeanne de Penthièvre, a niece of the late Duke of Brittany and wife of Charles de Blois, a nephew of Philip VI of France. John had the support of his army and William Lord Latimer, the King's lieutenant who had remained not only to serve John but also to see that he fulfilled his financial obligations to the King. What John probably valued most of all was the advice and encouragement he received

71

from the Black Prince who was also able to promise additional troops. The Prince had tried to solve the disputed Brittany succession by proposing a partitioning of the Duchy between the two claimants but his efforts had foundered largely because of Jeanne de Penthièvre's intractability. The result of this defiance was the siege and battle of Auray, in which Charles de Blois was killed, and later the Treaty of Guérande in which the competing ducal families were at last brought to terms. It contained a settlement which satisfied Jeanne de Penthièvre and acknowledged that John de Montfort was the rightful successor to the Dukedom.

Despite his acceptance, John was placed in an unenviable position. On the one hand he knew well his obligations to Edward III and the control the English King had over his actions. On the other hand, he needed to come to an agreement with Charles V, King of France. To pay homage to Charles was not easy without upsetting Edward but, in the end, a simplified form of homage was performed in Paris which John felt able to accept "as it was performed in the manner and form in which it used to be offered and rendered by his ancestors". The French King accepted the form of homage rather than drive John back into the hands of Edward III. Despite this arranged homage, John's problem remained that he must give priority to the interests of his own subjects in the Duchy and improve his government yet contend with two powerful sovereigns who were at war with each other.[44]

John's friendship and dependence on the Black Prince was to result in a treaty of alliance agreed between the two in 1365 which promised John much valued support. A year later, he married the Prince's stepdaughter Joan Holland but, as he had not first consulted Edward III, the wedding was frowned on by the King and given only luke-warm approval. In 1369, John's position became more difficult following an appeal by the noblemen of Gascony to the French Parliament, which set off renewed preparations for war between England and France. Edward III again adopted the title of King of France, troops were mobilised and alliances negotiated. The English King then put pressure on King Charles of Navarre to form an alliance and, though an abortive Anglo-Navarrese treaty resulted, it had little support from John of

Gaunt. Sandwiched between the Anglo-French combatants, John de Montfort did his best for the next two years to preserve the independence of his Duchy but his commitments to Edward III were such that, in the end, he was to have little alternative but to favour the English camp.

By 1372, the English influence in Northern France had begun to wane as did John's support from the noblemen of the Duchy, though they were at one with him that the integrity of the Duchy should be maintained. John's weakness was that he had misjudged his subjects who placed little trust in the English and believed that favouring the French would be more to their advantage. During 1369 and 1372 John's relations with the French King had been superficially polite but the opinion that he was an English sympathiser had gained strength. A major problem had been pressure from French sympathisers to canonise de Blois which, if adopted, would have labelled John a murderer. At this stage, it is likely that, had the French chosen to do so, they could have attached Brittany firmly to the French Crown. What prevented this was Charles V's failure to appease the Penthièvre family who still retained their claim to the right of succession to the Duchy and insisted on independence.

John was then put under pressure by Edward III to complete an Anglo-Breton treaty of alliance and, being well aware of the strengthening French position, John now recognised the increasing danger that he might lose his Duchy. Perhaps as a form of insurance, he asked that any alliance should give him possession of the Richmond estates with their valued income. This was agreed by Edward and a treaty was finally completed in July 1372. At the same time, John was granted the Richmond Earldom and the Lordship of the Honour which had been relinquished by Gaunt.

In October, English troops landed in Brittany to support John de Montfort's own army which by then was greatly weakened, but the French had already taken Poitou and the presence of the English soldiers not only served to confirm John's double dealing, they arrived too late to remedy his position. By the end of

April in the following year, John had little alternative but flight to England and, when he presented himself at Edward's court in May 1373 his sorry plight as a landless and poverty-stricken exile stirred the King to pity and prompted thoughts of revenge.

Gaunt was about to cross the channel to Calais with another expedition and the exiled John de Montfort was encouraged to join him. The plan was to give aid to the few remaining English garrisons but, harried by French troops, Gaunt changed his plan and began moving southwards. At this stage, Gaunt temporarily quarrelled with John who decided to leave the expedition and pay a brief visit to Brittany, though this proved of little benefit to his popularity. His affairs in Brittany were still being directed by lieutenants whose main problem was to defend the remaining Anglo-Breton garrisons, now becoming increasingly isolated. Defending Brest was particularly important and ducal resources there were exhausted. John's financial state had by then become so difficult that he had to mortgage his Richmond income in order to pay the wages of his troops.

Though further efforts were made to strengthen the garrisons, negotiations for another Anglo-French truce were in progress and, though John was not asked to take part, a truce was signed in 1375 which, for a time, put an end to further fighting. By the beginning of 1377, a revival of the war seemed inevitable but the death of Edward III ended all immediate plans for a further expedition into France. The heir to the English throne, Richard II, was only ten years old when he succeeded. He was crowned King at a Coronation ceremony organised by Gaunt in his capacity as Steward of England, and attended by John de Montfort, Earl of Richmond. There followed a period of several years during which John was involved in a to-and-fro situation as between England and Brittany. He was said to be in an impoverished state and in exchange for his castle in Brest, which he delivered to King Richard, he was given several manors in England.

A development in John's favour came with a build-up of Breton resistance to French interference in the internal running of the Duchy and it was not surprising when, in 1379, a coalition of Breton lords, clerics and townsmen, many of them supporters of Jeanne de Penthièvre who lent her own tacit approval, made an appeal for John's return. Envoys were sent from Brittany to England and agreement reached for John's return with a promise from Edward III of support from an army of 4,000 men. When word of this reached the French King he decided his best course was to await events and negotiate rather than attack the Duchy.

John took some time to become fully convinced that the Bretons were sincere in their wish for his return, but he finally left Southampton in July 1379 and on landing in Brittany he was given a genuine welcome. Even the Constable of France, who then controlled a number of forts in north-eastern Brittany, made no move to prevent his return. Once back in the Duchy John was faced again with the perpetual conflict of ducal allegiance but this time the conditions were different. He had not regained his position because of English aid, or for that matter with help from the French, but at the wish of the seigneurs and people of Brittany. Yet he still had to respect English demands and provide a refuge in Brittany for any force sent to France. On the other hand, the death of Charles V of France and the accession of Charles VI opened the way for new negotiations with the French and John was able to use the good offices of the Count of Flanders and even Jeanne de Penthièvre to come to an understanding which resulted in the signing in 1381 of the second Treaty of Guérande. It involved paying homage to the French King and accepting an indemnity liability of 200,000 francs. Though the Treaty restored legal relations with France, his homage to Charles VI did not please the English and resulted in the confiscation of John's Richmond titles.

Relations with the English deteriorated further when they continued to insist on retaining Brest. John's primary aim was the full reoccupation of the Duchy which he largely achieved but the port and surrounding area of Brest were always important to the English and, apart from a ten-year period between 1362 and 1372, the castle, town and immediate environments continued to remain in the hands of English or Anglo-Breton troops.

Although John had ceded Brest during his exile, he laid siege to it without success during 1386-7 and it was not until 1397 that it was eventually returned to the Duchy by Richard II.

Whatever the Duke's personal feelings, his subjects made it plain that they did not want an English alliance and preferred a subordinate position under France on the understanding that Breton affairs were a domestic concern. John's wife Joan Holland, who had been allowed to return to the Duchy from England, died in 1384. Her death released John from his personal tie with England and allowed him to use his new freedom for political ends. Jeanne de Penthièvre also died in the same year leaving her son John de Bretagne as a claimant for the ducal title, though he remained a hostage in English hands until a ransom was finally agreed.

In the last ten years of his rule, John de Montfort had to contend not only with problems arising from the continuing Anglo-French war but also with domestic opposition from the Penthièvres and Olivier de Clisson, a long-term opponent who had been an ambassador in the French court. Yet despite these difficulties, some indelicate diplomatic dealings and a variable foreign policy, John managed to maintain a degree of independence for the Duchy which brought a welcome period of economic prosperity. There was a growing confidence not only in Anglo-Breton relations but also in Breton friendship with France. In the spring of 1398, he visited England for the first time since 1379 and he was re-invested with the Earldom and Honour of Richmond as well as taking up his stall as a Knight of the Garter.

At the beginning of November in the year 1399, John de Montfort, Duke of Brittany and Earl of Richmond, died in his Duchy. So ended the life of a man given the immensely difficult task of ruling a small country which became a buffer state between the two major contestants of the Hundred Years War. Tied very much to England which was the country of his upbringing, he was obliged to show respect for the Kingdom of France yet work to maintain independence for his subjects in the Duchy. In the words of his biographer Michael Jones, "the diplomatic and military relations of Brittany with England and France between 1364 and 1399 were influenced largely by the actions and aspirations of one man, John de Montfort." What is certain is that he played a major role in the conduct of the Hundred Years War during the latter part of the 14th century.

Though the titles and the Honour of Richmond were returned to John before his death, the revenue from the Honour of Richmond had been granted for a term to John's second wife Joan. This arrangement was then cancelled because of John's alliance with France and the benefits of the Honour were given to Richard II's queen Anne who proceeded to lease her castles and other Richmondshire possessions to a Mr. Henry Fitzhugh for twelve years. She died in 1394 and the King then granted her possessions to the Archbishop of Canterbury, Edward Earl of Rutland and John Earl of Salisbury. John's third marriage was to Joanna of Navarre and when a son and heir was born, the third of eight children, fears that Jeanne de Penthièvre's son, John of Bretagne, would succeed to the Duchy were allayed.

King Richard II was murdered in Pontefract Castle in February 1400, and the lease to Henry Fitzhugh having expired, the new King Henry IV agreed the lease of the Castles of Richmond and Bowes and the remainder of Richmondshire to Robert Neville, Lord of Westmorland. Neville was never granted the Earldom however and, on his death, possession of the Honour passed to John Duke of Bedford. The long and troublesome connection between Brittany and Richmond was broken at last.[45]

CHAPTER 12

John of Lancaster
Duke of Bedford and Earl of Richmond
(b.1389 - d.1435)

JOHN OF THE HOUSE of Lancaster who became Duke of
Bedford and Earl of Richmond was a man of royal blood and
an understudy for the Kings of his time. His elder brother was
that great warrior Henry V whose reign of only nine years was
certainly one of spectacular achievement and included the great
English victory at Agincourt. It was during Henry's demanding
campaign to conquer France, and in the years immediately
following his death, that Bedford's name came to the fore, firstly
as Guardian and Protector of the Kingdom of England, and then
as Regent of France.

He was third son of Henry of Bolingbroke and Mary Bohun
and they gave him the name of John after his grandfather John
of Gaunt. Though Henry was rarely at home to see his family,

Mary is known to have been a gracious, gay and lovable mother to her children but she died in childbirth when John was only five. The children were then sent to live in Bytham Castle under the watchful eye of the Bohun grandmother, the Countess of Hereford. Despite his absences, Bolingbroke saw to it that his children were properly educated and John grew up with a great love of literature

During the reign of the unpredictable Richard II, it became apparent that Bolingbroke was one of the King's critics, and he was imprisoned for ten years. Yet the King took care to protect the children and John spent a happy period at Waltham. After John of Gaunt's death however, Richard alienated many of his subjects and certainly John's elder brother Henry by seizing the estates of the Duchy of Lancaster at a time when property was sacrosanct. When Bolingbroke then claimed his inheritance, he received such widespread support that, when Richard eventually returned from dealing with unrest in Ireland, he was trapped into renouncing his throne and sent as a prisoner to the Tower.

On the 13th October 1399, ten-year-old John escorted his brother Henry to Westminster Abbey where their father was crowned. He was an astute man of dynamic energy and, facing many problems in the early days of his reign, he made full use of his family in filling the great offices of state. John was only fourteen when he was appointed custodian of Berwick and Warden of the East March which entailed fortifying Berwick as well as keeping the peace in the eastern border area. He had been knighted on the eve of his father's coronation and, having received the Order of the Garter, he was made Constable of England, an office of which the Earl of Northumberland had just been deprived. As John grew old enough to take a larger share of his responsibilities his duties as Warden of the East March became more onerous. He had the support of the experienced Ralph Neville, Earl of Westmorland, from whom John learnt many lessons of government which stood him in good stead in later years. Yet his role as Warden in East March continued to be an unenviable one with discontent in the border area and an uprising centred in York led by Richard Scrope and Thomas Mowbray.

As March Warden, he had been given all the Northumbrian Percy properties in Calais, as well as those in York, Carlisle and Newcastle. Yet the income provided for John did not allow sufficient to pay his troops and not surprisingly, they became mutinous. His problems were only relieved by borrowing money from a friend, Lord Furnival. Eventually, more money was provided and he was able to continue keeping the peace as best he could until his father died in 1413. Soon afterwards, having complained again that he had to use his own money to maintain the King's defences, he resigned the Wardenship and surrendered his Northumbrian estates.

It was in August 1415 that the new King Henry V made his first expedition into France and the great battle of Agincourt was to follow in the autumn of that year. Henry was to spend most of the next five years completing his French conquests and he was away from England for very long periods. There were long costly campaigns and sieges which not only stretched the financial resources of England but cooled some of the martial ardour which had built up in the aftermath of Agincourt. During the King's absence, John was appointed to act firstly as Guardian and then Protector of the Kingdom of England. In 1417, thinking to take advantage of the King's absence, the Scots laid siege to Roxburgh and Berwick but John marshalled his forces and went northwards with 6,000 men to break the siege. He was joined by the forces of the Duke of Exeter as well as those of the Earls of Northumberland and Westmorland. Needless to say the Scots soon retreated.

One by one, every stronghold in Normandy was taken by King Henry and his men. There had been a reconciliation between the two opposing French factions, the Burgundians and the Dauphinists, but when the hot-headed supporters of the Dauphin murdered the Duke of Burgundy it did much to cement an alliance between Burgundy and the English. In 1419, John went to France where he accompanied the King to Paris, but two years later he was back in England and, though he resumed his office of Lieutenant, he had to return to France as an escort for the Queen who was joining her husband in Normandy.

In May 1420, Charles VI of France signed the Treaty of Troyes in which Henry V was acknowledged as being heir to the French Kingdom, and as Regent in the meantime. As part of this arrangement, Henry then proceeded to marry Charles's daughter Catherine and she bore him a son, destined to be heir to the throne. Two years later however, in the full tide of power and success, Henry's life came to an end for he died in 1422 probably of dysentery contracted in the fields of war.[46]

With Henry's death, Catherine's baby son was proclaimed King of England and, when the death of the French King Charles VI was announced two months later, the infant Henry VI was also named as King of France, apparently without dispute. Sooner or later however, with the Dauphin ruling most of Southern France except Gascony, the whole concept of the Treaty of Troyes was bound to lead to trouble, particularly because it allowed for France to be ruled by an infant English King.

Though for a time the dual monarchy worked reasonably well, it was dependent on the support of the Burgundians, that is to say those Frenchmen who preferred to be governed by the Duke of Burgundy and his allies rather than the Dauphin. As Henry had planned, his brother John, Duke of Bedford was appointed Regent of France and Commander in Chief. Though John was probably less brilliant than Henry, he had become a respected military man with a reputation of being clear-sighted, brave and resourceful; qualities which came to be needed in the troubled times which lay ahead. Moreover, he was a man who genuinely loved the French and their country. He was fortunate in having the support of the Earl of Salisbury, a great general and professional soldier and also of Richard Beauchamp, Earl of Warwick, an experienced soldier who was regarded as one of the pillars of the Anglo-French state.

There was little sign of an end to the long years of conflict between France and England and, though the Dauphinists had the more financial backing, the English with their archers continued to show their superiority in battle. In 1423 the English and Burgundians reaffirmed their alliance and a marriage was arranged between John and the Duke of Burgundy's sister Anne.

Though this could be described as a political match it was nevertheless to prove a very happy marriage despite reports that the lady was "as plain as an owl".

Increasingly, the English and Burgundian forces joined in raids and skirmishes though in Guyenne the English had to fight for themselves. In 1424, John felt sufficiently confident to strike south and, at Verneuil, he met the main body of the Dauphinist army which was supported by some 6,000 Scots. The Scots were animated by their hatred of the English and, though the French retreated after much hand-to-hand fighting, Douglas and Buchan with the other Scottish chieftains forced a further battle only to find that they had no answer to the English archers. They were nearly all destroyed by the storm of English arrows.

In England, Humphrey, Duke of Gloucester was acting as Regent and Protector of the child-King in the absence of John of Lancaster but he was a poor statesman and his marital affairs were to drive a new wedge between England and Burgundy. He became associated with and subsequently married Jacqueline, Princess of Hainault, a lady who had deserted an unsatisfactory husband and settled in England. Humphrey then proceeded to call himself Count of Hainault, Holland and Zeeland, which territories he then invaded with a force of 4,000 men. The invasion was a disaster and Humphrey hastily returned to England where he continued to make further trouble. His actions caused deep offence to the Duke of Burgundy who wanted Jacqueline's territories for himself. Humphrey created so much unrest in England that Henry Beaufort, Bishop of Winchester, pleaded to John to return and take over the Regency in a situation which could well have developed into civil war. When John came he found it necessary to stay for fifteen months and to repair the divisions caused by Humphrey's administration.

Fortunately, the Dauphinists did not take advantage of John's absence but the damaged relations with Burgundy were made the worse when the Duke of Brittany detached himself from the English and gave favour to the French. On his return, John did his best to make English rule popular but he was so desperately short of money to finance the armed struggle with the Dauphines that he was obliged to impose heavy taxation on his subjects. Particularly high taxes were imposed on those in Normandy and their lives were made the worse by gangs of highwaymen, as well as by deserters from the English garrisons, who plundered and looted the countryside.

Whilst in England, John had tried with little success to obtain money for fresh troops but the endless war with France was becoming unpopular and when he returned he took with him only a pitifully small new army. In an effort to restore good relations, he then went with his wife to visit Duke Philip of Burgundy. By then, John's task was made easier because Humphrey had abandoned Jacqueline and arranged for his marriage to be declared invalid; apparently he had tired of her and wished to marry her lady-in-waiting. By the end of 1427 the alliance with Burgundy had been restored.

The English continued to be restricted by lack of money however and it was clear that, as the conquered territories were taxed to the hilt, they could not provide more. John sent Salisbury to England to plead again for help and eventually Salisbury's persuasion brought aid to the extent of £24,000 though he had lent part from his own resources. A difference of opinion then arose between John and Salisbury as to their future objectives. Salisbury's priority was an assault to capture Orléans but John felt that such an attack would be against the rules of chivalry and a breach of a previous treaty. Yet despite his powerful position as Regent, John decided to let Salisbury have his way but, during the army's attack on Orléans, Salisbury was fatally injured. His place was taken by the Earl of Suffolk, but the walls of Orléans remained unbreached.

It was then that the situation in France became transformed with the appearance of a saintly peasant girl who became known as Joan of Arc, and as the Angel of Deliverance. She told the Dauphin that she had seen a vision and was "sent on the part of God to aid you and the Kingdom". Inspired by Joan, a new army was formed and, led by her, the besieged town of Orléans was relieved and the English attackers dispersed. It was the start of a French revival and, by her presence, Joan of Arc did much to restore the morale of the French troops and their leaders resulting in a weakening of the English dominance. At Joan's instigation, a new French King, Charles VII, was crowned at Reims and came to be accepted as head of the French army.

Joan now felt that her mission was exhausted and she asked to be allowed to go home, but the French captains were all too aware of her value to the French cause. In an advance on Paris, she was severely wounded and the French had to retreat. To her troops, her image as an invincible leader was tarnished and the attitude to Joan of both the Church and the French Court was changing. Their feeling was that she was intent on serving God rather than the Church and France rather than the Orléans party. When in May 1430 she led an army of only 600 men in an attempt to support the town of Compiègne she was taken prisoner by the Burgundians, and sold for a paltry sum to the rejoicing English who held her as a prisoner of war.

To John and his army, Joan of Arc was regarded as a witch and to the ecclesiastics she was a sorceress and heretic. Yet it was not easy to frame a charge against her and for a whole year she suffered inquisition by the Church which pursued her for heresy. Though her fate hung in the balance, the ungrateful French King Charles lifted not a finger to help her. In the end she was declared a relapsed heretic, condemned to the fire and burnt at the stake by Warwick's soldiers in the market place of Rouen.

Throughout the length and breadth of France Joan of Arc is regarded as a national heroine but in her lifetime her contemporaries regarded her in a very different light. The landed gentry detested her because she was a peasant girl, the church was bitterly hostile and it was extraordinary that King Charles who had gained so much from her presence, did nothing to help in her time of need. It may be that John could have saved her but, at the time she was taken prisoner, he was no longer Regent of Normandy and had relinquished his powers as head of the government. Joan of Arc perished in May, 1431 and the impetus to the Dauphinists which she had generated soon ground to a halt.

The English continued to need money desperately to retain their position but it was not forthcoming. In November of that year, John decided to play what he thought was his trump card and he arranged for the young Henry to be crowned King of France at a grand ceremony in Paris. Henry rode on a white charger through the icy streets and was given a great welcome by a population obviously expectant that his arrival in the city would bring an end to their misery but the ceremony of anointing Henry as King and the banquet which followed were badly managed and ended in disaster with an attack by a mob of starving Parisians. There was indeed little apparent support in the rest of France for the young King's enthronement and the English position continued to deteriorate.

At the end of 1432, John's wife, Anne of Burgundy fell ill and died. Despite his sorrow, John engaged in a further marriage, this time to Jacquetta of Luxembourg but his wedding angered Duke Philip of Burgundy as it was arranged without his consent and Jacquetta was the daughter of one of his richest nobles. Though he married twice, John had no children.

In the summer of 1434, the Norman peasants began an uprising against the English garrisons and as winter approached conditions for the starving people of Paris were appalling. By then, John had become seriously ill and he died in Rouen the following year. As Duke of Bedford and Earl of Richmond, he had served France as Regent during an important period of its history. He has been described as the most outstanding soldier and statesman of his time and it is evident that, with his death, the English lost much of their military direction.[47]

In contrast to the English, the French finances were in good order and King Charles was able to spend large sums of money on military reform. In July 1449, he sent 30,000 troops into Normandy and gradually he took possession of all northern France with the exception of Calais. It was the end of the Hundred Years War, a war which bankrupted the English government and, in the end, fatally discredited the Lancastrian dynasty. In its aftermath came the domestic but bitter feud known as the Wars of the Roses.

CHAPTER 13

Edmund Tudor (b.1430 - d.1456) and Margaret Beaufort (b.1443 - d.1509) Earl and Duchess of Richmond

THOUGH THE TUDORS are regarded as an English dynasty, their founder was in fact a Welshman with the name of Owen Tudor. Though some doubt exists about his relationship with Catherine, widow of Henry V, he is thought to have married her, and they had two sons named Edmund and Jasper. The Tudors were Lancastrians and Edmund's father Owen was eventually to suffer execution by the Yorkists. Edmund was only six when his mother retired to the Abbey of Bermondsey and he and Jasper were placed in the charge of the Abbess of Barking where they remained until 1440. The Abbess then decided that her charges should be brought to the notice of the King Henry VI and this led to them being taken away to be educated. Of the two, it was Edmund who played the more important role in our history.

When Edmund grew up, he was well favoured by the King who kept him in his court and knighted him. In 1452, he was summoned to Parliament, declared to be legitimate and created Earl of Richmond. The Honour of Richmond had lapsed to the Crown after Bedford's death and, though Henry VI had kept it more or less in his hands, he had made many grants from the Honour of annuities, manors and lands. The Lordship of the Honour, including Richmond Castle, now passed to Edmund and, moreover, Henry continued to favour him with large grants as well as making him a member of the Privy Council. Probably with

86

the intention of nominating Edmund as his heir, the King instigated his marriage to Lady Margaret Beaufort, daughter of the Earl of Somerset. Margaret had previously been married at the tender age of six to John de la Pole but, at that age she never understood or recognised the significance of the ceremony and the marriage was subsequently dissolved. She was only twelve when she married Edmund and, after the wedding, the couple travelled down to Wales and took up residence in Pembrokeshire.

Margaret soon became pregnant and there seems little doubt that Edmund's wish to secure an heir and a life interest in Margaret's estate took priority over any concern for his wife's safety and well being. The marriage was soon to be cut short for, while acting as King Henry's lieutenant in the region, Edmund was captured by the Yorkists. Though he was later released, his health was impaired and he died the following year having succumbed to an outbreak of plague. He was buried initially at Carmarthen in South Wales but, after the dissolution of the monasteries, his remains were removed to the choir of St David's cathedral.

Lady Margaret, widowed and six months pregnant, was able to avoid the plague but as she was quite unable to travel, she took refuge with her brother-in-law Jasper at Pembroke Castle. It was there on 28th January, 1457 that she gave birth to a son she named Henry who was destined to become Earl of Richmond and eventually Henry VII King of England. It was a difficult birth for a girl not yet fourteen and it left her with lasting physical damage which prevented her from having any further children. Only a year after young Henry's birth, arrangements were completed for her to wed the Duke of Buckingham's son Henry Stafford and this proved to be a successful marriage which provided a long and harmonious relationship lasting fourteen years.

Margaret Beaufort, Countess of Richmond, was a woman possessing both courage and foresight, shrewd in her decisions and very intent on preserving the life and inheritance of her son Henry. She herself had some title to the throne but she was happy to abdicate this to her son bearing in mind the practical impossibility for a queen to reign at that time. Her grandfather had been the bastard son of John of Gaunt and his mistress Catherine Swynford but, as already mentioned in a previous chapter, the two were married after the death of Gaunt's wife Constance, apparently with the Pope's blessing, and Gaunt originated the name Beaufort which he gave to all the children of his union with Catherine Swynford.

In 1453, Henry VI suffered the first of the bouts of insanity which were to recur at intervals throughout the rest of his life but, shortly afterwards, Margaret the Queen gave birth to a male heir. Though the King recovered from this early bout, it was necessary to appoint a Protector during the period that he was unfit to govern. The Queen was to prove a powerful force in politics and Henry's ineffective nature placed him very much under her control. She was a quick-tempered lady, courageous and passionate both in her likes and dislikes. She had a strong dislike for the Duke of York but could not prevent his appointment as Protector though he was soon dismissed in 1455 when the King was once again able to govern.

The Wars of the Roses began when the Duke of York led a rebellion at St Albans against the King which triggered off an entrenched hatred and suspicion existing between the Yorkists and the Lancastrians. In the north particularly, the bitter opposition between the important Percy and Neville families could only lead to confrontation and bloodshed. War historians have rightly pointed out the connection between the Hundred Years War and the internal struggle which followed in England. In France, English noblemen and men-at-arms had become accustomed to fighting as a way of life and, as Philippe de Commynes commented, "Their fathers and their followers pillaged and destroyed the Kingdom of France" whereas in the Wars of the Roses "they all killed each other".

Though the Queen raised an army which defeated the Yorkists at Ludlow, a Lancastrian army was later defeated at Northampton but this was followed by a reconciliation whereby Henry continued as monarch but recognised the Duke of York as his heir. Henry also seems to have acquiesced in the disinheriting of his son but not so the Queen who, having eluded capture at Northampton, had sought refuge at Harlech Castle. She went north to Berwick and, having raised a new army, moved down into England to do battle. When news of this reached the Duke, he hurried north with Warwick's father Salisbury and a small force, committing themselves to battle without waiting for reinforcements. The two armies met at Wakefield and not only were the Yorkists heavily defeated but both the Duke and Salisbury were killed.

The year 1461 was the last in Henry VI's first period of reign; and it was nine years before he was able to return. In February, the Queen marched on London and overcame Warwick and his Yorkists at St Albans where the King was restored to his wife. She expected to be able to march on into London but the citizens were fearful that her northern troops would resort to looting and the gates of London remained closed. However, they allowed entry to the Duke of York's son Edward with his army as well as the mauled troops Warwick was able to bring from St Albans. Edward then proceeded in triumph to St Paul's where he was acclaimed as King, and later to Westminster Hall and the Abbey where he took his seat on the throne. Though Edward was crowned King later that year, this was not a coronation but a recognition of his title by the soldiers and citizens of the capital.

Henry and his wife could do little but withdraw and went to York with the prisoners they had captured at St Albans. The Lancastrians re-formed but Edward did not dally long in London and he was soon moving his army northwards on the heels of his opponents. It was at Towton, not many miles from York, that the two armies met in a major and bloody engagement fought on a plateau in snowstorm conditions. The Yorkists were at first heavily outnumbered and seemed destined for defeat but, with the arrival of reinforcements, they eventually routed the Lancastrians and massacred many of the Queen's soldiers. Henry and his Queen were able to escape to Scotland with their son, but this was a battle which placed the Yorkists firmly in power for a while despite pockets of opposition which remained, particularly in Northumberland.

These were troubled times for the Lancastrian Lady Margaret Beaufort, and her husband Stafford decided that their best course would be to make peace with the Yorkists to protect Margaret's estates. The Duke of Buckingham had settled four hundred marks worth of land on the Staffords but their main source of landed wealth was derived from Lady Margaret's estates which enabled them to enjoy an aristocratic life rather than a gentry lifestyle. Henry Stafford had fought at Towton on the Lancastrian side but he was able to obtain a general pardon for both himself and his wife though the price to be paid was a long term separation for Lady Margaret from her son who was placed under the wardship of William Lord Herbert in Pembroke Castle.

It must be said of the new King that he did his best to effect a reconciliation with the Lancastrians. He realised that, at the crucial Battle of Towton, the majority of the English peerage had remained loyal to Henry VI and he was intent on securing the long term future of his dynasty. To this end, he made overtures to the Beaufort family and began to build up a friendly relation-ship with Henry Beaufort whose younger brother he released from prison. Yet his efforts were undermined when Henry Beaufort suddenly broke away and defected to Scotland. This was a major blow to Edward who was furious and took it as a personal insult. It resulted in a renewal of divisions between the two sides and, when Henry Beaufort was subsequently captured at Hexham, he was summarily executed. This signalled a perma-nent breach with the Beaufort family and, as Stafford became more and more associated with the Yorkist cause, Lady Margaret found she was being cut off from other members of the Beaufort family.

There is no doubt that, throughout these traumatic years of the Wars of the Roses, Margaret's over-riding purpose was to ensure her son's well-being, preserve his title to the throne and safeguard her own estates. Whilst her role as Stafford's wife was very much a supportive one, she benefited from her husband's connections as he increased his alignment with royal policy. On the other hand, Stafford benefited from the large income which her paternal inheritance and the dower portion of the Earldom of Richmond provided. The Richmond Earldom had lapsed in 1461, the year Edward IV was crowned King, and the Honour of Richmond had been passed to the King's brother, the Duke of Clarence. It was important that, as an act of goodwill, Edward had safeguarded Margaret's dower rights and, though it became clear that the King was cautious in his patronage of Stafford, Margaret and her husband were able to obtain the Beaufort manor at Woking, a substantial manor house with access to the Thames.

In 1469, the War flared up once more when Richard Neville, Earl of Warwick, who had been a leading Yorkist, changed sides and staged a rebellion against the King. Lord Herbert was called upon by King Edward to assist him in putting down this new rebellion and Herbert marched out of Raglan with a formidable array of young Welshmen to support the King's forces. The two armies met at Edgecote but in the battle which followed Warwick's men inflicted a heavy defeat on the King's army. Lord Herbert was taken prisoner and subsequently executed and the King was captured and placed in the custody of Neville at Warwick Castle. Lord Herbert and his wife Anne Devereux, who were in charge of the young Henry Tudor, had taken him to Edgecote but, to Margaret Beaufort's great relief, Henry had been safely led away from the battlefield and taken to the Hertfordshire home of Lord Ferrers, Herbert's brother-in-law.

Despite these uncertain times, Lady Margaret was prompted to re-enter the political scene. With the King a virtual prisoner of Warwick, she began negotiations with the Duke of Clarence to ensure that the benefits of the Honour of Richmond would ultimately pass to her son Henry. It was a dangerous move because Clarence was one of King Edward's captors and though he was subsequently pardoned and released, Margaret's approach clearly angered Edward IV who was soon allowed to regain freedom of movement.

In the end, Lady Margaret came to an arrangement with Clarence, but her husband's allegiance to the King was now under scrutiny. As a test, Edward called upon him to take part in dealing with a series of popular risings in Lincolnshire which resulted in the execution of a member of Lady Margaret's family, Richard Lord Welles. This was to say the least a distasteful task for him to perform and it revealed the ruthlessness and cruelty of Edward IV. Stafford had then to join the King's troops in dealing with an insurrection stirred up in Yorkshire by the Nevilles and afterwards move rapidly to Exeter to try and intercept fleeing insurgents.

The Earl of Warwick had gone with his supporters to France where he received support from Louis XI who engineered an alliance with Margaret of Anjou. This made possible an invasion of England at a time when the King was again concerned with uprisings in the north of the country. He was ill-prepared for warfare with Warwick whose forces landed in the west country and gained a rapid accumulation of fresh support. Edward had been outwitted and was forced to flee to Holland leaving Warwick able to release Henry VI from the Tower and restore him to the throne.

The period of Lancastrian Restoration which followed made Margaret and Stafford look again at the future of her son Henry Tudor. At that time, they were still concerned to reach an agreement with Clarence about the passing of Richmond's Honour and also to discuss the future role the young Henry could play in healing the divisions of war. Henry himself was brought to London with Jasper and given an audience with the King but the return of Henry VI to the throne was a brief one.

Having been provided with money and ships by the Duke of Burgundy and with the support of Clarence, Edward returned to England and marched on London to regain the crown. In April 1471, he led his troops to do battle with Warwick and another fierce struggle ensued in a swirling mist at Barnet. Warwick was killed and though Stafford had decided to fight with the Yorkists, and survived, he received wounds from which he later died.

Edward's campaign came to its climax on the 4th May, 1471 when the Lancastrians and Yorkists faced each other at

Tewkesbury. The Lancastrians had been divided in their approach to this encounter for Edmund, Duke of Somerset wanted to attack the Yorkists while others were against any immediate engagement and advised waiting until the arrival of Jasper Tudor with reinforcements. In the end Somerset's reputation and standing prevailed but the result was a crushing defeat for the Lancastrians and disaster for the Beaufort family. Henry VI's son Prince Edward as well as Somerset's brother John Beaufort were amongst the dead and Somerset with several other leaders was taken prisoner and later beheaded. Queen Margaret arrived too late to save the Lancastrian cause and had intended to link up with Jasper Tudor in Wales but she was caught hiding in Little Malvern Priory and taken by the Yorkists. Edward's triumph was complete and he returned to London on 21st May, the day on which Henry VI was put to death in the Tower by Edward's order.

As the King consolidated his authority after Tewkesbury and began to punish those who had supported his enemies, Lady Margaret Beaufort was able to make use of Stafford's support for the King at Barnet and safeguard her mother and some of her family. Henry Tudor and Jasper were holding out in Pembroke Castle and, though there was a possibility of a pardon from King Edward, Margaret knew only too well of his breaches of faith and advised her son to leave the country. He took her advice and with Jasper, escaped from Pembroke to Tenby in South Wales from where they set sail for France. Though they were blown off course, they eventually arrived in Brittany. It was the start of a long exile for Henry and a considerable question mark hung over his political future.

Margaret's further widowhood was brief and despite the deep affection she had for Stafford, she soon married again, to Thomas Lord Stanley, a member of a prominent family and a steward in Edward IV's royal household. As events were to prove, it was largely a marriage of convenience, but it offered Margaret valuable protection and an enhanced influence in the Yorkist court. It also gave her the opportunity to negotiate the return of her son from exile. Though Edward IV adopted a conciliatory attitude to

Henry Tudor's return, Margaret still had doubts about Edward's intentions and these doubts were conveyed to Henry who decided to stay in France. A new and unexpected opportunity to return was to arise however when, on the 9th April 1483, Edward IV died and Richard, Duke of Gloucester was crowned King.

Margaret now sought an alliance with the new King Richard for her son's return using the Duke of Buckingham as an intermediary but this failed, apparently because Richard did not completely trust Margaret's husband Stanley. Moreover, Margaret began to realise the extent of opposition building up against Richard and she took the calculated step not only of throwing in her lot with those who were plotting against the King but of encouraging her son Henry Tudor to claim the throne of England. It is not widely recognised that she took part in an attempt to rescue the princes in the Tower and, though this failed, there was an increasing build-up of opposition to Richard. With Lady Margaret's encouragement, Buckingham then led a rebellion in Wales and south-west England but this failed. When Margaret's role in the conspiracy came to light it placed her in considerable personal danger and she was only saved by the fact that her husband Lord Stanley had remained loyal to King Richard during the crisis. Although she was spared attainder she forfeited her right to all titles and estates and Stanley was instructed to keep his wife confined in some secret place without her household servants. The time had come for Henry Tudor's return from exile and the story of Richard's death in battle, the crowning of Henry as King of England and the reinstatement of Margaret Beaufort is told in the following chapter.

A major factor in the life of Margaret Beaufort was the extent of her properties. Long before her death, her estates had become a major source of income underpinning her religious patronage and her subsequent educational foundations. The development of her properties was based not only on inheritances from her father and mother but to a considerable extent from the marriage market. Apart from her marriages to Edmund Tudor and Henry Stafford, she derived a considerable release of capital on the death

Margaret Beaufort.

of Thomas Lord Stanley in 1504 even though, at the time of his death, they were living apart. Over the years, Margaret became an efficient administrator and developed her own system of estate management. As a great landowner she was well aware of her obligations to charity but, whereas she was capable of great acts of sensitivity and kindness, her estate management could at times be harsh and severe.

In her later years Margaret devoted much of her time to religious and educational patronage. She had a particular interest in Oxford and Cambridge universities, particularly the latter, and she became the greatest in a line of female benefactors. Her first major university benefaction was the foundation of an endowed lectureship in theology at each of the two universities, the modern Lady Margaret Professorships. At Cambridge, she had a local presence as the Honour of Richmond included properties and land in the surrounding villages. It was at Cambridge University that she came under the influence of John Fisher, Chancellor of the University and Bishop of Rochester. She donated to the completion of Christ's College, previously known as God's House, and instituted a series of foundations which earned her a lasting name as a benefactor. Perhaps her greatest monument is St John's College, on the walls of which her portrait hangs to this day. She died on 29th June 1509, little more than two months after her only son for whose welfare and success she devoted much of her life. She has been described as one of the few worthy and high-minded members of the aristocracy in an essentially selfish and cruel age.[48]

CHAPTER 14

Henry Tudor (b.1457 - d.1509)
Earl of Richmond and
King of England

HENRY TUDOR WAS the only Earl of Richmond to become King. He was born in 1457 in Pembroke Castle where his mother Margaret Beaufort had taken refuge while the Yorkists were in power and it was in Wales that Henry spent his difficult boyhood years. His father had died two months before he was born and he was placed under the care of his uncle Jasper Tudor. Henry became Earl of Richmond from birth and, as heir to the House of Lancaster, his life was always in danger from the Yorkists. From the remarkable Margaret Beaufort, he could trace his descent not only to Edward III but to Cadwallon and the old British Kings.

The Yorkist Edward IV became King in 1461 when Henry was only four and though at the time the Lancastrians held various castles in Wales, Harlech was surrendered in 1468 and Henry, who seems to have been there at the time, was made a prisoner in the castle. His guardianship was then taken over by Herbert, Duke of Pembroke but in 1470 Edward IV was driven from the throne and King Henry VI restored after nine years exile. The young Henry Tudor was then reclaimed by his uncle Jasper after which he was taken to London and presented to the King. Though exile and privation had been Henry's lot and had stamped themselves on his character, he is said to have possessed a wise and commanding mind and an amiable presence.

The Wars of the Roses continued unabated and when Edward IV returned to London after the Lancastrians were routed at Tewkesbury in one of the bloodiest of battles, King Henry VI was put to death by the Yorkists after being made captive in the Tower of London. In the same year, Edward Prince of Wales was also killed in battle and the young Henry Tudor, Earl of Richmond, then became head of the House of Lancaster. It soon became apparent that he was an object of jealousy to Edward IV who had regained the throne and it was clearly unsafe for him to remain in the country. It was in this situation and on the advice of his mother that Jasper took Henry to France.

Though Edward applied to the Duke of Brittany to have Henry returned to England, he was able to remain an exile in France for the whole of Edward's reign. In April 1483 King Edward contracted a fever and, on his death, the crown passed to his twelve year old son Prince Edward. There followed the well recorded imprisonment of Prince Edward with his younger brother by Edward's uncle, Richard Duke of Gloucester, the seizure of the throne by Richard and the subsequent death of the two young princes in the Tower of London.

The Duke of Buckingham was related to the Beauforts on his mother's side and Margaret Beaufort consulted him about the possibility of a marriage between her son Henry and Elizabeth, a daughter of King Edward, an arrangement which Buckingham agreed would surely bridge the gulf between the Lancastrians and the Yorkists. There is no doubt that Buckingham had done much to place Richard on the throne but, from being his chief supporter, he soon became his mortal foe, and planned a conspiracy against the King, as well as giving support to the succession of Henry, Earl of Richmond.

With the assistance of the Bishop of Ely, he organised a rebellion against Richard which would be aided by the landing of troops from Brittany. However, Richard was conscious of the danger of his position and stationed his army to withstand any attack. Although a general rising against the King took place in October 1483, it could not be developed because of a great flood of the

River Severn and storms at sea which prevented troops from landing. Henry Earl of Richmond intended to land from France and join with Buckingham's forces but the weather made this impossible and he returned to Brittany. Buckingham's uprising had then collapsed and he was captured by Richard's forces and executed at Salisbury on the 2nd of November. Many of his conspirators escaped however and took refuge in Brittany. On Christmas Day, 1483, they all congregated at Rennes Cathedral where they swore allegiance to Henry who, for his part, undertook to marry Princess Elizabeth as soon as he obtained the Crown.

Richard's reaction was to demand from the Duke of Brittany the surrender of Henry and the exile only saved himself by escaping to Anjou disguised as a page boy. Though opinion in England was gradually moving in his favour, his problem was to raise sufficient resources to build up an invasion force. With help from several sources including the French regency and the Earl of Oxford, he was able to equip half a dozen ships at Rouen and recruit 1,800 French mercenaries but hopes for further support rested on the Welsh and on the Stanleys whom he could approach through his mother, Margaret Beaufort, the Lady Stanley.

Henry was greatly alarmed by news that King Richard intended to marry Princess Elizabeth and this spurred him on to build up an invasion force without delay. From Wales came further offers of support and, on 7th August 1485, Henry landed at Milford Haven with what Richard referred to as "some beggarly Britons and faint-hearted Frenchmen."[49] Help from the Welsh was slow in coming but it gradually built up though, even with other well-wishers and eventual support from the Stanleys, Henry's force numbered only about 5,000 against Richard's army of some 10,000. Many of Richard's followers were suspicious of each other's loyalty however and this was to Henry's advantage. The opposing forces met at Bosworth Field and it is thought that Richard tried to win the day by killing Henry in personal combat. With a loyal squadron of his household, he swept through Henry's personal bodyguard striking down his standard bearer and engaging Sir John Cheyney, Henry's close attendant. At this point Richard's horse is said to have died under him and he was killed "fighting manfully in the press of his enemies".[50] With the timely arrival of Sir William Stanley's men, the Yorkists were overwhelmed and victory for Henry and his followers was then assured. Henry Earl of Richmond was to be King, the first monarch of the House of Tudor, a dynasty was being born and ever since, the crown of England has remained in the line of the heirs of Henry Tudor.

At the beginning of September 1485, Henry and his victorious army reached the capital and, after a fortnight at Baynard's Castle, Henry went to Margaret Beaufort's home at Woking where there was an emotional reunion between mother and son. The events of the previous years had deeply affected Margaret not only because of the dangers and duress she had experienced but also the problems of loyalty and allegiance she had faced during her three later marriages. There is no doubt that Henry fully appreciated the important part which Margaret Beaufort had played in his rise to the throne. In the arrangements for the coronation and in the years which followed, she was to play an important and influential role. Indeed, her status in Henry's new royal court and the precedence and honour accorded to her were to become semi-regal. At the coronation of Henry's queen Elizabeth of York in 1487, she accompanied her at the procession and sat at her right hand in the parliamentary chamber. In the following year, Margaret and Elizabeth were issued with liveries of the Order of the Garter which was a sign of special standing. In one of his earliest grants, Henry had provided his mother with a splendid London residence at Coldharbour overlooking the Thames.

On the last day of October 1485 Henry was crowned as King Henry VII in a magnificent ceremony which had probably not been equalled at the coronation of any previous English monarch. Despite the grandeur of the occasion however, both Henry and his mother were only too aware of the transient nature of political fortune. It was important that when Parliament assembled, it gave approval to Henry's coronation and re-enacted a statute

Henry Tudor.
REPRODUCED BY COURTESY OF THE NATIONAL PORTRAIT GALLERY

101

of 1397 which declared the Beaufort family legitimate, omitting a clause that had barred them from succession. The new King chose to portray himself as a symbol of continuity, a rightful successor to Edward IV as well as legal heir of Henry VI. He rewarded the trusted followers who had supported him at Bosworth by making them members of his council and he also remembered some of Buckingham's supporters who took part in the unsuccessful revolt against Richard III in October 1483. Experience of government was at a premium however and he had to choose many former Yorkists as councillors and officials.

At Coldharbour, rooms were made ready for Henry's intended bride, the Princess Elizabeth of York, and he entrusted her to his mother, in accordance with etiquette. It was natural enough to rely on her advice and experience in the arrangements leading up to the marriage. The wedding took place early in 1486 without waiting for papal dispensation though the Pope later acknowledged that the marriage would unite the rival houses and offered hopes for future peace. Margaret was eight years younger than her husband and a woman of considerable beauty, tall and possessing a fair complexion. There was no role for her to play in politics beyond becoming Henry's queen and the mother of his children. It was a political marriage, not a love match, but they grew close to each other and Henry remained faithful to her. He had built a sumptuous residence on the banks of the Thames which was named Sheen Palace but it was burnt to the ground and then rebuilt with greater magnificence than before. He called it Richmond perpetuating the title of the Earldom and Honour of Richmond in Yorkshire which had been his until he became King.[51] Richmond Palace and his Chapel in Westminster Abbey served to exemplify his dynastic success.

Henry was very much a child of the wars between Lancaster and York. Though his marriage to Elizabeth did much to heal the wounds between the two factions, the cause of the Yorkists was never far below the surface and, throughout his reign, Henry was troubled by Yorkist claims to the throne and by pretenders. After Bosworth, he had imprisoned the young Earl of Warwick as being the main Yorkist competitor for the throne, and another claimant, the Earl of Lincoln, was also placed in custody. However, with aid from Margaret of Burgundy, an implacable foe of Henry, a rebel force including 2,000 German mercenaries, headed by a certain Lambert Simnel impersonating the Earl of Warwick, landed in Lancashire from Ireland in 1487. At the Battle of Stoke the pretenders were routed by Henry's forces but another Yorkist, known as Perkin Warbeck, was to be a thorn in the side of King Henry for six years. Warbeck claimed to be Richard of York, the younger of the two princes in the Tower and said that he had been spared by the murderers of his brother. Most people regarded him as an imposter but his bearing, dignity and good looks brought him a number of followers and his activities encouraged English malcontents. The Yorkists gave him encouragement and the Dowager Duchess Margaret is said to have favoured his claims after closely examining his title. Moreover, Warbeck was accepted by the Netherlands and even gained support from Maximilian of Rome. King Henry was so annoyed by the Netherlands' decision that he demanded a halt in the trade between the two countries.

The King had become aware of Warbeck's part in the build-up of a conspiracy against him and Henry made full use of his intelligence services in having the more important conspirators arrested. They included the Dean of St Paul's, two Dominican friars, and two priests. The churchmen were spared but others like Sir William Mountford and Lord FitzWalter were beheaded. The most distinguished of Warbeck's recruits was Sir Robert Clifford but he was given a free pardon. Perhaps the most surprising personage to be charged with conspiracy and treason was Sir William Stanley, a man who had set the battered crown on Henry's head at Bosworth. It must be assumed that the evidence against him was good or the King would not have dared to condemn to death the brother of the Earl of Derby and the brother-in-law of his own mother.

The embargo on trade with the Netherlands imposed by Henry was hurting both sides, and certainly English exports, yet the King's prohibition remained in force and Maximilian and

Archduke Philip of the Netherlands replied by imposing an embargo on English wool and iron. Maximilian believed that "the Duke of York" could easily establish himself in England and a considerable expedition was prepared which resulted in Warbeck appearing off Deal on the 3rd July 1495 with fourteen ships. The attempt was a failure for Warbeck did not dare to land and the adventurers he had hired who did land were soon either killed or taken prisoner. Perkin then sailed to Ireland but there he received only a cool welcome and, having been rebuffed, he went to Scotland where at first he was well received. In November 1495 King James even honoured "the Duke of York" with a state welcome in Stirling and the attention paid to the pretender soon attracted the eyes of Europe towards Scotland.

James IV of Scotland had been planning to make a large-scale invasion of England but this degenerated into border raids. King Henry's intention was to humble the Scots and force them to surrender Warbeck. When James and his men eventually crossed the border and began a siege of Norham Castle they were easily repelled by a strong royalist force. By mid-summer 1496 Perkin Warbeck had became an embarrassment to his northern protectors and he was prompted to leave Scotland. He then sailed with thirty of his followers to Cork where he was not at all welcome and then left for Cornwall hoping to profit from the local unrest. He landed at Whitesands Bay and, leaving his wife at St Michael's Mount, set himself to fan the smouldering embers of revolt. With some 8,000 men he set off to besiege Exeter but his men were poorly armed and their attempt was doomed to failure. Leaving their dead, they went to Taunton but the King's army was now approaching and Warbeck left his men and galloped for his life towards Southampton Water where he hoped to find a ship. Perkin was captured however and then taken to Taunton where he made a full confession of his imposture. King Henry showed him great clemency but Perkin abused the freedom he was given and was ultimately executed together with the Earl of Warwick.

At the beginning of 1497 the King had to suppress further trouble when he summoned Parliament to vote for additional war taxation. This so angered the people of Cornwall that they decided to march to London with a petition against the tax for which they blamed the King's ministers. They had left intending to make only a peaceful protest but, at Wells, they were joined by a new recruit, James Touchet, seventh Baron Audley, who became their formidable leader. They went to Kent where they gained no real support and eventually encamped on Blackheath. Dismayed by the lack of recruits, but now an insurgent army of about 15,000 men, their entry into the capital was blocked by 25,000 Royalist troops. Early in the morning the Royal army attacked and, in the end, numbers and experience prevailed, leaving the insurgents defeated and in a dismal rout. Many were killed and three of their leaders were taken prisoner; of these Audley was beheaded and the other leaders Thomas Flamank, a lawyer, and Michael Joseph, a resolute blacksmith, were hanged at Tyburn.

With the Battle of Bosworth, the Wars of the Roses reached their final milestone. For this, Henry must take considerable credit. He was a diplomat and peacemaker and he revived the ancient strength of the English monarchy. His domestic rule was noted for its harsh financial direction, for efficient administration and for the importance he gave to commercial trading. His foreign policy was one of mediation and, despite having to send protective forces to Brittany, he completed agreements with France and treaties with Burgundy and the Holy Roman Empire which resulted in a new pattern of European alliances.

Though Henry's marriage to Elizabeth was a political one rather than a love match she was able to bear him three sons and two daughters, but their eldest son Arthur died tragically in 1502. He had been married at St Paul's to Catherine of Aragon in a prestigious ceremony followed by a spectacular banquet and festivities. Though regarded as the high point of Henry's reign, the celebrations were forgotten only eight months later when Arthur suddenly died at Ludlow. His death came as a horrific shock but despite his sorrow, Henry is known to have shown his wife exceptional tenderness and consoled her in a most moving way. Their daughter Princess Margaret was to marry James IV of Scotland but as their third son Edmund had died in infancy two years before Arthur, the male line depended on the remaining son Prince Henry who at that time was not in robust health. The dynasty's future had therefore become dogged with uncertainty and, in 1503, tragedy again struck with the death of the Queen in childbirth. Henry was stricken with grief and became almost a recluse.

With the King's health gradually deteriorating, Margaret Beaufort took up residence in the palaces of the south-east to be near her son but Henry died in April 1509. He had reached the age of fifty-two and, though never a popular King, he achieved much during the years of his reign. Most of all he is remembered for rescuing England from a civil war and, having achieved internal peace and prosperity, giving her a reputation in Europe that she had not enjoyed for some time.[52]

Bibliography

PART 1

1 Churchill, W.S., *The Birth of Britain* in "A History of the English Speaking Peoples" Vol.1 (Cassell 1956) p.135.

2 Galliou, P. and Jones, M., *The Bretons* (The Peoples of Europe Series).(Blackwell 1991) pp.181/6.

3 Churchill, W.S., *The Birth of Britain* p.127.

4 *D.N.B.* Vol.XXI pp.293 et seq.
   Musgrave, F., *The North of England* (Blackwell 1990) p.81.

5 *V.C.H. (North Riding)* Vol.1. p.1 The Honour and Castle of Richmond (Topography). *E.Y.C.* Vol. IV Part 1 p.94. The date of the grant of lands to Alan Rufus is uncertain; the year 1069 has been quoted but some of the lands forfeited by Edwin of Mercia may have been passed to him earlier.
   Gales Registrum (Cotton MS FaustinaB VII) depicts Alan kneeling before the King receiving some form of charter. However, no original charter is said to remain and it is questionable whether land comprising the Honour would have been conveyed by charter.
   A full description of the lands comprising the Honour of Richmond is given in *Registrum Honoris de Richmond* (London MDCCXXII) which assumes that the drawing, a copy of which is included in Chapter 1 of this book, depicts the handing over of some document of title to Earl Edwin's lands.

6 *D.N.B.* Vol.XXI. pp.293 et seq.
   Jones, M., *Ducal Brittany 1364-1399* (Relations with England and France during the reign of Duke John IV.) (Oxford Historical Monographs 1970) pp.174/5.

7   Ibid p185.

8   Clarkson, C., *A History of Richmond* (Bowman 1821) p.14.
V.C.H. (North Riding) Vol.1 p.1 et seq.

9   *E.Y.C.* Vol. IV. Part 1 (Introduction) pp.VIII XXXIV.

10   Clarkson, C., *A History of Richmond* p.14.
V.C.H. (North Riding) Vol.1 p.1 et seq.
E.Y.C. Vol. IV. Part 1 p.98. "There is no evidence that Alan or his brothers possessed an English earldom" (Refer also to Spencer's Guide c1898).

11   Wilson, C., and Burton, J., *St Mary's Abbey, York* (edited by Elizabeth Hartley and published by The Yorkshire Museum 1988).
V.C.H. (North Riding) Vol.1 p.1 et seq.
Poole, A.L., *Domesday Book to Magna Carta* 2nd ed. (Oxford 1955) p.18.
Stenton, Sir Frank, *The First Century of English Feudalism* (Oxford 1961) pp.194/6, 210.

12   *Y.A.S.* Vol.5 pp.295/6.

13   Clarkson, C., *A History of Richmond* p.20.
V.C.H. (Norfolk) Vol.2 p.17.

14   *E.Y.C.* Vol.IV Part 1 p.87.

15   Clarkson, C., *A History of Richmond* p.20.

16   Chron. Stephen & Hen. II. - (Rolls serv. iii) pp.64/72.

17   Churchill, W.S., *The Birth of Britain* pp.148/50.

18   Stenton, Sir Frank, *The First Century of English Feudalism* pp.241/3.
V.C.H. (North Riding) Vol.1 pp.2/3.

19   Poole, A.L., *The Oxford History of England* p.385.

20   Symeon of Durham *Opera Historica* Rolls Series ii p.312.
Clarkson, C., *A History of Richmond* p.21.

21   Ibid pp.1136/45.

22   *V.C.H. (North Riding)* Vol.1 p.3.
E.Y.C. Vol.IV Part 1 p.92/3.
Galliou, P. and Jones, M., *The Bretons* pp.94/5.

23 *E.Y.C.* Vol.V. Pt II pp.8/9.

24 Clarkson, C., *A History of Richmond* pp.22/3.

25 *C.P.E.* Vol.4 p.797.
    Galliou, P. and Jones, M., *The Bretons* pp.196/7.
    Poole, A.L., *Domesday Book to the Magna Carta* pp.318/9.

26 *C.P.E.* Vol.4 Part 1 pp.797/8.

27 Poole, A.L., *Oxford History of England* 2nd. ed. p.485.
    Fraser, A., *The Lives of the Kings and Queens of England.*
    (Book Club Associates 1975) p.65.
    D.N.B. Vol.I. pp.601/2.
    Churchill, W.S., *The Birth of Britain* pp.191/3.

28 Powicke, Sir Maurice, *The Thirteenth Century* (Oxford 1962)
    p.15n.

29 Ibid p.93.

30 Stenton, Sir Frank, *The First Century of English Feudalism*
    p.26.
    C.P.E. Vol.4. Part 1 pp 79 and 93.
    Galliou, P. & Jones, M., *The Bretons* pp.198/200.

31 *C.P.E.* Vol 4. p.805.
    D.N.B. Vol. XV. pp.46.et seq.

32 Clarkson, C., *A History of Richmond* p.39.
    Galliou, P. & Jones, M., *The Bretons* Ch.8 and 10.
    Seward, D., *The Hundred Years War (The English in France
    1337-1453)* (Constable 1996) p.79.

33 Poole, A.L., *The Oxford History of England* p.485.

34 Clarkson, C., *A History of Richmond* p.31.

35 Lubimenko, I., *Jean de Bretagne* (1908) pp.66/70.
    Clarkson, C., *A History of Richmond* p.34.
    McKisack, M., *The 14th Century 1307-1399* (Oxford 1959)
    pp.1 et seq.

36 Clarkson, C., *A History of Richmond* p.35.

37 McKisack, M., *The 14th Century 1307-1399* p.131.
    Galliou, P. and Jones, M., *The Bretons* pp.222/4.

38   Goodman, A., *John of Gaunt (The Exercise of Princely Power in Fourteenth-Century Europe)* (Longman 1992) pp.78/82.

39   Ibid pp.32/34.

40   Ibid p.312.

41   *C.P.R.* 1358/61.

42   Goodman, A., *John of Gaunt* p.358.

43   Ibid p.185/6.

44   Jones, M., *Ducal Brittany* pp.67/8.
     Galliou, P. and Jones, M., *The Bretons* pp.234/239.

45   Ibid pp.114/142.
     V.C.H. (North Riding) Vol.1 p.9.
     Hector & Hervey. *Westminster Chronicle* (Clarendon 1982).

46   *C.P.E.* Vol.4 p.824/5.
     Seward, D., *The Hundred Years War* Ch.8. pp.172-195.

47   Churchill, W.S., *The Birth of Britain* Ch.IV pp.325/333.
     C.P.E. Vol. 4, p.825.
     D.N.B. Vol.X pp.864 et seq.
     Seward, D., *The Hundred Years War* Ch.8 pp.172/195.
     Jacob, *The Fifteenth Century* (Oxford 1961) p.241 et seq.
     Galliou, P. and Jones, M., *The Bretons* pp.231 et seq.

48   *D.N.B.* Vol.II p.48.
     Jones, M.K. and Underwood, M.G., *The King's Mother* (Cambridge 1992) Ch.2 pp.35/65.
     Jacob, *The Fifteenth Century* pp.562 et seq.

49   Mackie, J.D., *The Early Tudors* (Clarendon Oxford 1952) pp.48/52.

50   Guy, J., *Tudor England* (Oxford 1988) p.3.

51   Fraser, A., *The Kings & Queens of England* (Weidenfeld & Nicholson 1975) pp.168 et seq.

52   Jones, M.K. and Underwood, M.G., *The King's Mother* Chapter 3. pp.66/92.
     Guy, J., *Tudor England* Chapter 3. pp.53/79.
     Mackie, J.D., *The Early Tudors* Chs. 5 and 7.

PART 2

THE DUKES OF RICHMOND

CHAPTER 15

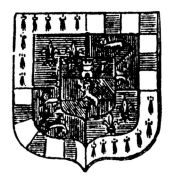

Henry Fitzroy (b.1519 - d.1536) Duke of Richmond

KING HENRY VIII wanted a son and heir and, though his marriage to Catherine of Aragon brought them a son they named Henry, the young Prince was only to live some eight weeks. Thereafter, there was an unhappy sequence of miscarriages until Catherine presented the King with a daughter, the Princess Mary, but with the passing of years it became clear that there would be no further children. Before his marriage to Catherine, the King had been shy of women but she had given him confidence and he now began to cast his eye around the beauties of the court.

He became fascinated with Catherine's maid Elizabeth Blount who "for her rare endowments, nature, ornaments and education" was thought to be the masterpiece of her time. His fascination with the beautiful "Bessie" led to the birth of an illegitimate son who was given the name of Henry Fitzroy. The King clearly saw the baby as his ultimate successor though he desperately wanted a son born in wedlock who could succeed to the throne unchallenged. He began to think that his marriage to Catherine had been against God's law because she had been his deceased brother's wife and he asked Wolsey to use his influence with Rome to have the marriage declared invalid. It was not to be; Rome would not agree and it was only when the King acted on Cromwell's advice and broke away from papal allegiance that Henry's marriage to Catherine was made null and void. There followed the King's well-known sequence of marriages to Anne Boleyn, Jane Seymour, Anne of Cleves, Catherine Howard and then Catherine Parr, but it was Jane Seymour who gave the King the legitimate son he so desired, Edward Prince of Wales who became Edward VI. Henry's first wife, Catherine of Aragon, for whom there was much sympathy, reverted to her former title of Princess of Wales and lived out her remaining days at Ampthill and Kimbolton manors where she died in January 1536.

When Henry Fitzroy was only six, he was appointed Knight of the Garter and created the first Duke of Richmond and Somerset at a ceremony of installation which took place at Bridewell on 18th June, 1525. He is also recorded as being made Lord of the Honour of Richmond but, in 1532, the King recovered possession and, apart from Richmond Castle, the remainder of the Honour has been held by the Crown ever since. For Henry Fitzroy, other titles were soon to follow and he was made Lord Warden of the East, West and Middle Marches of Scotland and Lord Lieutenant of Ireland, these high offices being recognised as part of a preparation for kingship. As Receiver of Middleham and Sheriff Hutton he was taken north to Wensleydale and he lived there for a time, as well as at Pontefract where his council transacted all the business of the border country.

The King was concerned that his son should receive a good education and, by the time Fitzroy was ten years old, he was well advanced in his studies as well as showing a natural liking for

FITZROY, Duke of Richmond. *The royal arms of HENRY VIII with the difference of a sinister baston argent in a border quarterly ermine and checky or and azure and over all a scutcheon quarterly gules and vairy or and vert a lion argent and a chief with a castle between two harts' heads caboshed or therein.*

singing and playing on the virginals. When he returned to the south he lived for a time at Hatfield and went with the King to France where he stayed in Paris with his close friend the young Earl of Surrey. This was a prelude to his marriage for, on his return to England, he was married to Mary, the young daughter of Thomas Howard, the second Duke of Norfolk.

Mary's childhood was spent at Tendring Hall in Suffolk and at Hunsdon in Hertfordshire and dispensation for her marriage to Henry Fitzroy was given in 1533. Owing to her tender age, she continued to live with her friends after her wedding and her husband probably lived in Windsor Castle. He was not a robust young man and when he had to cancel a planned visit to Ireland it became clear that he was far from well. His health continued to deteriorate and the King's aspirations for his son came to an end when Henry Fitzroy died, apparently of consumption, when he was only seventeen. There was some suspicion that he had been poisoned but this seems never to have been substantiated. He was buried in the Church of St Michael in Framlingham in the County of Suffolk where a spacious tomb was erected in his memory.

There had been no children of the marriage and Mary, Duchess of Richmond, who had become a strong supporter of the

113

reformed church, was made lady-in-waiting to Anne of Cleves. She had some difficulty in obtaining a dowry but, eventually, she was given the manor of Swaffham in Norfolk for life. For a while she remained a widow after her husband's death but, in 1546, she was offered in marriage to Sir Thomas Seymour and this gave the prospect of future alliances between the two families, the Norfolks and the Seymours.

In December of that year her father, the Duke of Norfolk and his brother Henry Howard, the Earl of Surrey, were arrested and three commissioners were sent to her father's mansion in Norfolk to examine her and a certain Elizabeth Holland, described as "an ambiguous friend" of the Duke. The two ladies were brought to London for interrogation. The Duke of Norfolk and his son, described by some as a reckless and haughty catholic, were charged with acts of high treason. Henry Howard was also brought to account for trying to persuade Mary, Duchess of Richmond, to offer herself as mistress to the King so that she could exercise some power over him. In this, Mary was required to give evidence and she resolved to hide nothing. She screened her father from the charge but confirmed that her brother had indeed made the proposal when he was angry that she considered marrying Sir Thomas Seymour. She spoke of her brother's abominable advice, his deep hate of "the new men" and her strong abhorrence of his proposal.

Both the Duke and his son were convicted of acts of high treason and sent to the Tower. Henry was executed on 21st January, 1547 and though his father's execution was pending, it did not proceed because of the death of the King the following day. The Duke began a term of imprisonment but he was released on the accession of Queen Mary in 1553. Mary Duchess of Richmond took up residence in Knightsbridge and became friendly with John Foxe, the Protestant martyrologist. Henry Howard's children had been taken from their mother and committed to Mary, their aunt, and she had immediately appointed Foxe as their tutor. It is apparent that her father, the Duke, held no grudge against his daughter and on his death she benefited from his

The Lady of Richmond from the original drawing by Hans Holbein.
REPRODUCED BY PERMISSION OF ROYAL COLLECTION ENTERPRISES

115

Henry Fitzroy – Duke of Richmond by Lucas Hornebolte.
REPRODUCED BY PERMISSION OF ROYAL COLLECTION ENTERPRISES

estate. Mary who became known as the Lady of Richmond died in 1557 and her portrait remains in the royal collection.

References:
Clarkson, C., *The History of Richmond* (Bowman 1821) p.42.
D.N.B. Vol. X pp.23/5 and 204/5. Vol. XIX p.108.
Guy, John, *Tudor England* (Oxford 1988) pp.116 and 142.
V.H.E. p11.

CHAPTER 16

Ludovic Stuart (b.1574 - d.1624) Duke of Richmond and Lennox

IT WAS NOT UNTIL 1613 in the reign of James I of England (VI of Scotland) that the Earldom of Richmond was revived and it was ten years later that Ludovic Stuart, already the Earl of Richmond and 2nd Duke of Lennox, was created Duke of Richmond and Lennox. An important link was thereby established between the Richmond and Lennox families and, as will be noted in a later chapter, with the Stuarts, the Darnleys and also the Seigneurie of Aubigny in France.

Ludovic was born in 1574 in Paris, the eldest son of Esmé, the 1st Duke of Lennox and his wife Catherine. His father, a friend of King James, died there in 1583 and Ludovic succeeded to the Lennox title. In Scotland, James was reported to be "without all quietness of spirit till he should see some of his posterity to possess him in his father's honours and rents". He therefore arranged for the young Duke to be conveyed to Leith where he arrived with his escort in November of that year. He was received into the King's special favour and James issued instructions for "the virtuous nature and honourable education" of the young Duke, who was to remain in the King's own house and company, to be placed at the end of the table and "served forth of his kitchen and cupboard". Fontenay, writing to the Queen of Scots, referred to Ludovic as "le petit Duc de Lennox qui est un très gentil enfant et qui promet beaucoup de la bonne nature".

Ludovic was welcomed to the Scottish court and, though a mere boy, he was sent to bear the crown at the opening of the Scottish Parliament. The King clearly intended to give him a taste of the problems of government. and made him not only the member of a commission for executing the laws against the Jesuits and Papists but also gave him what seems a strange task of keeping watch in Dumbarton for the Spanish Armada. The Duke was only fifteen when the King left Scotland to collect his bride, Anne of Denmark, and appointed Ludovic as President of the Council in his absence.

Ludovic's first marriage was to Lady Sophia Ruthven, daughter of the Earl of Gowrie, but he upset the King by taking her from Wemyss Castle where she was being "warded". There were no children of the marriage and, when Sophia died, Ludovic entered into what history describes as a "troublesome" marriage with Jane the widow of the Hon. Robert Montgomery by whom he had a daughter. Jane was indeed a pronounced rebel and when Ludovic complained that she was detaining their daughter from him and giving no care to the daughter's upbringing she was summoned to appear before the Council of Scotland but refused to do so. Ludovic is reputed to have said "I shall ever think of her as a cross" and "there is no earthly thing I wish more than to be rid of her". His wish was granted and he married a third time, with more success, to Frances, the widow of the 1st Earl of Hertford.

King James who had to contend with several rebel leaders in the North clearly valued Ludovic as a lieutenant and took him to Perth in 1600 where the Earl of Gowrie and the master of Ruthven were killed. Ludovic had taken an active part on behalf of the

Ludovic Stuart, Duke of Richmond and Lennox.
FROM THE GORHAMBURY COLLECTION AND REPRODUCED BY PERMISSION
OF THE EARL OF VERULAM

119

King against Gowrie, who was his brother in law. A year later, Ludovic was sent to the embassy in France and, on his return through London, he was entertained for three weeks with great splendour by Queen Elizabeth. It was late in December 1602 and Elizabeth's health was beginning to fail. The Duke returned to Scotland with a letter from Elizabeth to James and, in the following March, she died, the last of the Tudors and certainly one of the greatest of Queens. On her death, James VI of Scotland was acknowledged as the ruler of England. Ludovic had been intimately associated with James' arrangements for securing the English crown and the King directed that the Duke should accompany him on his journey to London.

King James' major objective once he was established in England was to complete the union of the two crowns by a union of states. This could only be done with the support of the two parliaments. The Scottish assembly was unlikely to raise objections but, in England, parliamentary debates on the issue made clear the depth of English prejudice against the Scots which was a factor of which Ludovic was soon made aware.

On the 18th June 1603 Ludovic was naturalised in England and became a gentleman of the bedchamber and a privy councillor. His income was no doubt increased when he was granted the manor of Settrington in Yorkshire. This had been held by the Crown since 1600 though, some sixty years earlier, it formed part of the possessions of Sir Frances Bigod and passed to the Crown following his attainder and execution for high treason in 1537. In 1544, it was granted to Matthew Earl of Lennox by Henry VIII but returned to the Crown before being granted to Ludovic in 1603 together with the manors of Temple-Newsam and Wensleydale in Yorkshire. In a different sphere, Ludovic was granted the alnage of "New Draperies". The knitting trade was becoming all important at that time and the alnager not only inspected draperies produced, he enforced the payment of duty. It was clearly a role which Ludovic as well as his wife fulfilled with some vigour and, even after her husband's death, his widow is known to have prosecuted several Yorkshire merchants for evasion of alnage payments.

During the years 1604-5, Ludovic served as ambassador to Paris and, back in England, he accompanied the King to Oxford, where he received his M.A. and this was followed by his appointment as High Commissioner to the Scottish Parliament, perhaps an astute move to offset the considerable power of the General Assembly of the Scottish Church. It is apparent that he was a great supporter of the King's ecclesiastical policy in Scotland and his biography records that he voted for the obnoxious ecclesiastical articles known as the four articles of Perth.

In October 1613, Ludovic became Earl of Richmond and Baron Settrington and, in the following year, Deputy Earl Marshal. Ten years later, he was created Duke of Richmond and Lennox as well as Earl of Newcastle-Upon-Tyne. He had also taken possession of the seigneurie of Aubigny in opposition to the rights of his nephew Charles who was eventually recognised as seigneur by decree in 1668.

Ludovic's life was to come to a sudden end for, in February 1624, when he had reached the age of fifty, he died in bed at his lodgings in Whitehall. It was the day fixed for the opening of parliament, which was then deferred. His body was conveyed "with all magnificence from Ely House to the Holborn" for interment in Westminster Abbey where a magnificent tomb was erected in Henry VII's chapel by his widow.

Ludovic was mourned both in England and Scotland. He was a man who had gained a high reputation and many honours, always retaining respect for his courtesy, meekness and liberality to his servants. Though married three times there was no male issue or successors though the Dukedom of Lennox passed to Ludovic's brother Esmé who had become naturalised as an Englishman but survived only until later in 1624 when he died of fever leaving his widow, six sons and three daughters. Ludovic's widow, his third wife Frances, died in 1639 and was buried next to him in the tomb she erected for her husband in Westminster Abbey.

References:
C.P.E. Vol 4. No.829.
D.N.B. Vol. 1 pp.85/86 and Vol. X1X pp.107/8.
Hartley, M.and Ingleby, J., *The Old Hand Knitters of the Dales* (Dalesman 1951) p.10.
PRO E134, 2 CARI Mich 38. re payment of alnage.
King, H. and Harris, ed. *A Survey of the Manor of Settrington* (Yorks. Arch. Society - 1962).

CHAPTER 17

The Lennox Dynasty

T O DELVE INTO THE history of the Lennox (or Levenach)
family is to unveil an extraordinary dynasty with its origins
in Celtic if not the Saxon period. Legends tell of a Saxon baron
with the name of Arkill who was descended from the King of the
Picts and Scots and came to Scotland in 1069 or 1070 where he
married the daughter of a Mormaer of the lands around Loch
Lomond. The marriage produced a son, given his father's name,
and after him came Alwin who was created the first of the Earls
of Lennox in 1130. Under Alwin, the ancient and immensely
powerful Celtic Mormaers of Lennox, high-ranking chiefs, developed control of an extensive area of Scotland which included the
whole of Dumbartonshire, as well as Renfrew, Stirlingshire and
Perthshire. By the end of the 13th century, the Earls of Lennox
had become the most powerful nobles in the realm.

The second Earl of Lennox who was named Alwin like his
father, married Eva, the daughter of the Earl of Monteith. It was
a marriage which produced a number of sons whose achievements
did much to extend the Lennox dynastic connections. At a time
when the King of Scotland called upon his lords to send men to
defend the realm, the Earl refrained from sending his eldest son
but another son Donald went in his stead. In a battle which
followed, things went badly with the Scots who were being forced
to retreat but Donald seized his father's standard and jumped
into the breach turning the tide to win a great victory. For his
valour, the King granted him lands in Gosford and Fife and bade
him change his name to "Naepeer". The Napier clan was established and, though one of the smallest, it has produced several

THE LENNOX CLAN
The link with the Stewarts and the Richmonds

EGFRITH (or AYKFRITH) (d. 1064)

ARKILL (or ARCHILL) (c. 1064 - d. 1100)

ARKILL (or ARCHILL) (c. 1100 - d. 1130)

EARLS OF LENNOX

ALWIN MACARCHILL (c. 1130 - d. 1155) 1st Earl

ALWIN (c. 1155 - d. 1217) 2nd Earl. Married Lady Eva, daughter of Gilchrist, Earl of Monteith

MALDOUEN (c. 1217 - d. 1270) 3rd Earl. Married Elizabeth Stewart

MALCOLM (predeceased his father in 1248)

MALCOLM (c. 1270 - d. 1292) 4th Earl

MALCOLM (c. 1292 - d. 1333) 5th Earl

DONALD (c. 1333 - d. 1364) 6th Earl

MARGARET   Married   WALTER OF FASLANE
(only child of Donald)   (Her cousin and heir male of the Lennox family)

DUNCAN (c. 1385 - executed 1425) 8th Earl

ELIZABETH
married 1391 Sir John STEWART who
fought in France against the English and was made Seigneur of Aubigny

SIR ALAN DARNLEY   JOHN STEWART
(c. 1429 - d. 1439)   Seigneur of Aubigny
                                    (c. 1439 - d. 1482)

JOHN (c. 1460 - d. 1495) 9th Earl of Lennox   BÉRAULT STEWART
(1st Earl of new creation). Created Lord Darnley in 1460   Seigneur of Aubigny (c. 1483 - d. 1508)

MATTHEW (c. 1495 - d. 1513) 2nd Earl, killed at Flodden   ROBERT STEWART
                                                                 Seigneur of Aubigny (c. 1508 - d. 1543)
JOHN (c. 1513 - d. 1526) 3rd Earl, slain by Sir James Hamilton

MATTHEW (c. 1526 - d. 1571) 4th Earl   JOHN - Seigneur of Aubigny (c. 1560 - d. 1567)
Married Lady Margaret Douglas   Captain of the Archers of the Scots Guards

HENRY - Lord Darnley (c. 1545 - d. 1567)   ESMÉ STEWART Earl of Lennox (c. 1579-1580)
Married Mary Queen of Scots,   Seigneur of Aubigny,
became King of Scotland. Murdered 1567   1st Duke of Lennox (c. 1581 - d. 1582)

                                              LUDOVIC STEWART (c. 2nd Duke of Lennox 1583)
KING JAMES VI of Scotland and 1st of England Earl of Richmond 1613, Duke of Richmond and
                                              Earl of Newcastle 1623. (b. 1574 - d. 1624)

KING CHARLES I - beheaded 1649
                    (Lennox records use the spelling "STEWART" in preference to "Stuart")

124

leaders of note including John Napier, 7th Laird of Merchiston, the inventor of logarithms.

Another of the second Earl's sons, given the name of Gilchrist, created the Macfarlane clan which became the ruling clan in the Arrochar district. His brother Christian became the hereditary judge of the Lennox, and his descendants had much to do with the resettlement of the Isle of Man after Scotland won it back from Norway. There were also Lennox dynastic connections established in 1200 with the MacAulays of Ardencaple who claimed descent from the ancient royal house of Munster in Ireland and several Alwin sons gained high positions like Anley who became Baillie, or chief magistrate, of the Lennox. Other famous Scottish families like the Colquhouns, Haldanes and the Pattersons were all founded through Lennox connections.

The Lennox dynasty continued to prosper and Maldouen, who became the third Earl, married a Stewart, Elizabeth the daughter of the High Steward of Scotland, and became a great benefactor of the Church. In 1225, he granted the Island of Clarinch, occupied by the Buchanan clan, in return for a pound of wax to be rendered annually each Christmas. Maldouen's successor Malcolm, the fourth Earl, gave a charter to the Buchanans confirming the use of their clan lands and granting them the right to hold courts with the baronial powers of life and death. The Buchanans were probably related to another Lennox clan, the Galbraiths, who married into the Lennox family as early as 1193 and also had their origins in the ancient Britons who escaped into Scotland. The Hamiltons, who became great Highland landowners, are also believed to be connected by marriage with the Galbraiths, but in 1526 they fought and defeated the Stewarts of Lennox in a dispute about succession to the throne. Sir James Hamilton, who led the Hamiltons and killed his cousin John Stewart, became known as "the bastard of Arran" and was later beheaded for treason.

Malcolm, the fourth Earl, was a Wallace follower and a great supporter of Princess Margaret of Norway who laid claim to the Scottish throne. Margaret's mother was a Lennox and the

Princess could well have become the Queen of Scotland if she had not died on the voyage from Norway. The fifth Earl was another Malcolm and he was an ardent supporter of Robert the Bruce. He led his Lennox men into England to besiege Carlisle and, though he swore fealty to the English King Edward I, he was at the forefront of Scottish independence, which he emphasised in a celebrated letter which he wrote to the Pope in 1320. He was to die with three other earls in the Battle of Halidon Hill, resisting the English invaders in 1333.

The Lennox title then went to Donald, a supporter of King David against Edward III but he had no male heir and it was left to his daughter Margaret to assume the title of Countess of Lennox. She married her cousin Walter of Faslane and they decided to resign the title in favour of their son Duncan who then became the eighth Earl though his period as the title holder was to end in disaster. He was executed by James I in 1425 together with his three brothers and also his son-in law Murdoch, with his two sons. Murdoch was the son of the Duke of Albany who had acted as Regent of Scotland but had shown no desire to ransom James I who was imprisoned by the English. Though the Duke died before James was released from captivity, James so hated the Regent and all who had been opposed to him that, on his return to Scotland, he was driven to commit this murderous attack on all the Duke's family.

The succession to the title was then disputed. The Lennox lands became divided and the Stewart line separated from the followers of the ancient name of Levenach who became Earls of Balcorrach. The ancient MacFarlane chiefs claimed to be chiefs of Lennox as male heirs of the old Earl and it was not until 1473 that the dispute was settled. Duncan and his wife Helen had a daughter Elizabeth who married Sir John Stewart of Darnley. It was Sir John who went to France in joint command of a Scottish force being sent to aid the Dauphin against the English and, for his distinguished service, he was granted the Seigneurie of Aubigny in 1423. Four years later, he was sent on a special embassy visit to Scotland, firstly to obtain reinforcements, but also to gain the hand of the Princess Margaret for the Dauphin. It was during this visit to Scotland that he received from James I a charter granting him Torbolton. The Dukedom of Aubigny and the Barony of Torbolton are of course included in the current titles of the Duke of Richmond as is the Barony of Settrington.

In 1460 Elizabeth's grandson John Stewart became Lord Darnley and the first Stewart Earl of Lennox of the second creation, sitting in the first Parliament of James IV. MacFarlane opposition was overcome by the marriage of their then chief Andrew MacFarlane to the daughter of the new Earl. The title then went to Matthew who repossessed Dumbartonshire, the hereditary land of the Lennox family, but he was killed at Flodden in 1513 leaving his son John to take the Earldom of Lennox. John married Elizabeth Stewart but he met his end at the hands of Sir John Hamilton. and the title passed on to their eldest son Matthew, who became the fourth Earl.

Lady Margaret Douglas, daughter of the 6th Earl of Angus and Margaret Tudor and sister of Henry VIII, became Matthew's wife, but her husband was assassinated at Stirling in 1571. She was an ambitious lady however and, in the time of Mary Tudor, came next in line to the throne. When Elizabeth I became queen, she regarded the Lennox family and Lady Margaret in particular as being a threat to the throne to such an extent that she had Margaret arrested and put in the Tower on more than one occasion. For a number of years Margaret was forced to live quietly at Settrington, which was a Lennox manor, where she was kept under surveillance, never being allowed to return to Scotland and she is said to have died in poverty at Hackney. When James I succeeded to the English throne, he erected an elaborate altar tomb for her in Westminster Abbey adjoining the tomb of Mary, Queen of Scots.

Matthew's eldest son Henry took the title of Lord Darnley, married Mary Queen of Scots and became King of Scotland. Though the marriage produced a son who was to become James VI of Scotland, Mary tired of his bad behaviour and love intrigues which may have led to his apparent murder in 1567 when the house in which he lay ill, was blown up.

The youngest son of the 3rd Earl of Lennox and his wife Elizabeth Stewart was given his father's name John. He went to France where he made a name for himself as Captain of the Scottish Archers of the Guard and became naturalised as a French subject. He was created Seigneur of Aubigny in 1560 and was succeeded by his only son Esmé Stewart on whom the Earldom of Lennox was conferred by James VI. Esmé had been living in France but, at the invitation of King James, he went to Scotland where in 1581 he was created 1st Duke of Lennox. Whereas on Esmé's death, his son Ludovic became the 2nd Duke of Lennox, his second son, also Esmé, inherited the title of Seigneur of Aubigny, though Ludovic took possession on the grounds of his being a French subject. The seigneury of Aubigny passed subsequently to Charles Stewart and, on his death, reverted to the French Crown thought it was revived and became a dukedom in the days of Louise de Kéroualle.

Ludovic had inherited the important Stewart connection and became Duke of both Richmond and Lennox but he was to die without issue. Esmé, his brother, then became the 3rd Duke of Lennox and he had five surviving sons, the eldest being James Stewart. James succeeded to the title of 4th Duke of Lennox and he was followed by another Esmé, the 5th Duke, and then Charles Stewart who became Duke of Richmond and Lennox as well a Seigneur of Aubigny. The Richmond and Lennox titles then continued into the present day.

References:
Scottish Clans and Family Encyclopaedia p.192/3.
Dodsworth, J., *All Saints' Church, Settrington* - A History and Guide with additional notes.
Moncrieffe, Sir I.B., *Highland Clans* (Barrie & Jenkins 1967) pp.32 et seq.

CHAPTER 18

Aubigny Sur Nère – the City of the Stuarts

T HE CREATION OF Ludovic Stuart as Duke of Richmond established a link between Richmond and the City of Aubigny sur Nère in France, which was to be further cemented in the reign of Charles II and continues to the present day. The history of Aubigny goes back to the Gallo-Roman period when it was only a small town given the name of Albiniacum. In the Middle Ages, it gained some importance, mainly as a religious centre, but its ecclesiastical leaders found they had difficulty keeping out the neighbouring feudalism and they called on help from Louis VII and then Philip Augustus. From then on it was annexed to the Capetian domains and with Philip Augustus as chief organiser, it became a city of growing importance with the Gothic Church of St Martin at its centre.

In the early period of the Hundred Years War, Aubigny was sacked and burned by the English on two occasions. The Dauphin Charles, who used nearby Bourges as his strategic capital, asked for and received help from the Scots. The extent of the support which came is shown by the size of the contingents which arrived after considerable journeys from Scotland in Castilian ships. After an initial party of 450 men which landed in May, 1419 there came an expeditionary force of 7,000 followed by the arrival of a further 5,000. With them came Sir John Stuart of Darnley and other leaders; it was truly a revival of the "Auld Alliance" between Scotland and France. They joined the Dauphin's army which proceeded to inflict a notable victory over the English at Baugé in

Anjou but a great many Scottish lives were lost in the ensuing conflicts.

As far as Aubigny was concerned, the links then established with Scotland were particularly with the Stuarts, and to this day, Aubigny regards itself as the town of the Stuarts. When Sir John Darnley arrived in 1419 he was appointed Constable of the army of Scotland and he was soon to distinguish himself at Baugé. In recognition, the Dauphin Charles conferred on him the Seigneurie of Concressault in Berry and, when the Dauphin became King in October 1422, the Seigneurie of Aubigny. There were further awards for Sir John later and he became Comte de Évreux in Normandy as well as being granted the privilege of bearing the arms of France on the 1st and 4th quarter of his shield. He was to die serving France at the Battle of Herrings at Rouvray-Saint-Denis, probably in 1428, and he was buried at the Cathedral of Orléans. Though a Stuart, he had married the daughter of Gillespie Campbell of Lochawe and she was buried at Orléans with her husband in 1429.

After Sir John there followed a succession of Stuarts, the first being his second son who was named after his father and inherited the seigneuries of both Concressault and Aubigny. He became Chamberlain of the King of France, a Knight of the Order of St Michael and Captain of the 100 Scottish Men-at-arms, the "Life-Guard" of the Dauphin. Then there was Béraud (or Bérault) Stuart who continued to support the French cause and commanded the French contingent at the Battle of Bosworth in 1485. Appointed Captain of the Scottish Archers, he accompanied Charles VIII and Louis XII on their Italian campaign after which he was made Governor of Calabria and was created Duke of Terranuova and Marquis of Girace by Louis XII for service against the Spaniards. Despite his years in France and Italy, he died when at Corstorphine in Scotland and was buried in Black Friars, Edinburgh.

Robert Stuart was Béraud's second cousin and brother to Matthew, the 2nd Earl of Lennox, and and, through Béraud's daughter Anne Stuart, he was the next to become Seigneur of

Aubigny. In 1512, there was a major fire in Aubigny and it destroyed all the houses except one. Robert is remembered as being generous in his help and he allowed the townspeople to take timber from his forests to rebuild their homes. He rebuilt the Château at Aubigny and installed a Scottish clock with an inscribed bell and an hourly chime. He was also responsible for the greater part of the construction of the Château La Verrerie started by his father-in-law.

Robert took part in the Italian wars; Louis XII rewarded his military ability by naming him Marshal of France and in 1520 he was entrusted with an Embassy in Scotland. He lived until 1543 and, though he married twice, there were no heirs. The seigneurie of Aubigny then passed to his grand-nephew, another John Stuart who was a brother of Matthew the 4th Earl of Lennox. He was a Captain of the Scottish Guards like his forebears and became a naturalised French subject. His only son and heir was Esmé Stuart who was brought up in France but went to Scotland in 1579 where he was created firstly the Earl and then Duke of Lennox.

He was succeeded by his son of the same name who, like his father, was brought up in France and then succeeded him as Duke of Lennox. He married Lady Catherine Clifton and, of their many children, James Stewart, the eldest, became the 4th Duke of Lennox. The remaining five sons are said to have cared little for the Aubigny seigneurie, preferring when in France to live in a mansion in Paris. However, Henry, the eldest, succeeded to the seigneurie when his father resigned in his favour in 1619, and he was sent with two of his brothers to Aubigny where they were brought up in the Catholic faith and became naturalised subjects "that they might be capable to inherit the lordships of Aubigny and the rest of their father's lands in that kingdom which otherwise they could not do, being born in England and therefore aliens in France". Henry died in 1632 whilst in Venice, where he was buried, and the next Seigneur was his brother George Stuart, who did the unexpected and secretly married Katherine daughter of the 2nd Earl of Suffolk. Yet he was soon to die at the Battle

The Château de la Verrerie, built by the Stuarts at the end of the 15th century.

of Edgehill in 1642 while commanding a body of three hundred horsemen which he himself had raised for King Charles. He was buried at Christ Church Cathedral in Oxford and his epitaph refers to him as "a gentleman of great hopes, of a gentle and winning disposition, and of very clear courage". His widow "Katherine Lady Aubigny" subsequently married the Earl of Newburgh but she died in exile in The Hague.

After George's death in 1642, the seigneurie eventually passed to his son Charles Stuart, George's brothers John Stuart and Bernard having been killed in battle and Ludovic, the remaining son having become a canon of the Notre Dame Cathedral in Paris. It was not until 1668, however, and after long negotiation, that a decree was issued confirming that Charles was recognised as the Seigneur d'Aubigny. When he died four years later, the English King Charles II and his brother James were the only remaining descendants in the male line of Sir John Stuart of Darnley, the original grantee of Aubigny. Although Charles II proceeded to claim the Seigneurie, Louis XIV would not allow the King of England to hold land in France though, as a compromise, he made a grant of "le fonds et propriété de la dite terre d'Aubigny" to Charles' mistress Louise de Kéroualle, the Duchess of Portsmouth.

In 1734, after Louise had died, the second Duke of Richmond inherited the Aubigny Dukedom but, though the title had been given by letter patent in 1684, it had never been registered with the Parlement in Paris. After an unsuccessful effort by Charles Lennox to obtain registration he became convinced that it was impossible to do so, at least during the lifetime of Louis XV, mainly because he was not a Catholic. It was not until 1777, in the time of the 3rd Duke of Richmond, three years after the succession of Louis XVI, that registration was completed and the holder of the Richmond Dukedom was finally accepted as Seigneur of Aubigny. The third, fourth and fifth Dukes of Richmond were all much concerned to retain this Aubigny inheritance and many of the works of art at Goodwood came from Aubigny but, during and after the Revolutionary wars, the Château d'Aubigny was confiscated and it was sold by auction in 1812. Though some settlement was agreed after the death of the fourth Duke of Richmond, the situation for the heirs of Louise de Kéroualle became impossible and, when the Château de la Verrerie was disposed of in 1841, it was the last of the Richmond inheritance of Aubigny. The title of Duc d'Aubigny remains however and continues to be held by the present Duke of Richmond.

The Aubigny known to Louise de Kéroualle and greatly loved in the later years of her life remains a place of much interest. The Château d'Aubigny with its gardens so much favoured by Louise is now the Town Hall and a museum, and the Château de la Verrerie which she frequented, was bought by the Marquis Leonce de Vogüé, a direct ancestor of the present owner Count Béraud de Vogüé. This stately Château with its extensive grounds and lake is now being promoted by the family.

The Château d'Aubigny.
REPRODUCED BY KIND PERMISSION OF M. JACQUES GUARANT

The Stuarts' Scottish dynasty left an imprint on Aubigny and its surrounds by introducing Renaissance-style architecture in the more recent construction of manor houses and private dwellings. During the Revolution, Aubigny was elevated to the rank of chief city of the district and its land was divided into two districts or communes, Aubigny-Ville, being the town centre, and Aubigny-Village, the surburbs of the City. At the beginning of the 20th century the two communes were rejoined and Aubigny was once again unified.

References:
Aubigny-sur-Nère - The Stuarts' Chateau - Published in France from the work of Jean-Yves Ribault.
C.P.E. Vol. XVIII pp.326/329.
D.N.B. Vol. XI pp.921/2.

CHAPTER 19

James Stuart (b.1612 - d.1655) Duke of Richmond and Lennox and Esmé (b.1649 - d.1660)

IN JAMES STUART, Charles I had one of his greatest supporters. Not only did he voice strong support for the King, he contributed some large sums of money for the monarch's upkeep and even sold him some valuable land at a "knock-down" price. Born at Blackfriars in London, James was to become the third of the early holders of a Richmond Dukedom, but he was first and foremost a Stuart and the son of Esmé, the third Duke of Lennox. Ludovic Stuart, the second Duke was his uncle. and he had a brother named Bernard Stuart who became titular Earl of Lichfield.

James succeeded his father in 1624 to become the fourth Duke of Lennox and his nearest male relative was then King James VI who, until he died the following year, acted as tutor and guardian according to Scottish custom. Honours soon came the way of the young Duke, he was made a gentleman of the bedchamber and in 1630 he was knighted. After a period of study at Cambridge he began travelling and went to France, Italy and Spain where he was treated as a nobleman of high status. On his return to England in 1633 he was made a Privy Councillor and then accompanied King Charles on a visit to Scotland.

When James married the only daughter of the Duke of Buckingham in 1637, the King attended with the Queen to give the bride away and it was soon evident that Charles I regarded his young cousin as a close confident. When the King resolved to

James Stuart.

137

endow the bishopric of Edinburgh, James sold him some land for that purpose at a much cheaper price than he could otherwise have obtained. The Scots felt that the Duke's views had been tutored to look upon episcopacy and all British ceremonies with an evil eye and, when he again went to Scotland in 1637 for the funeral of his mother, the ministers of the Church entrusted him with making "supplications and remonstrances" against the service book. Charles I however was a high Protestant churchman and his insistence on enforcing the Anglican Prayer Book, with government by Bishops, on the Presbyterian Scots, was ultimately to lead to the conflicts known as Bishops' Wars. The Duke's position regarding episcopacy was clearly a difficult one and, though he ultimately signed the Presbyterians' National Covenant of 1638, his feelings for the Scots were outweighed by his devotion to the King and his policies. Though he seems to have acted perfectly honourably in the dispute with the Scottish Presbyterians it is worth noting that James was soon to receive grants of land in various counties bringing him a quite substantial income.

In 1638, he was confirmed as keeper of Richmond Park and his appointment as warden of the Cinque ports came at a time when the King gave him exclusive rights to levy dues on shipments of raw wool from London. The intention of the dues, and of the appointment of staple towns, was to deter the export of raw wool and to conserve supplies in England for the benefit of spinners and weavers in the country. Wool exports however brought a profitable trade to the Merchant Adventurers Company, an organisation which caused trouble with James Stuart when he asserted his rights and co-operated with the King's navy to impound all cargoes of wool in ports throughout the Kingdom. Some relaxation of this interference in trade became inevitable. In 1641 James was given added status when he was created Duke of Richmond, a specific reminder being given that, failing any immediate male heir, the title was to pass to his younger brother.

During the long drawn-out civil war between Charles I and parliament, the Duke of Richmond continued to be a generous supporter of the King. His attachment to Charles was unequalled, so much so that after Naseby, and the events which finally led to the trial of 1648, he is said to have offered his own life to save that of his master. The King was condemned to die for "the freedom and liberty of the people of England" and despite the reluctance of members of the court to sign the order, Charles was executed on 30th January 1649.

James, Duke of Richmond and Lennox was one of the mourners who attended the King's funeral at Windsor. He had immediately gone into mourning and though he lingered for a few years, he is said to have died a victim of grief in March 1655 and was buried in Westminster Abbey in the Chapel of Henry VIII with other members of the family. He had never been regarded by the Scottish covenanters with hostility and in the History of the Rebellion, Gordon affirms that, as regards Scotland, "he never declared himself one way or the other, never acted anything for the King or against him, and was never at any time quarrelled or questioned by any party, but lived and died with the good liking of all, and without the hate of any".

James Stuart's marriage to Mary, daughter of the Duke of Buckingham produced a son who was given the family name of Esmé and he became Duke of Richmond as well as the fifth Duke of Lennox. He was a young man thought to have great promise but because of the difficult times of the civil war, his mother took refuge with her son in France. There, Esmé developed smallpox and he died in Paris when aged only eleven. The new King Charles II and his court were said to be much grieved and, according to Westminster Abbey records, Esmé's heart was placed on a pyramid adjoining the massive tomb of Ludovic with his wife Frances, and above the vault containing the remains of his father.

References:
D.N.B. Vol. X1X pp.85/86.
Wedgewood, *The King's Peace* (Collins 1955) pp.117/8.

CHAPTER 20

Charles Stuart (b.1639 - d.1672) Duke of Richmond and Lennox and Frances Teresa (b.1647 - d.1701)

CHARLES STUART WAS always looking for favours. Born in London in the time of Charles I, he was the only son of George Stuart, Ludovic's younger brother, and though titles seemed to come his way from an early age he was always looking for more, and spending much of his life hoping for further benefits from the Crown. When he was aged six he became Baron Newbury and Earl of Lichfield, titles said to be intended for his uncle, Bernard Stuart. He went to France and took up residence at the house of his Uncle Ludovic but there he incurred the displeasure of the Council of State and warrants were issued to seize his person, goods and chattels. This upset him considerably and he returned to England.

When his cousin Esmé died in 1660, Charles Stuart succeeded him as Duke of Richmond and Lennox and as an insatiable petitioner for favours from the new King Charles II, he became hereditary Great Chamberlain and Admiral of Scotland as well as Lord Lieutenant of Dorset and also of Kent. In 1662 he was made a member of the Order of the Garter and his income increased considerably when he became a Gentleman of the Bedchamber. There is little doubt that he benefited most by the King's profusion but it was only after much negotiation that he was recognised as Seigneur d'Aubigny and his favoured relationship with the royal family was somewhat damaged when he

Charles Stuart.
IN THE COLLECTION OF LENNOXLOVE HOUSE

141

had a difference of opinion with the King and spent several weeks incarcerated in the Tower of London. Perhaps the most important event in the life of Charles Stuart was his marriage to Frances Teresa, a lady who became known as "La Belle Stuart".

Frances was the elder daughter of Walter Stuart M.D. who was the third son of the 1st Lord Blantyre and is said to have taken refuge in France some time after 1649 and become attached to the household of the Queen Dowager, Henrietta Maria. Her younger sister Sophie married the master of the household to Charles II and James II, but Frances, having been educated in France, became imbued with French tastes, especially in matters of dress. Her extraordinary beauty attracted wide attention in the royal circles of England as well as France. Pepys relates that the French King, having cast his eyes upon her "would fain to have had her mother, who was one of the most cunning women in the world, to let her stay in France" as an ornament to his court. However, the Dowager Queen Henrietta and Frances' mother were determined to send Frances to England and in 1613 procured for the young beauty, "la plus jolie fille du monde", a letter of introduction to the English monarchy; whilst Louis XIV had to content himself with giving Frances a farewell present.

Early in 1663, she was appointed maid of honour to Queen Catherine of Braganza and it was doubtless the Queen's influence which procured for her sister Sophia a place as "dresser" to the Queen Mother. Whilst Lady Castlemain affected to patronise Frances, King Charles is said to have noticed her when she was sleeping in that lady's apartment. Early in 1663 Pepys noted that the King had "become besotted with Miss Stuart and will be with her half an hour together kissing her". Pepys himself viewed her "with her hat cocked and a red plume, sweet eye, little Roman nose, and excellent taille" as the greatest beauty he had ever seen. He "fancied himself sporting with her with great pleasure".

The French ambassador was amazed at the artlessness of her prattle to the King and it was thought hardly possible for a woman to have less wit and more beauty. Her favourite amusements were blindman's buff, hunt the slipper and card building. Buckingham

and others in the court were also entranced by the lady and hope-
less passions were aroused amongst several notable young men
of the day. The most hopelessly in love with her was probably
Francis Digby, younger son of the Earl of Bristol, whom her
"cruelty" drove to despair, but he died in a sea fight with the
Dutch. This seems to have prompted Dryden to express the
lovelorn Digby's feelings for her in a song depicting Frances
Teresa as the sorceress Armida.

> Farewell fair Armida, my joy and my grief.
> In vain I have loved you and hope no relief;
> Undone by your virtue, too strict and severe,
> Your eyes gave me love and you gave me despair:
> Now called by my honour, I seek with content
> The fate which in pity you would not prevent:
> To languish in love were to find by delay
> A death that's more welcome the speediest way.

> On seas and in battles, in bullets and fire,
> The danger is less than in hopeless desire;
> My death's wound you gave me though far off I bear
> My fall from your sight - not to cost you a tear:
> But if the kind flood on a wave should convey,
> And under your window my body would lay,
> The wound on my breast when you happen to see,
> You'll say with a sigh - "it was given by me".

These lines were parodied in some verses put into Armida's mouth
by Buckingham in his play "The Rehearsal".

At a time when the Queen's health gave cause for alarm, the
King's feelings towards Frances Teresa led to gossip that he
intended to marry her and his courtiers formed "a Committee for
the Getting of Mistress Stuart for the King". Yet Frances Teresa
exasperated him by her unwillingness to yield to his importuni-
ties. She refused titles but was smothered with trinkets.
Temporarily, her obduracy seemed to be overcome with the arrival

at court of a calash from France and the honour of the first drive was eagerly contested by the ladies of the court and even the Queen herself. Needless to say it was Frances Teresa who was the first to be seen in the new vehicle.

In January 1667 she received a proposal of marriage from Charles Stuart, Duke of Richmond and Lennox. Hearing of this, the King sought leave to divorce his own wife but, before any decision could be given, Frances Teresa and the Duke took matters into their own hands. On a dark and stormy night she eloped from her rooms in Whitehall and joined the Duke at London Bridge. They then escaped to Kent where they were married. The King was beside himself with rage but blamed his chancellor Clarendon for divulging news of the divorce plans rather than the Duke who suffered less than might be expected for his temerity. The new Duchess of Richmond returned jewels the King had given her and, with the Queen acting as mediator, Frances Teresa returned to court and settled with her husband to live in Whitehall.

In 1668 she became ill with smallpox and, though she recovered, her face was badly disfigured. The Duke was sent off to Scotland to be out of the way and then made ambassador to the Danish court to persuade Denmark to join England and France in an attack on the Dutch. In 1672, however, Frances Teresa was widowed when the Duke was drowned at Elsinore. It is said that, on a visit to a British frigate, where he had a particularly good dinner, he fell between the warship and the boat that was to take him ashore. There seems good reason to consider whether or not this incident was pre-arranged, the more so when the King of Denmark sent the Duke's body back to England with a mourning present "in a new ship richly adorned, the sails and ship all in black".

The Duke's titles reverted to the Crown and, though Frances Teresa was granted a small bounty it is said that she disposed of it to a trust. She continued in court for many years but she died in 1702 and was buried next to her husband in the family vault in the Henry VII Chapel of Westminster Abbey. Her effigy in wax,

Frances Teresa Stuart.

145

modelled by Antoine Benoist, may be seen in the Abbey dressed in robes worn by the Duchess at Queen Anne's Coronation. However vacuous she appeared in her youth, Frances Teresa developed a fair measure of discretion in her later life. In her letters to her husband when he was in Denmark, she gave evidence of good sense and affection and she made bequests to several poor gentlewomen friends. She left a large sum of money to her impoverished relation Alexander Stuart, Lord Blantyre and it was used to purchase the Castle and lands of Lethington which were then called Lennoxlove, a name also given to the Scottish country dance, Lennoxlove to Blantyre.

"La Belle Stuart", as she was called, has figured on numerous medals and currency notes, notably as Britannia seated at the foot of a rock with the legend "Favente Deo". A special medal was struck in her honour in 1667 with Britannia on the reverse. She was certainly a remarkable lady whose beauty and uninhibited approach to royal circles enlivened the history of her time.

The following Elegy to Charles Stuart, Duke of Richmond, was printed for Philip Brooksby in 1673. The original is held in the British Library and is included in the Luttrell Collection of Eulogies and Elegies.

AN ELEGY
ON HIS GRACE THE ILLUSTRIOUS CHARLES STUART
DUKE OF RICHMOND AND LENNOX
Ambassador Extraordinary to the Crown of Denmark

Is this the News we expected from the Frost,
The Fatal Tidings that Great Richmond's lost?
Behold! how Britain's Genius shivering lies,
And trickling Icicles drew from its Eyes;
A sudden Damp has seized its spirits, and all
Our hopes are Frostnipt in his untimely fall;
Did Northern Stars there so severely Reign,
Not to be Counterchecked by Charles Wain?
Could not the Sovereign Star so guard his Heart
To gain some little respite from Death's Dart?

Twas subtly done, O Fate! thus to surprise
Him out of reach of his chaste Consort's eyes;
From her Life-breathing Lips had one Kiss come
That had call'd him back, and so reversed his Doom;
Grief's sables now surround the gloomy Room,
And sighs like Incense cloud it with Perfume
From her sweet breath; whilst her two Panting Breasts
Like little mournful birds, droop in their Nests;
The Funeral Tapers burn, but with dim Light;
Nought but her eyes, beneath her Veil, shine bright.
To rugged Charon she makes gentle moan,
Calmly to waft the Dearest Reliques home
From cruel Denmark's Shore; Hark! how she charms
The Churl, to the Elysium of her Arms,
To bring the twice cold Corpse, that her Sighs may
With Floods of Tears soften his stiffened Clay
Let none into her presence dare to Intrude
Once to disturb her graceful solitude;
She needs none of your help; let her alone,
The Turtle by herself loves to bemoan.
She has no leisure yet t'adhere to Fame,
Who must high Stories tell of his Great Name;
For Fame herself must court her lofty Ear,
For a fit time when she is pleased to hear
Her large Discourse of all that he hath done,
Since the first Scene of his great part begun.

Yet give me leave, Great Duchess! to let fall
The shady Curtain of his Funeral;
And draw in brief to the World's wond'ring Eye
Your Noble Duke's still living Effigie.
He was a Man – ('s Death! That I could not say
He was a Man) but moulded of the Clay
Of Nature's purest Mass, fraught with a mind
For his so brittle body too Refin'd;
And therefore unto Denmark was he sent,
As none more fit, His King to Represent,

Yet would not Death veil his High Character,
To show that SUCH, like KINGS still Mortal are;
Though in His Death he has as much to Boast,
As those that seem'd at Home to serve him most.
Thus left he all his SERVICES on score
Unsumed, Denied by Fate, to make them MORE.

(For easier reading, this Elegy has been somewhat modernised, mainly in spelling and punctuation but retaining throughout the meaning,verse form, flavour and tone of the original.)

References:
D.N.B. Vol. XL pp.80/81.
Moncrieffe, Sir I.B., *Highland Clans* (Barrie and Jenkins 1967) p.225.
The Oxford Companion of English Literature - ed. M. Drabble (Oxford 1985) p.41.
The Illustrated Pepys ed. Robert Latham (Bell and Hyman 1978) pp.8, 105 etc.
The Poetical Works of John Dryden (F. Warne London 1893) p.257.
The Poems and Fables of John Dryden ed. J. Kinsley (Oxford 1958) p.136.

CHAPTER 21

Charles Lennox (b.1672 - d.1723) The 1st Duke of Richmond in the Present Line

A N ACCOUNT OF THE life of Charles Lennox, 1st Duke of Richmond in the present line, must surely begin with his mother Louise de Kéroualle who came from France and became the long-term mistress of Charles II. She outlived both Charles and their son and played an important though not always popular role during a troublesome part of the King's reign and in Anglo-French history of that time.

King Charles' sister Henrietta had lived in France since childhood and had become involved in an unhappy marriage with the brother of Louis XIV. Louise de Kéroualle was twenty years old when she became a Maid of Honour to Henrietta and, at the celebrations for the signing of the Treaty of Dover, and on his visits to Henrietta, Charles was to meet Louise and become infatuated by her beauty. He was very close to Henrietta, calling her "his Minette", and without doubt she was an intelligent woman with a natural wit and diplomatic ability. Rather than use the normal channels of diplomacy she worked with Charles to complete the secretive personal negotiations which in 1670 led to the Treaty of Dover. The intention of the Treaty was to provide for a perpetual alliance between the Kings of England and France and to allow for King Charles to convert to Roman Catholicism when he saw fit to do so. It has been described as a camouflage Treaty, being more concerned to ensure England and France should work

Charles Lennox, 1st Duke of Richmond.
REPRODUCED BY COURTESY OF THE NATIONAL PORTRAIT GALLERY

together in preparing for a Dutch war rather than to establish any serious long-term state of unity between the two countries. Nevertheless, it was an agreement which held until the revolution of 1688 brought William of Orange to the English throne.

In June 1670 a tragedy occurred which greatly upset King Charles. News reached him of Henrietta's sudden death at her home in France. She had bathed in the River Seine on a very hot day and, after drinking a glass of chicory, she was taken ill and died. Overcome with grief, Charles became so bitter against the French that some feared the Anglo-French Alliance was in jeopardy. There was some suspicion that Henrietta had been poisoned but this could not be proved and today it is believed that she died of acute peritonitis. For Louise, the death of her generous mistress seemed disastrous for she had lost a powerful protector and her impulse was to think seriously of entering a convent in France.

King Charles had reached the age of forty and was tiring of his overbearing mistress Lady Castlemaine. Louise had so fascinated him that he was heard to say "She is the only jewel I covet". With the reluctant consent of Queen Catherine, the services of the 2nd Duke of Buckingham were used to invite Louise to come to England and become one of the Queen's Maids of Honour. After obtaining her parents' permission, Louise consented and came to England knowing that her decision had the full approval of the French King who clearly thought the move would provide an excellent opportunity to exert influence over Charles and the English court.

Queen Catherine and her close friend Frances Teresa, Duchess of Richmond, soon became concerned with the way Charles was swept off his feet by the attractions of Louise. Yet she was certainly not an easy conquest and it was many months before she succumbed to his advances despite diplomatic and ministerial encouragement. On 29th July, 1672 she gave birth to an infant son who was given the name of Charles Lennox. Initially, the child was not publicly acknowledged by King Charles but he soon developed a great liking for his son and, when aged three,

the young Charles Lennox was given a plethora of titles suppos-
edly to cover his bastardy. He was created Duke of Richmond and
given the titles of Baron of Settrington and Earl of March, as well
as High Steward of the City of York. In the Scottish peerage, he
not only succeeded to the Dukedom of Lennox, he became Baron
Methuen of Torbolton and Earl of Darnley.

Louise proved to be a good and loving mother though she was
very ambitious both for herself and her son. A Scottish lady was
appointed governess and Charles Lennox grew up a handsome
little boy, resembling his father in appearance, beloved and rather
pampered by his parents. Though he was brought up as a
Protestant, his father was always secretly inclined towards
Catholicism whilst Louise came from a strong Catholic family.
They were both well aware however of the strong anti-Catholic
feeling in England and complaints in Parliament of the growth
of popery. Religious divisions were to play no small part in the
life of the young Duke.

The King was attracted to Louise not only by her considerable beauty but also her knowledge and love of art and music. He
gave her the pet name of "Fubs". As time went on, he became
increasingly reliant on her ability to listen sympathetically to his
problems and suggest solutions. Yet Charles II was his own man
and, though he valued her opinions, he was never a puppet in her
hands and in the end, invariably followed his own counsel.
Nevertheless, Louise had a presence and the role she played as
an intermediary between the Kings of England and France at
difficult times gave her a status unusual for a King's mistress.

After the birth of Charles Lennox, Louise petitioned the
French King for permission to become an English subject so that
she could benefit from the gifts and honours which King Charles
wanted to lavish on her. She soon learned to spend money and
became greedy for rewards and honours. As well as her apartments in Whitehall, Charles assigned to her a pension of £10,000
a year and created her Duchess of Portsmouth. However, Louise
had to accept that she certainly had no monopoly over Charles II
in matters of sex for he also had the popular Nell Gwynn as a
mistress as well as the beautiful Italian Lady Hortesse.

Louise de Kéroualle.

153

The favours the King granted to Louise were unpopular with the mass of the people who liked Nell Gwynn and felt that she was not being adequately rewarded for her services in the King's bedroom. Louise was not generally popular, partly because she was French, Popish in her views, and regarded as a spy in the service of Louis XIV. She was foolish enough to believe and make known that Queen Catherine had only a short period to live and had visions that, after the Queen's death, she might be her successor. She liked to support the view that Charles wanted to be rid of his childless consort though, in fact, the King was very fond of his wife. Contrary to Louise's predictions, which had greatly antagonised the Queen's friend Frances Teresa, the Duchess of Richmond, Catherine did not die until 1705 when she was aged 67.

When he was only three, Charles Lennox was taken by Louise on a visit to France. She had great ambitions for him and hoped that he would eventually become a Catholic. She was concerned about his financial prospects, but King Charles was generous and provided him with an annuity of £2,000 together with a grant of Richmond Castle, a fee of £20 per annum for the support of the dignity of an Earl and £40 per annum for the support of the dignity of a Duke. By that time, the Castle and its land seemed all that remained of the great Honour of Richmond. Some thirty years later, Charles Lennox claimed that the grant included the houses built up against the Castle but legal opinion was against him and he had to withdraw his claim. The Richmond family retained full possession of the Castle until 1910 when it was leased to the Ministry of Works and later to English Heritage, though the ownership remains with the Duke of Richmond.

In 1677, the King granted Charles Lennox and his heirs a duty of one shilling on every chaldron of coal exported from the port of Newcastle upon Tyne. As manufacturing increased so did the number of laden barges leaving the Tyne and the benefits of the coal duty to the Richmond family of those days became very considerable. Even in the time of the 1st Duke, the annual payment reached £14,000 and, by the end of the 18th century, it had risen to an average of £21,000, a sizeable slice of the crown's total tax revenue. Though their expenditure on property building and maintenance was considerable and eventually led them into difficulties, the Richmonds had the income of an extremely rich family. The coal duty arose from a tax agreed by the burgesses of Newcastle as a substitute for paying the arrears of an ancient duty due to the crown on all coal sold to persons not franchised in the port of Newcastle Upon Tyne. It applied not only to pit coal but also stone and sea coals though coals destined for Hartlepool were exempt (see Chapter 22).

In 1681, the King made his son Master of the Horse and also Knight of the Garter which gave great satisfaction to Louise. Three years later she became seriously ill and expressed the fear that should she die, Charles Lennox would be quite unable to inherit her French assets because he was regarded as a foreigner. She sent a message asking King Louis XIV to issue letters of naturalisation to her son and this was quickly granted. Thinking no doubt of her old age, King Charles had appealed to the French King to revive the Duchy of Aubigny, the estate some 100 miles from Paris described in Chapter 18, and to gift it to Louise. Louis XIV knew well the service she had given to the English Court in the interests of France and he granted her the Duchy which included the Château de la Verrerie, later to become a favourite shooting lodge of the second Duke of Richmond. Louise recovered from her illness and in her later years, she did indeed settle in the Château of Aubigny though by then she was plagued with heavy debts because of her extravagant life style.

Charles II was aged fifty-five when he died following a stroke on Friday the 6th February 1685. On his death bed he spoke with special affection to the Duke of Richmond and blessed the rest of his family. His final request was to be able to die in the Catholic faith and, at the instigation of Louise de Kérualle, the last rites were administered by Father John Huddleston, a Benedictine monk who had saved Charles' life after the Battle of Worcester. The death of the King came as a great blow to Louise who knew well that it meant the loss of her political importance. The new

King, James II visited her within an hour of his brother's death assuring her of his protection and friendship but the truth was that James disliked her and she knew it.

Though James seemed to respect the late King's wish that Charles Lennox should become a Catholic, both Louise and the French King were indignant when James took away the position of Master of the Horse from the thirteen-year-old Duke of Richmond on the grounds that he was too young. In August 1685, Louise took her son to France and there the Duke was well received by Louis XIV and accepted as a Catholic. He came to England a year later but returned to France where he served with some distinction in the French Army as a volunteer in the army of Marshal d'Humières and as aide-de-camp to the Duke of Orléans. Louis XIV was pleased with him and, though Charles Lennox was only seventeen, he was given a company in the cavalry regiment. In England, his uncle King James was making preparations to invade Ireland to restore it to his kingdom. Charles Lennox was keen to take part but on being told he was too young he became frustrated and rebellious.

By temperament, the young Charles was proving unstable in character and liable to shift his political allegiance at will. In many ways he was like his mother who seldom pursued consistent policies. Yet he had an eye for the main chance and realised that, in England, his titles and the coal dues would make him someone of far greater influence than he could ever achieve on French Army pay. The young Duke left France in February 1692 without saying a word to anybody and travelled through Switzerland on his way back to England. His mother was in despair when she was told of his defection and though the French King was very angry he felt he could hardly blame Louise. William III, now the English King, regarded the young Duke with some distrust but Charles successfully petitioned the King for his titles, income and property. By way of payment he became a Whig and a supporter of the Hanoverian succession. He also declared himself to be a Protestant and his re-conversion to the Anglican Church took place in Lambeth Palace on 15th May, 1692. He also involved himself in Freemasonry and took his seat in the House of Lords. William III had by then become impressed by the young nobleman and made him one of his aides-de-camp.

Charles Lennox was barely twenty when he married a very attractive young widow. She was Anne, the daughter of Lord Brudenell and she was to prove a loyal and devoted wife. They had three children, two daughters, the eldest of which was named Louisa after the Duchess of Portsmouth, and a son who became Earl of March and later, the second Duke of Richmond. Anne developed a friendly association with her mother-in-law and, in her later years, Louise became a lonely woman who took great consolation in corresponding with her grandchildren.

The Duke of Richmond was fond of riding and in 1697 he bought Goodwood for use as a hunting lodge at a cost of £4,100, a property referred to in the Domesday Book as Godinwood. It consisted of a residence, described as a "mansion house", with a small estate of parkland and two farms. The original house of Goodwood is believed to have been built for £550 by the 9th Earl of Northumberland, whose steward had purchased it for him at a time when the Earl was "resident" in the Tower of London. Later generations of Richmonds altered and enlarged Goodwood to make it their family home and it is now no longer just a shooting lodge but an historic house at the centre of a 12,000 acre estate.

Though the Duke of Richmond had returned to marry and make his home in England, which his mother came to accept, she was very critical of his lifestyle. He favoured the French in his outlook and, perhaps because of this, he found it difficult to obtain a job at Court or any military commission. Consequently, he spent a great deal of his time hunting and his frequent drinking bouts and gambling were well known though his loyal wife always did her best to fend off criticism. He had the easy pleasant manners of his father but he lacked strength of character and was an unprincipled adventurer throughout his life.

In 1702, by the death of the Dowager Duchess of Richmond, he came into possession of the Lennox estates which he sold to an unknown purchaser who then sold them on to the Duke of Montrose. In 1713, he visited Paris again and he was mysteri-ously wounded in an attack near the Pont Neuf. Though he appeared to recover, he died at Goodwood in May 1723, his wife Anne surviving him by only a few months. The Duke was buried in King Henry VII's Chapel at Westminster Abbey but his body was later removed to Chichester Cathedral.

Greatly saddened by the death of her son, Louise became very pious and religious. She founded a convent in the grounds of her estate and during the last few years of her life she occupied herself in performing charitable deeds in her town of Aubigny. In her letters she was always seeking sympathy from her grandson for her straitened circumstances and indifferent health. In 1734, when she was eighty-four, she visited her doctors in Paris but died in November of that year. On her death, Charles Lennox, the 2nd Duke of Richmond, succeeded to the Dukedom of Aubigny.

The following poem inscribed to the 1st Duke of Richmond was printed in London for J. Wilcox at the Green Dragon in Little Britain, S. Chapman, at the Angel and Crown in Pall Mall; and sold by J. Peele at Lock's Head in Paternoster Row. The author is unknown but may have been Thwaits, the "merry witty" innkeeper and Proctor of Richmond mentioned in the poem. (*British Library Ref. 1161 and Camdens Britannia enlarged by Richard Gough (1806 edition)*)

A POEM HUMBLY INSCRIBED TO HIS GRACE
CHARLES DUKE OF RICHMOND 1721

Phoebus, descend, on thy own[a] RICHMOND shine,
Her fruitful Hills, and Stream that is[b] Divine,
Her ever rolling Flood; thrice happy[c] Swale,
Blest are thy Banks, and doubly blest thy[d] Dale.

In pious Times, when Vertue was rever'd,
Religion practised then, as well as heard:
Some Venerable Piles[e] were founded here,
Whose sacred[f] Ruins now too plain appear;
Where on a rugged[g] Rock, of old there stood
A Castle, to defend the Norman[h] Blood;
From whence an Ancient Race of Kings we Date,

Enroll'd within the Book of Time and Fate;
Whence by Descent the Illustrious[i] Stuarts came;
And gave to[k] Lenox RICHMOND'S greater Name.
Then Martyr'd CHARLES began his Sacred Reign,
CHARLES the Delight at once of Gods and Men:
His Royal SON of never dying Fame
Of CHARLES and RICHMOND gave this Shining Name
To Thee! - - - - - - - - - - - - - - - - - -

a) Richmond is a large town in the North Riding of Yorkshire, situated upon three hills, which give three different prospects of it, with large hills on all sides. This gives title to the present Duke of Richmond.
b) Camden tells us that the River Swale was called "Divine"; from Paulinus, a Bishop, who in the times of paganism converted at one time some thousands to the Christian religion and baptised them in this stream.
c) Swale in the Saxon language signifies any sudden flush or rapid current of water.
d) The whole valley on each side of the River for many miles together, is called "Swaledale".
e) In and about this place have been many religious houses, abbeys, priories and nunneries, founded and endowed by the Earls of Richmond.
f) Here is a beautiful tower, the remains of a church that belonged to the Friary, called now the Friary in the town.
g) The rock is very cragged, steep and inaccessible on the south side, where it is almost perpendicular to the River Swale,betwixt the bridge and the mills; on the other side, the ascent is gradual from the east and north-east part of the town.
h) The first Earl of Richmond was Alan, surnamed "the Red".
i) Margaret, daughter of Henry VII, who was last Earl of Richmond, was married to the Scots King, from whence descended James I, King of England.
k) The Duke of Lenox, who came from Scotland with King James. and was afterwards created Duke of Richmond.

From such exalted Birth who claims Descent
Can want no Praise, no fulsome Compliment;
Your Regal[l] SIRE for you made this his Choice,
As Heaven did Canaan, next to Paradise.
This does as that, with Milk and Honey flow,
And Rocks[m] and Cliffs their Bounteous Gifts bestow;
Round all her Walls is one continued[n] Mine,
And Sacred Metals in her Bowels shine.
The Noble Pile the lofty Turrets show,

Her Strength we from the Vale survey below;
But when upon the mounting Cliff we stand,
And take a Prospect of the Neighbouring Land;
Where Hills and Vales and Shady Banks appear,
Rich flow'ry Meads, sweet fertile Pastures there;
Where the swift Stream o'er Rocky Pavements rolls,
Here foaming Surges no fierce Wind controls;
But Cascades, like the rapid Currents, flow
And form the harmonious Cataracts Below.

l) King Charles II, father to the present Duke of Richmond.
m) The town of Richmond, and the neighbourhood, have of late, by digging into
    the rock called Castle Hill, discovered a treasure of various sorts of Roman,
    Saxon and English silver coins; one of these, by the letters and inscriptions,
    seems to be a dedication in remembrance of some Abbot or Prior of the
    Cistercians. They are reckoned to be of some thousand pounds value and
    are undoubtedly the property of his Grace the Duke of Richmond.
n) In all the hills about the town, copper or lead is found and the very stones
    in some of the rocks are full of copper.

Then see at Distance from each Mountain Side,
Pure Streams of Rich Metallic Juices Glide;
Here lies a bed of Massy Copper Ore,
The Cyprian Goddess[o] treasur'd up in store
For happy Thee, in ev'ry Hill and Grove,
Where we still trace the Beauteous QUEEN of LOVE;[p]
And Plenty stretching forth her lib'ral Hand,
To bring in Saturn's Reign[q] to RICHMOND's Land;
For, Search the Bowels of the Teeming Earth,
Here Lead and Coal and Stone are brought to Birth;
And wholesome Streams, with Springs of Chrystal Hue
Present their Fountain-Heads at ev'ry View,
There with their Salutary Influence flow
Around thy Walls, and healing Gifts bestow.

o) The Cyprian Goddess is Venus, the planet to which copper is assigned.
p) The beauteous Queen of Love is the same thing.
q) Saturn's reign signifies the many lead mines that have been discovered of
    late years about Richmond.

Now let my Muse survey the Town within,
And see the Kitchens[r] dirty, and the Streets lie clean;
But this is owing to thy Product Swale,
The fruitful Fields and Pastures of[s] Wensleydale,
Where lowing Oxen glad the Breeder's Eye,
And Neighing Steeds the well-fenc'd Mounds defie,
But turn Melpomene, turn back and see,
RICHMOND of high Parnassus an Epitome;
Phoebus thy Sire, disdains not here to Shine,
For there we find a Helicon Divine;[t]
We may thro' a much larger Country look
For Hills like these, a Steam and such a Brook;[u]
But for a POET, Muse be[w] THWAITS thy Song,
Thou will die too soon, or he will live too long.

r) "Dirty", a word not introduced to discredit the good housewifery of the ladies in this part of the country, but to show that plenty was so great of all manner of provisions that it was no easy matter to keep their kitchens clean.
s) Wensleydale is a very fruitful part which is famous for breeding of black cattle and excellent horses.
t) An incomparable school is here that was founded and endowed by Queen Elizabeth with an industrious and able Master.
u) The Reverend and worthy Rector of the place Mr Brook.
w) A merry witty fellow that keeps an inn and is Proctor in Richmond.

(For easier reading, the wording has been somewhat modernised mainly in the spelling and punctuation but retaining throughout the meaning, verse form and tone of the original.)

References:
Clark, Sir George. *The Later Stuarts* (Oxford 1934) pp.76/78.
C.P.E. Vol. 4 No.836.
D.N.B. Vol. XL p.920.
Olsen, A. *The Radical Duke* (Oxford 1961) pp.1/2
Tillyard, Stella. *Aristocrats* (Vintage 1994) p.9.
Waggett, R. *The Duke of Richmond's Claim* in The Richmond Civic Society Review No.12 pp.29/30.
For the life of Louise de Kéroualle refer:
Bevan, B., *Charles II's French Mistresses* (Hale 1979) and Hardy, A., *The King's Mistresses* (Evans 1960).

THE LINEAGE OF THE DUKES OF RICHMOND

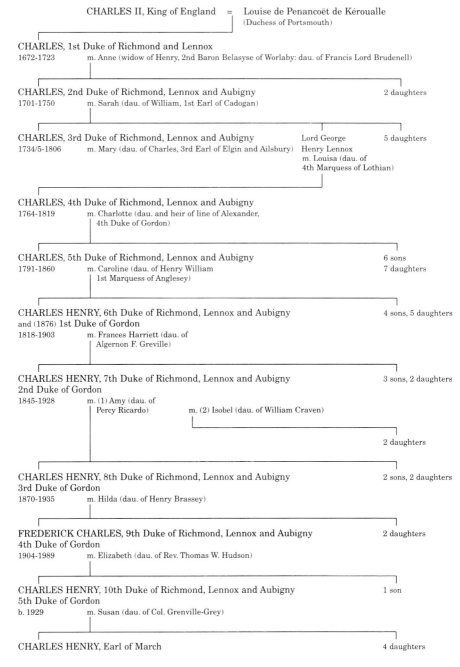

CHARLES II, King of England = Louise de Penancoët de Kéroualle
(Duchess of Portsmouth)

CHARLES, 1st Duke of Richmond and Lennox
1672-1723   m. Anne (widow of Henry, 2nd Baron Belasyse of Worlaby: dau. of Francis Lord Brudenell)

CHARLES, 2nd Duke of Richmond, Lennox and Aubigny   2 daughters
1701-1750   m. Sarah (dau. of William, 1st Earl of Cadogan)

CHARLES, 3rd Duke of Richmond, Lennox and Aubigny   Lord George   5 daughters
1734/5-1806   m. Mary (dau. of Charles, 3rd Earl of Elgin and Ailsbury)   Henry Lennox
                                                        m. Louisa (dau. of
                                                        4th Marquess of Lothian)

CHARLES, 4th Duke of Richmond, Lennox and Aubigny
1764-1819   m. Charlotte (dau. and heir of line of Alexander,
              4th Duke of Gordon)

CHARLES, 5th Duke of Richmond, Lennox and Aubigny   6 sons
1791-1860   m. Caroline (dau. of Henry William   7 daughters
              1st Marquess of Anglesey)

CHARLES HENRY, 6th Duke of Richmond, Lennox and Aubigny   4 sons, 5 daughters
and (1876) 1st Duke of Gordon
1818-1903   m. Frances Harriett (dau. of
              Algernon F. Greville)

CHARLES HENRY, 7th Duke of Richmond, Lennox and Aubigny   3 sons, 2 daughters
2nd Duke of Gordon
1845-1928   m. (1) Amy (dau. of
              Percy Ricardo)   m. (2) Isobel (dau. of William Craven)

                                                        2 daughters

CHARLES HENRY, 8th Duke of Richmond, Lennox and Aubigny   2 sons, 2 daughters
3rd Duke of Gordon
1870-1935   m. Hilda (dau. of Henry Brassey)

FREDERICK CHARLES, 9th Duke of Richmond, Lennox and Aubigny   2 daughters
4th Duke of Gordon
1904-1989   m. Elizabeth (dau. of Rev. Thomas W. Hudson)

CHARLES HENRY, 10th Duke of Richmond, Lennox and Aubigny   1 son
5th Duke of Gordon
b. 1929   m. Susan (dau. of Col. Grenville-Grey)

CHARLES HENRY, Earl of March   4 daughters

CHAPTER 22

The Richmond Shilling

A MAJOR AND PERHAPS unexpected factor in the lives of the early Dukes of Richmond was the income they received from a duty on coal shipped from the River Tyne. Coal was indeed the major source of their income and it not only paid for their lifestyle, it also enabled them to build and develop their property at Goodwood and Richmond House in London. To learn more about the history of this important duty on coal production we must go back at least to the reign of Queen Elizabeth I and even as far as the Plantagenet Edward III.

Edward was the first monarch to allow a charge to be made on coal production though at the time he probably thought it of no great significance. He agreed that the burgesses of Newcastle upon Tyne could levy a charge on all coal sold to "the natives of this country" though he reserved for himself a tax on all the coal sold to foreign buyers. The burgesses made the most of their freedom to make a charge and they benefited considerably from a rapid increase in coal production. In Henry V's reign the charge appears to have been two pence on every chaldron of coal and, by the end of the sixteenth century, an increase to four pence per chaldron brought in £10,000 a year, a very considerable sum in those times.

Queen Elizabeth seemed well aware of "the Newcastle bounty" and clearly felt that coal should be properly taxed for the benefit of her Exchequer. In 1599, she demanded a payment in arrears from the Mayor and burgesses of Newcastle but they pleaded inability to meet her demands. They agreed however

163

that, in future, a duty of one shilling would be imposed on every chaldron of the coal which passed through their hands. It was a compromise arrangement peculiar to the Tyne and it was the origin of what later became known as the Richmond Shilling, a tax which was to exist in one form or another until 1831. It was a tax which Parliament acknowledged as being part of the inheritance of the Crown to be disposed of as the monarch saw fit. An additional burden imposed by Elizabeth was the requirement to pay a duty of five shillings per chaldron on all coal transported overseas. This applied to all ports including Liverpool but there were so many protests that relief from the tax had to be provided.

The sale of coals on the Tyne had always been in the hands of a guild or fraternity of persons known as hostmen or oatemen, and they acted as middlemen between the owners of the coal mines and the merchants who frequented the port. The origin of the hostmen appears to date from 1404 when it was ordained by statute that, in every city, town or seaport to which foreign merchants repaired, "hosts" should be appointed with whom the merchants might dwell during their stay. On the 8th of April, 1600, the Company of Hostmen of the town of Newcastle received a charter of incorporation and then exercised the exclusive privilege of vending all coals shipped on the River Tyne imposing a duty of one shilling for every chaldron of coal, Newcastle Measure, except overseas shipments. The term "Newcastle Measure" is important for the weight of a chaldron of coal at Newcastle in the 18th century was about 53 cwts, twice that of the London weight. The extent of the coal leaving the Tyne can be gauged by the shipping that was involved. In 1615, 200 boats were engaged in carrying coal to London and another 200 were used to supply other parts of the country.

As a result of the rapid growth of the coal trade by the end of the sixteenth century, the Newcastle hostmen rose to a position of much influence and importance, particularly because some were colliery owners as well as hostmen. Nevertheless, they had to undertake to pay the shilling tax and a recognised system of tax collection was developed which appeared to bridge the gap between the colliery and the ship which loaded the coal. The owner of the colliery employed a person free of the hostman's company, who was usually called a coal-fitter, and his job was to pay the coal owner a stipulated price for every chaldron of coal he received. He then sold the coal to the ship's master and, when the ship was laden, the fitter made up his account including the amount due to the Duke of Richmond and his own expenses and costs, and charged the total to the ship's master. The Richmond Shilling money was then paid to the agent in the Customs House so that, in practice, the ship's master paid the duty although it was due to be paid by the fraternity of hostmen.

It was in 1677 that King Charles II decreed that the duty on coal was to be paid to his natural son Charles Lennox, Duke of Richmond and, failing him and his heirs, to Louise, Duchess of Portsmouth and thence to the heirs of her body. In effect, King Charles was giving the young Duke a substantial slice of the Crown's revenue which increased in direct proportion to mining and manufacturing. At the beginning of the 18th century, the coal dues already produced £5,000 a year which was sufficient to enable an aristocrat and his family to live very comfortably. By the end of the century, payment had increased enormously and exceeded £20,000. An examination of the annual shipments from the Tyne in that century indicates that payments may have peaked at a figure as high as £30,000.

Payments of the Richmond Shilling continued but there was a private act in 1757, when George II allowed the 3rd Duke of Richmond to make a jointure on his marriage to Lady Mary Bruce providing her with £3,000 annually. In the year 1799, during the life of the 3rd Duke, agreement was reached for the surrender of Richmond's coal dues to the Government and, as compensation, an annuity of £19,000 was to be paid from the Consolidated Fund. This was commuted later for £633,333.6.9d of 3 per cent stock and, in 1831, the collection of the duty was discontinued after representations from the Newcastle hostmen.

References:
Act of Parliament ES523 relating to Coal Dues.
Brand, J., *The History of Newcastle* (B. White & Sons 1789) p.298
Bunning, Tho. Wood., *An Account of the Duties on Coal* (Andrew Reid 1883)
Surtees Society Vol.19 pp.25, 211, 223/5
The Chronicles & Records of the Northern Coal Trade in Durham and Northumberland, in *North of England Institute of Mining Engineers Transactions* Vol.XV pp.185-6.
The Rise and Fall of the British Coal Industry (Cass 1966) ii. pp.306/7.

CHAPTER 23

Charles Lennox (b.1701 - d.1750) the 2nd Duke of Richmond

WHERE HIS FATHER had weakness, Charles Lennox the 2nd Duke of Richmond had strength. He held high rank in the Army, was elected a Member of Parliament and, after his succession, became a member of the Court and a political figure much involved in the affairs of Government. Yet he was a respected family man, ambitious for sobriety and dignity rather than advancement, a lover of the countryside with a liking for sports including cricket and a particular interest in maintaining and improving his properties which included Goodwood and Richmond Castle, an interest which involved him in a considerable financial commitment.

He was born at Goodwood on the 18th May 1701, a grandson of Charles II and with the title of Earl of March, heir to the Dukedom of Richmond. He was only a year old when William of Orange died and Queen Anne came to the throne. The Earl's early years were spent peacefully at Goodwood with his sister Louisa Lennox and, as he grew up, he learned to ride and enjoy the many country pursuits that were available. A hunting accident when he was about twelve gave concern to his mother and served as a reminder of the dangers of horse riding. For some unknown reason he was never sent to school and was given a private and probably imperfect education at home by a tutor, Thomas Hill, who became his guide, philosopher and lifelong friend. Though wayward in his lessons, the Earl was a likeable young man endowed with good looks as well as agreeable qualities which always enhanced his popularity.

His father made frequent trips to London and Europe and, apparently to stave off boredom, indulged in long bouts of gambling often playing for large stakes. When he visited The Hague in 1719, he built up a large debt to the Irish Earl of Cadogan who was one of Marlborough's staff officers and a confidant. To settle the debt and seal his friendship, the Duke gave his son and heir, the Earl of March, as husband for Cadogan's daughter Sarah, accepting a reduction of five thousand pounds in her marriage settlement to make up the difference. Sarah was hardly thirteen years old and the young Earl of March only eighteen and, when told of this extraordinary arrangement, the little girl was speechless and the Earl, who was not exactly impressed with his future bride, was heard to mutter "Surely you are not going to marry me to that dowdy". However, the two young people were brought together in The Hague and a marriage ceremony was solemnised. Afterwards, Sarah returned to her family and the Earl set off with his friend and tutor Tom Hill on a three-year tour which had been arranged to visit Holland, France, Austria and Italy.

Three years elapsed and, on his return to London, Lord March was in no hurry to visit his young bride. He went one evening to the opera and, looking around him, he noticed a beautiful young lady in a box surrounded by admirers. He asked his neighbour "Who is that lovely young creature in the box?". "You must be a stranger in London not to know the reigning toast of the Town. That is the beautiful Lady March". Lord March lost no time in claiming his wife and it proved to be a very happy marriage.

In view of the gambling debt arrangement, the success of the union came as a considerable relief to the couple's relations and to none more than to Sarah's father Lord Cadogan. He became concerned however when March and his wife left England for another visit to Holland. He wrote to his son-in-law encouraging them to return to London where they would be greatly welcomed by their friends and reminded March that he should be present when the King reviewed the Horse Guards. There was also implied criticism in the letter of the young Earl's financial extravagance. The couple did return to London and in that way the letter had some effect, though their financial excesses continued to give some concern. They settled down to make their home at Richmond House overlooking the Thames. Later, the Earl became a patron of Canaletto who painted his famous views "The Thames from Richmond House" and "Whitehall from Richmond House", both of which still hang at Goodwood.

In 1722, the Earl was elected Member of Parliament for Chichester having been returned unopposed for the seat which had been kept open for him whilst he was on his three-year tour of Europe. The mentor for the Earl's election was Thomas Pelham-Holles, 1st Duke of Newcastle, then Lord Chamberlain. Richmond had to give up his seat when he succeeded to the Dukedom in the following year, but a long-lasting friendship then developed between the two Dukes based on their mutual interest in politics. They were concerned with local Sussex politics and their relationship was founded on a mutual support for Whig principles. Both became Privy Councillors and national figures with the wealthy and powerful Duke of Newcastle relying on Richmond's advice on military matters. They corresponded frequently on national and more local matters over a period of twenty-five years and later Richmond corresponded with Henry Pelham, the Duke of Newcastle's brother, who became Member of Parliament for the County of Sussex and for eleven years held the position of 1st Lord of the Treasury. These historic letters held by the Sussex Record Society and at the British Library have been edited and published for the Society by Timothy J. McCann.

It was in March 1723 that Sarah gave birth to the young Richmond's first child, a daughter they named Georgina Caroline. Caroline, as she become known, was to be the first of twelve children, though only seven survived. Two months later, Charles, the 1st Duke of Richmond died at Goodwood. He had been in failing health for some time and the Earl had been warned by his mother that the Duke was "extremely decay'd". So the Earl became Charles, the 2nd Duke of Richmond and succeeded to all his father's titles. Other honours were to follow and, in 1725, he was created a Knight of the Order of the Bath and then became the recipient of the Most Noble Order of the Garter, both of these Orders having been revived by George I. The year 1727 saw the coronation of George II and Queen Caroline. This was naturally a major occasion and, having been appointed Lord High Constable of England for the day, the Duke took a prominent part in the ceremonial arrangements.

He had begun his service in the army on return from his European tour. Though his military career appears to have caused little interruption to his other activities and his active service life was comparatively short, he nevertheless played a significant part in some of the major campaigns of the day. His service record shows that in September 1722 he was made a Captain in the Royal Regiment of Horse Guards and having impressed as a particularly conscientious officer, he was soon promoted to the rank of Major.

In 1743, having by then been appointed as Master of the Horse, he accompanied the King throughout the campaign in Europe and was responsible for a baggage train of 662 horses as well as a complement of carriages and wagons. He gave service at the Battle of Dettingen, the last occasion in which a British sovereign led his troops into battle, and Richmond's presence there enabled him to defend his regiment against an unjust charge of cowardice. When Charles Edward Stuart, the Young Pretender, launched his invasion in Scotland in 1745, Richmond immediately offered his services in support of the Hanoverian dynasty and, having been made a Lieutenant General he was to attain the rank of General. He was in command of the forces which awaited the Scottish Jacobites on their march south and subsequently chased the retreating Scots as far as Carlisle before returning to his Goodwood estate. Late in his life he was appointed Colonel of the Royal Horse Guards and this reunited him with officers he had served under as a young man. It was this final appointment which is believed to have given him the greatest pleasure of his army career.

His inheritance of Goodwood, where he spent much of his youth gave him a great interest. Though the house provided a good and well-appointed home he soon began to make improvements and before long extended the estate by buying the adjoining manors of Singleton and Charlton. He had a great love of trees and obtained and planted oak and beech trees, a plane tree from the Caucasus and a great variety of exotic species, notably pines, cedars of Lebanon, tulip trees and thujas. On a hill behind the House the Duke built Carné's Seat. a stone temple from which there are panoramic views of the coats of Sussex and Hampshire. One of Goodwood's attractions is the shell house which was decorated by Charles' wife Sarah and their two elder daughters with shells brought mainly from the West Indies. Shells cover the walls like stuccoed plaster and were woven into ribbons and bows, twisted into ropes and written in the initials of the Duke and his daughters. It is thought to have taken seven years to complete and remains today as probably the finest surviving early 18th-century shell work in the country.

One of the Duke's loves was animals and he proceeded to establish a menagerie in part of the Goodwood estate. It contained animals and birds from many parts of the world and included a lion, two tigers, leopards, five wolves and a jackal while amongst the bird population were eagles and vultures. Its fame spread and zoologists as well as curious sightseers travelled from far and wide to see it. Apart from the cost of building his menagerie the Duke had to meet a food bill which included 70 lbs of meat a day. It was clearly an expensive undertaking and provided a considerable extra burden on the Goodwood housekeeping.

His early years in the countryside of Goodwood had given the Duke a great love of cricket which he learned to play and which provided him with a lifetime interest even though his friends seemed apt to criticise his own performance with the bat. Though there are references in history to cricket games in which the Duke played, including a challenge match against Sir William Gage, M.P. for Seaford, he is remembered particularly for agreeing a first set of rules with a Mr Brodrick of Peper Harow in Surrey. The game of cricket was becoming deeply rooted amongst men living in the southern part of England, particularly in Sussex, and the Duke was regarded as a pioneer responsible for building up a successful county team. Recognition is certainly due to him for his part in formulating the Laws of Cricket as we know them today.

For most of his life the Duke was involved in some sort of building work, with consequent expense. Apart from other work at Goodwood, he built a hunting lodge when he was made Master of the Charlton Hunt. In London, work to rebuild Richmond House had obliged the Richmonds to rent other London properties. They moved to a house in Pall Mall, another in Arlington Street and then rented Vanburgh Castle for a time. Even there, the Duke could not resist building alterations. He was always planning alterations or improvements to his properties and made entries in his notebook about his intentions. Of work he intended to arrange at Richmond Castle he noted "Repair the Tower so that it may not fall down" and "Repair the walls everywhere where they are undermined". He even had plans prepared to rebuild Goodwood but these, like some others, were never brought to fruition, though he added the south-west front.

When not at Goodwood or in London, the Duke and Duchess made numerous excursions to The Hague and to Aubigny where they visited the elderly and failing Louise de Kéroualle. With his building, travelling and many other activities, it is not surprising that their debts became ominously heavy. They had been mounting steadily towards the end of 1723 when the death occurred of the Duke's mother, Anne the widowed Duchess of Richmond. After the funeral, the Duke's uncle, Lord Cadogan, chose the moment to write to him saying how concerned he was at the extent of the debt that had built up and suggested that he should borrow £10,000 to repay his creditors, setting aside £2,500 each year to repay the borrowing. It was a forthright reminder to the Duke that he must mend his ways otherwise his creditors could "blast his reputation and character". The letter had considerable effect and the Duke at once acknowledged that he must economise and reform. However, he was a spender by nature and his life was never really free from financial problems.

In their early married life, the Richmonds had been obliged to spend much time in London because of their Court duties. The Duke had been appointed aide-de-camp to King George I and, after the succession of George II, he was confirmed as Lord of the Bedchamber, a position which he held for seven years. It was for this service that the King appointed him Master of the Horse, a position which involved considerable entertainment. The Duchess became for a time Lady of the Bedchamber to Queen Caroline but the Richmonds were to lose a son who lived only a few hours after birth and, for the benefit of his wife's health, the Duke decided to take her on a European tour, staying for some time with Louise de Kéroualle at Aubigny.

In 1731, another daughter named Emily was successfully born and four years later came Charles, the son the Richmonds had hoped for. The young Charles was destined to become the 3rd Duke of Richmond. but his birth came too late to bring pleasure to the Duchess of Portsmouth who died in November, 1734. In the following year, the Richmonds went to France for three months to claim their Aubigny inheritance and to pay homage to the French King. The Duke became very fond of France and enjoyed hunting in his estate. He began to visit France every autumn, often combining these visits with a journey to The Hague where he stayed with friends or with his wife's family. His knowledge of the European courts and his popularity made him an obvious choice for an Embassy in Paris and his appointment as special Ambassador in Paris in October 1748 came as no surprise.

Of the Richmond children who survived there was a second son named George and three other daughters Louisa, Sarah and Cecilia. As they grew up, the daughters were all much lauded for their beauty and particularly Sarah who was wooed by the young George III and was painted by Reynolds. All the daughters married except Cecilia, who died young, but the marriage of Caroline, the eldest daughter, created a major division in the Richmond family.

Caroline had met Henry Fox at Goodwood in the 1730's and on many subsequent occasions in Whitehall drawing-rooms. She found him an attractive, personable man and, in 1742 when they met again, she fell passionately in love with him. She was only 19 and he was aged 37, an ambitious Member of Parliament and a Lord of the Treasury. Though he was described as being short, stout and pear shaped, he was well read, friendly and domestic. Though the Richmonds were happy to entertain him as a friend, they thought him impossible as a suitor. Henry had been a Tory, a member of a party which had given some support to the Jacobean rebellion and, in consequence, Toryism was tainted with treachery and disloyalty towards the Hanoverian dynasty. As it offered little hope for an ambitious politician, Henry had just changed sides and become a Whig. He had inherited a fortune from his father but, with a propensity for gambling, had squandered it in a very short time. With support from a wealthy admirer however, he had been able to enter Parliament where he became a Walpole supporter. In the Richmonds' opinion, he was too old for Sarah and they recoiled from his ambition, thirst for power and money, as well as his atheism.

When, with Caroline's consent, Fox approached the Duke to ask for his daughter's hand in marriage there was firm refusal. The Duke then wrote confirming his decision and told Fox to forget the whole affair: if he persisted he would be ruined. The Richmonds could not understand why their daughter had fallen for such an unsuitable man. Fox was not giving up however and when, ultimately, he wrote suggesting that he knew Caroline better than the Duchess, the Richmonds were furious and planned to take Caroline to Goodwood where she could be kept apart from Fox and made to realise that marriage to him was not possible.

However, Fox decided that the time had come to act. He had a secret meeting with Caroline and, faced with making a decision, she agreed that they should be secretly married at the home of a well-wisher and that, afterwards, she would return home and remain there until her parents went to Goodwood. Everything went smoothly and they were married at the house of a friend, Charles Hanbury Williams. Caroline then returned home to break the news to her parents and Fox wrote to the Richmonds saying that as there was no hope that they would consent to the marriage, he and Caroline had taken the only course possible. He asked if Caroline could stay at Richmond House until the Richmonds went to Goodwood. The Duke was so angry that he refused to allow Caroline to stay one further night in his house. She returned to the home of Hanbury Williams having been banished by her mother and father from her childhood home.

THE LENNOX FAMILY

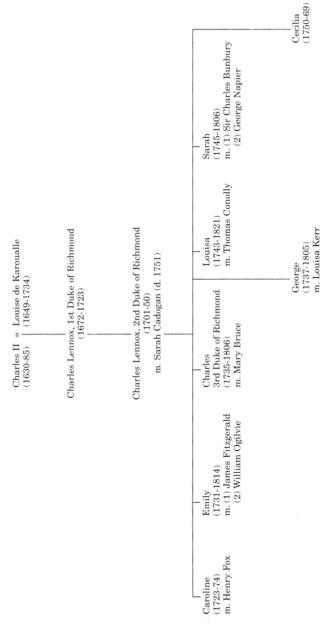

Charles II = Louise de Karoualle
(1630-85) (1649-1734)

Charles Lennox, 1st Duke of Richmond
(1672-1723)

Charles Lennox, 2nd Duke of Richmond
(1701-50)
m. Sarah Cadogan (d. 1751)

Caroline
(1723-74)
m. Henry Fox

Emily
(1731-1814)
m. (1) James Fitzgerald
(2) William Ogilvie

Charles
3rd Duke of Richmond
(1735-1806)
m. Mary Bruce

George
(1737-1805)
m. Louisa Kerr

Louisa
(1743-1821)
m. Thomas Conolly

Sarah
(1745-1806)
m. (1) Sir Charles Bunbury
(2) George Napier

Cecilia
(1750-69)

There was no doubt that Caroline and Fox had married for love and they presented a well matched and happily united couple but, despite sympathy and support from many quarters, they were outcasts from the Richmonds for the next four years. After a visit to Cheltenham, Henry and Caroline moved to a London house in Conduit Street where Caroline began to develop an interest in her husband's ambitions and became something of a political hostess. In 1745 Caroline gave birth to a son but a second son delivered the following year died from fever. Illness then drove Caroline to seek treatment in Bath both for herself and for her surviving son.

In London, Henry concentrated on furthering his political career in support of Robert Walpole. Yet in the four years between 1742 and 1746 there was political turmoil at home matched only by the turbulence of the European war. King George II fought and beat the French at the Battle of Dettingen, but the general drift of the war was in favour of the French and their allies. Walpole resigned and the King came to rely on the advice of Lord Carteret rather than that of the experienced Duke of Newcastle, long-time friend of the Duke of Richmond. With the war going badly, Carteret was eventually dismissed and patience with the monarch finally wore out. In February 1746 virtually the whole administration resigned including Henry Fox and the Duke of Richmond. In the new administration which followed, Fox was given the job of Secretary for War, an onerous task at that particular time but one which gave him a cabinet post.

Having been made Secretary for War, Henry began to look for a new house and decided to lease a large, old and decaying mansion known as Holland House. Though it suited Caroline who liked antiques, it seemed too cold a house for guests to stay, but its proximity to Westminster was a great advantage. The elevation in the role of Henry Fox marked the beginning of a reconciliation with the Richmonds. The Duke had been keeping a shrewd eye on the career of his son-in-law and as Fox rose in prominence, so he had risen in the Duke's estimation.

Caroline's sister Emily, to whom she had always been close, married the Earl of Kildare and went to live in Ireland. Again,

Charles Lennox, 2nd Duke of Richmond and Sarah, his wife.

the Richmonds were not fully in favour but time and the arrival of grandchildren clearly softened the feelings of the Duke and Duchess. In March, 1748, the Duke wrote a gracious letter of reconciliation to Caroline and Henry Fox. Though the Duchess still found it difficult to forgive Henry, the break in the Richmond family relationship had been mended and the Duke and Duchess happily assumed the role of grandparents. Only two years after the reconciliation, the Duke died. He was taken ill in the summer of 1750 and a planned visit to stay with his daughter Emily in Ireland had to be cancelled. He was travelling from London to his much-loved Goodwood but he broke his journey at Godalming and did not feel well enough to continue. His wife was called but despite her devoted nursing the Duke passed away a week later. He was buried in Chichester Cathedral where his father's remains were to be laid after removal from Westminster Abbey. A year later, the Duchess too was dead.

The Duke was a man always spoken of with respect and affection by his contemporaries and by his many friends in Sussex where he had been a Member of Parliament and High Steward of Chichester. In his later years he was particularly remembered for the way he used his local power and influence to try to defeat the notorious Sussex smugglers. Indeed, he spent the last three years of his life tracking down and recording their activities.

Many honours were given to him during his lifetime. He followed a number of intellectual pursuits especially art. As a great patron of Canaletto he commissioned two pictures of the London scene from Richmond House and he is known to have purchased two small views of Venice on copper. Using the services of the artist's agent Owen McSwiney, he also procured a series of allegoric tomb paintings. The Duke's interests included a study of medicine, science and antiquity. In April 1728, he was awarded a Doctorate of Law at the University of Cambridge which was followed by his election as a Fellow of the Royal College of Physicians and, as President of the London Hospital he gave outstanding service in the medical field. The year 1736 saw his election as a Fellow of the Society of Antiquities and later his appointment as Elder Brother of Trinity House. He became a

Governor of the Charterhouse and he was an enthusiastic Freemason who was Grand Master of the Grand Lodge of England in 1724.

The Second Duke of Richmond was indeed a man with an extraordinary range of interests who did not seek advancement yet achieved success and wide recognition for his integrity. Though he was a Privy Councillor and took part in the deliberations of the Cabinet he was not remembered as a statesman, but as a likeable and abnormally trustworthy man he gained the respect of the King who believed him to be one of the few genuine disinterested adherents of the dynasty.

Much publicity has been given to the five daughters of the 2nd Duke's marriage; to Emily who lived a life of luxury in Ireland yet produced no less than 22 children, to Louisa who was childless and discarded her wealth in favour of bringing up poor children and to Sarah who became an outcast after her affair with royalty but ultimately found happiness as the wife of a career soldier. These sisters were rebellious by nature and led complicated lives, often being involved in or on the fringes of the major political events of their time, yet they were essentially family minded and supportive of each other. When their father died, it was Emily, rather than her elder sister Caroline, who looked after the needs of the two younger sisters Sarah and Cecilia.

References:
D.N.B. Vol. X1 pp.921/2.
March, The Earl of, *A Duke and his Friends* (Vol. 1/2) (Hutchinson 1911).
Marshall, J., *The Duke who was Cricket* (Muller 1961)
The Correspondence of the Dukes of Richmond and Newcastle Ed. by Timothy J. McCann (Sussex Record Office 1982/3).
Tillyard, Stella., *Aristocrats* (Vintage 1995).

CHAPTER 24

Charles Lennox (b.1735 - d.1806) the 3rd Duke of Richmond

TO DESCRIBE CHARLES Lennox, the third Duke of Richmond, as a difficult and unsociable man would be to emphasise an aspect of his character which brought him unpopularity and limited his success in his political career. Yet he was capable of acts of great kindness and Horace Walpole described him as intrepid and tender, inflexible and humane.

He enlisted in the army when he was seventeen and gave distinguished service during the Seven Years War but he was not a born leader and decided to take up a political career. He did not work well with his political colleagues and, though the social side of life in London and Paris gave him little pleasure, a grand tour, taking in France, Germany, Italy and other countries, inspired him with an interest in art, architecture and sculpture. Throughout his somewhat frustrated political life and in his later years he found relaxation at Goodwood, the Richmonds' family home, where he enjoyed hunting and farming and devoted a great deal of time and money to improving the House and surrounding estate.

He was born in London in 1735 and, as Earl of March, was sent as a town boy to Westminster School where he was reputed to have "had his ears boxed". One of his fellow pupils at that time was Rockingham, later to be an important colleague in the political arena. The young Earl did not board at the School but lived at Richmond House and he had freedom to spend weekends and evenings to do as he pleased. At fifteen, he was was an amorous and pedantic schoolboy with an eye for young ladies and his lifestyle so troubled his brother-in-law Henry Fox that he felt the Earl's behaviour should be made known to his father. The news must have caused the Duke unwelcome concern but he was then far from well and in August of that year 1750 he died leaving his son to succeed him as the third Duke of Richmond. As well as taking the other family titles, the young Charles was to receive two-thirds of the total returns from the Newcastle coal duty granted to the Dukes of Richmond by Charles II.

It was going to be five years before he came of age and guardians were appointed to administer his father's estate and supervise his affairs. Those appointed were Henry Fox (Lord Holland) and James Kildare (the Duke of Leinster) who were his brothers-in-law, two of his uncles and also the Duke of Newcastle, who has been described as a sort of political godfather, yet it was to Henry Fox that Charles turned for support and guidance. Apart from succession to his father's titles, he knew that before long he would have to accept the age-old rights and considerable responsibilities that rested with the head of such a titled family. After the guardians had completed the task of clearing the affairs of the estate and paying outstanding debts there remained an accumulated fortune of some £19,000. When his mother died only six months after his father, he was given the ownership of Goodwood as well as the family's Richmond House in London and the remaining one third of the Newcastle coal income. At that time in his life he had become a young man of some wealth.

With the guardians looking after his affairs, it was decided that Charles should be sent to Geneva in the care of Abraham Trembley, a biologist and scholarly man whom the late Duke had named as a tutor to both his sons. In Geneva, he was instructed by several of Trembley's own tutors and they were pleased with his progress. In September, 1752, Trembley and Charles set out on a grand tour and apart from a stay in England in the following year and a short period at Leyden University, they moved from one centre to another until their return to England in January 1756. Trembley's intellectual interests ensured that this grand tour had an educational purpose. He and the young Duke travelled from the south of France to Belgium and Holland as well as visiting the main Italian cities, Berlin and Vienna, where they apparently spent fifty mornings studying at the museum of the Emperor Francis. Charles was overwhelmed by the richness of his experiences but it cannot be said that he had an intellectual bent. Nevertheless, his new interest in art and sculpture led him to acquire some pictures as well as superb French furniture, tapestries and porcelain for Goodwood, Richmond House and Aubigny.

He had always wanted to have a military career and, during the tour, he displayed considerable interest in military affairs. Excited by the prospect of war with France, he wrote to Fox reminding him that he wished to serve in whatever capacity he was needed. He had met Colonel Wolfe in 1752 in Paris and Wolfe had been greatly interested in his views on army organisation and discipline to such an extent that the two continued to correspond until Wolfe went to Canada. In 1756, at the conclusion of his tour, Charles was made a Lieutenant Colonel in what was to become the Duke of Wellington's Regiment.and spent some months with his men in Holland and Germany. He soon became restless because his regiment had not been posted to fight in France and was appeased only when he was asked to take part in a raid on Cherbourg. In 1759, opportunity came to fight in the Continental War and he served with his brother Lord George in support of Prince Ferdinand of Brunswick, distinguishing himself for bravery at the Battle of Minden. By the time he emerged from the Seven Years War he had attained the rank of Major General. Yet despite his promotion and bravery in action, he did not work well with troops and often quarrelled with subordinates. Though he could have remained in the army, he seemed to realise his own limitations and made the decision to take up parliamentary life and enjoy the family estate at Goodwood. With the support and prompting of his brother-in-law Henry Fox, Lord Holland, he was appointed Lord Lieutenant of Sussex and this gave him control of the Sussex militia which preserved his link with the military.

Having taken his seat in the House of Lords, there is no doubt that he had the wealth and extensive family connections to build up a high status in political life. Of his sisters, Caroline had married Henry Fox, the first Baron Holland and Emily's husband was the Earl of Kildare. The future King George III fell in love with Charles' younger sister Sarah but a marriage was felt inappropriate and George was persuaded to marry "a plain little German princess", leaving Sarah to enter into what proved to be an unsatisfactory marriage with Sir Charles Bunbury.

Charles was a young man whose appearance was always in his favour and he gave the impression of being both dignified and intelligent. Since his early years he had been known for his many casual affairs with the opposite sex but in 1756 he became devoted to the beautiful Lady Mary Bruce, daughter of the Countess of Aylesbury. They were married in the following year when he was twenty-two and his bride seventeen. Horace Walpole declared it to be a perfect match but Mary Bruce was a flirtatious young lady who took the opportunity to enjoy life while her husband was away on military service though she discarded her lovers on his return. On the other hand, the Duke had a mistress in France known as Madame de Cambis and several illegitimate children. Yet despite the fact that both Charles and Mary were unfaithful for a time, the marriage proved to be a success. The sadness was that Mary was herself unable to have children but, as time progressed, this seemed to draw them together and lead to a close but secluded married life.

At the Coronation of George III in 1760 Charles, as the Duke of Richmond, carried the Sceptre and the Dove and in November of that year he was appointed a Lord of the Bedchamber. This was a position of some status, yet in an impetuous manner he suddenly resigned, the only reason being that his brother Lord George Lennox had not been appointed an aide-de-camp to the King, others having been considered more suitable. To make matters worse, he appears to have argued with the King about the appointment and made him very angry. Within two days Charles repented his decision but the King never forgave him.

Though there were many factors in Charles' favour, one major reason why he rose to little more than a minor politician was his failure to gain the King's support. In character he was intensely nervous and driven by immense energy, yet his quick temper and frequent lack of respect for the ability of others made him unpopular amongst his associates. In the House of Lords, he often made personal attacks which were taken far more seriously than he intended and an example is quoted of an acrimonious discussion with the Marquis of Zetland during a debate on a commercial treaty. He was not a brilliant orator but his colleagues regarded him as a formidable debater, well able to argue the case for the opposition if he chose to do so. His close relatives considered him generous and affectionate though his sisters criticised his high-flown ideas of right and wrong. There was little or no agreement with his relations on political matters however, and his only family confidant in political affairs was his brother Lord George Lennox. This was not entirely of the Duke's own doing for his relations were themselves frequently divided in their political opinions. Nevertheless, there is little doubt that lack of political support from leading members of his family did little to help his advancement.

After the Coronation, the government came into the hands of several political leaders including George Grenville, whose ministry is remembered for the passing of the American Stamp Act in 1765. It was an Act which Charles strongly disliked and it provoked serious rioting in America. The King had little faith in Grenville however and, after he had been in office for two years, a new administration was formed under the leadership of the Marquis of Rockingham. Charles then sought ways of approaching the Marquis in an effort to obtain a government appointment but eventually, all he was offered was the Paris Embassy. It was something he did not want and at first he refused the appointment, but when he came to realise that it was the best he could hope for he accepted the position of Ambassador Extraordinaire.

Though he performed his Embassy duties with great efficiency he gained little popularity in Paris, mainly because of his social aloofness and lack of regard for French society. After a stay of only four months he travelled back to England, ostensibly to clear up his Sussex affairs but actually to take part in a debate on the repeal of the Stamp Act. He left the Embassy in charge of his brother, Lord George Lennox, who had originally gone there as a secretary but, in the Duke's absence, served as Minister Plenipotentiary. It cannot be said that Lord George and his wife found any more favour in French society than had Charles for they spent much of their time with the English residents and their attitude to the French people was considered far from acceptable.

In the following year there was a vacancy for a Secretary of State in the Southern Division and Charles offered his services to Rockingham. It was only when others had refused the position that Rockingham nominated him and was able to convince the King that there was no alternative. If anything, relations between Charles and the King deteriorated further during what proved to be a short term of office. In July 1766, Rockingham was replaced as Prime Minister by Pitt with the result that Charles was cast into involuntary opposition. There followed long periods of political opposition during which he was often left out in the cold and spent much of his time at Goodwood or in France. This was because Rockingham's supporters were mostly based in the north of the country and the Duke made no effort to go there or to try to meet Rockingham when he was in London. Another follower of Rockingham was Edmund Burke who despite living in the south, took the trouble to go north and attend meetings of the Rockingham Whig party. He became Rockingham's private secretary and an active politician as well as a writer of considerable repute. Though he was well aware of Charles' difficult temperament, he was one of the first to voice recognition of his political ability and debating skills. Indeed, for more than a decade, Burke was the Duke of Richmond's strongest supporter in the party and urged Rockingham to use him in government. As a result, during the years 1770-80, Charles came to be considered as one of the foremost Rockingham Whigs, especially in debate yet, largely through his own doing, he always remained on the periphery of the party.

It was not until Rockingham was asked to form a second administration that Charles received an appointment as Master-General of the Ordnance with a seat in the cabinet. He was a great supporter of Parliamentary reform and spent much time on the preparation of a Reform Bill. Despite considerable public desire for reform at that time, he was well aware that any general agreement was remote. His plan was rejected without a division but the presentation of his case was marred by rioting which flared up outside Parliament, not against his Bill but in opposition to any religious relief to the Roman Catholics. However, there is no doubt that his considerable work on reform was immensely useful and farseeing in its objectives. It paved the way for Charles Grey's 1832 Reform Act and subsequent changes.

Largely because of personality clashes with its leaders which were aggravated by the Party's failure to support several of his parliamentary motions, the years between 1780 and 1783 saw Charles become alienated from the Rockingham Whig party. Rockingham died in 1783 and though Shelbourne was a temporary successor, Charles developed a personal and political association with Pitt who became Prime Minister later that year. Having broken away from the Whigs and resigned his office, Charles was then re-instated at the Ordnance. He no longer persevered with his parliamentary reform plans and instead began concentrating his energies on reform of the military. To a limited extent the King began to view him with more favour but only after Charles had apologised for his earlier behaviour.

The cabinet formed by the young Pitt was one of mediocre talents and its members had little experience or interest in foreign affairs. Charles found himself in a strong position and there is no doubt that Pitt looked to him for military knowledge, ingenuity and encouragement. Yet they did not always see eye to eye and, as time passed, Pitt came to realise how unpopular Charles was in the House of Commons; this was emphasised by the defeat of his bill containing extensive plans for fortifications of the dockyards at Portsmouth and Plymouth. The political implications of the defeat were far more serious to Charles than they were to the military. In 1793 came the declaration of war against France and serious doubts then arose about the adequacy of the country's military organisation. A particular incident was cited involving the failure to provide infantry for the Duke of York's siege of Dunkirk. This and other failings reflected greatly on Charles in his capacity of Master-General of the Ordnance and the criticism levelled against him was strengthened by his continued inability to work amicably with men of standing like the Duke of York, Henry Dundas and other members of the cabinet. It was evident that as long as the Ordnance remained under Charles' control it was vulnerable to political attacks and by 1788 criticism of the administration involved him personally. His dismissal was inevitable and not a single cabinet colleague was sorry to see him go. All too often he had shown ill temper and lack of respect for the views of others. Yet he protested and was mortified by his dismissal. Some three months later, he retired to Goodwood where the Duchess was confined through illness. To all intents and purposes it was the end of his political career.

Though he had a miserly image the Duke was capable of impetuous generosity and spent as much money on art as on politics. He was elected Fellow of the Royal Society in 1755 and he built a theatre in Richmond House where he also set up a free studio for artists, subsidising several Chichester landscape painters as well as personally patronising George Romney, a young portrait painter whose work at the Richmond House studio met with his approval. At Goodwood, he had inherited the House and a park of 200 acres together with some 1,100 acres of land. With the help of Sir William Chambers and the young architect James Wyatt, he was largely responsible for transforming his inheritance into the fascinating flint building and estate which exists today. He bought large areas of additional land bringing the total estate to about 17,000 acres and, in 1760, he embarked on a huge planting operation, as had his father before him, making particular use of exotics, tulip trees, magnolias, cork oaks, and more than 1,000 further cedars of Lebanon.

The old Goodwood House had been built as a gentleman's residence but the 1st Duke used it as a hunting lodge. It had been

Charles Lennox, the 3rd Duke of Richmond.
REPRODUCED BY COURTESY OF THE NATIONAL PORTRAIT GALLERY

altered very little since the 1720s and the 2nd Duke used the services of Roger Morris, a surveyor, to remodel what is now called the Long Hall, giving it the present classical appearance with screens of columns and two Palladian style chimney pieces. The Duke also extended the House to the south adding a plain pedimented south façade looking down to Chichester. By 1771 the 3rd Duke planned a further enlargement and a North Wing was built to the design of James Wyatt. By 1800 there further plans for the conversion of the building into a grandiose octagon with a tower at each corner but this was a major undertaking and, through lack of finance, it had not been completed when the Duke died in 1806. His financial position late in life made it impossible to complete the tasks he had set himself but the Goodwood we know today rests very much on his achievements and particularly on his co-operation with James Wyatt whose outstanding interior work in the fascinating Tapestry Drawing Room has been given particular recognition. Many of the works of art at Goodwood came from Aubigny, which had been sequestered by the Republicans in 1795 but restored at the peace of Amiens in 1802. But Napoleon seized Aubigny in 1806, shortly before the third Duke died, and although the fourth Duke did homage to Louis XVIII, the French courts ordered that the châteaux be sold by auction and the proceeds distributed amongst the heirs.

During the 1750s, an impressive stable block had been built at Goodwood to the design of Sir William Chambers. It took the form of a fine quadrangle and attracts the deserved attention of visitors to Goodwood today. The third Duke used the building very largely as a training stables and at one time is said to have had over a hundred horses in training. It is now fully used during race meetings and is a feature of the facilities provided on those occasions. The Duke also built the Goodwood Kennels though these were closed with the end of the Charlton Hunt, re-established by the 6th Duke but now used as the Headquarters of the Golf Club. Hunting and horses have for long been a love of the Dukes of Richmond and the third Duke laid out the Goodwood Racecourse on a beautiful site high on the Sussex Downs where the land near the winning post rises to 700 feet above sea level. The first recorded race meeting at Goodwood was in 1801 and a three-day meeting was held the following year but sadly, the Duke died less than five years after building the course and before any of the races for which Goodwood was to become famous had been started.

Richmond House was regarded as the permanent London home of the Dukes of Richmond and, in the time of the second Duke, it was largely re-built using designs provided by Lord Burlington. In the 1780s the third Duke's architectural energies and income were largely directed towards further improvement work for which he commissioned James Wyatt. The Duke was anxious that the art collections and valuable furniture which he held in Richmond House should be properly presented but, in December 1791, disaster struck when the House was destroyed by fire.

It was clear from the subsequent report in The Times that the fire had started on the upper floor in the bedchamber of Miss le Clerk where a spark from the bedroom fire set alight the curtains. Miss le Clerk, a natural daughter of the Duke, was so alarmed by the fire that she was unable to move and had to be brought out in her bed. By the time the fire engines arrived the upper part of the building was in flames and the roof had fallen in before the fire could be extinguished. As the fire spread across the upper floors, a man climbed a ladder to rescue the Duke's favourite spaniel dog; needless to say both he and another man who held the ladder were suitably rewarded. The inside of the House was gutted but, as the fire started in the upper floor, it was possible to rescue most of the Duke's valuable collection of pictures, plate, furniture and family papers which were later taken to Goodwood. A number of privates from the Duke of York's Regiment had soon been called in to help in the rescue operation and they were also used to hold back the crowds of people attracted by the blaze. For the Duke, the fire was a disaster as the House was not insured and the heavy financial loss which he sustained brought his financial difficulties into focus. His capital expenditure was already considerable and his position deteriorated in the succeeding years to such an extent that, by 1799, he was over £90,000 in debt. According to the Duke's account books around 1800, he was spending £8,000 a year on interest and tax alone and £4,000 on the ordinary upkeep of Goodwood. There were various personal expenses shown in the accounts such as the upkeep of his own sloop, his militia and hunting but the considerable sum spent on capital projects included improvements and developments at Goodwood House, the building of two new houses, the race track and dog kennels. In order to reduce his taxes and because he feared that taxes would be levied on his coal income, he took the drastic step of selling his coal dues to the Government for an amount of £728,333.

There is no doubt that, from the year 1677 when Charles II granted the Newcastle coal dues to his illegitimate son the Duke of Richmond and his heirs, the considerable income which the grant generated not only provided for the life style of the early Dukes but largely financed the whole Goodwood complex. By the year 1800, the annual income of the third Duke may have averaged £23,000 yet, by then, he had already borrowed £95,000 to enable him to meet his commitments.

After his dismissal from the government, Charles retired to Goodwood and spent his time looking after his wife, entertaining occasional visitors and developing the new race track. In 1796 however, his wife died. She and the Duke had become very close in marriage and he was greatly to miss her companionship. She was buried in Chichester Cathedral, a widely respected lady possessed of great dignity and gentleness. After the shock of her death, it took a family crisis to bring the Duke temporarily out of his retirement and to involve him in the problems of Irish nationalism.

His sister Emily who had married James Fitzgerald, the Earl of Kildare, had a son Lord Edward who was always very attached to his mother. He went to Paris in 1792 where he met and married Pamela Seymour, a ward of the Duke of Orléans. In France he developed a revolutionary enthusiasm and on his return to Ireland sought French help for an Irish national uprising. Though a French force is said to have set sail, it never landed in Ireland and though the United Irishmen had built up in numbers the government became aware of their membership and intentions and many leaders were arrested. By 1798 Lord Edward had become an executive member of the organisation and he was wanted by the authorities in Dublin. To escape arrest, he moved from house to house ending up in the home of an Irish feather merchant. The police found him there in bed nursing a heavy cold but he violently resisted arrest and was shot in the shoulder. With his wound untreated and festering he was taken to Dublin gaol and with the bullets still in his shoulder he soon became critically ill with septicaemia. Visitors were not allowed to see him and it was some time before Edward's mother was told what had happened. Though she hastened to Dublin from London, only Emily's sister Louisa was able to visit Edward before he died on 4th June 1798.

The rebellion by the Irish nationalists, who demanded Catholic emancipation and parliamentary reform, causes which had been so near to Lord Edward's heart, brought about atrocities, reprisals, and the death of many rebels, but the ultimate outcome was Union with Great Britain. Though Charles had been strongly opposed to Edward's ideas he accepted the obligation to help and support not only his sister Emily but also Lord Edward's wife Pamela. He immediately offered temporary refuge to Pamela at Goodwood and arranged for her to visit relations she had in Hamburg. If Edward had lived, his trial for treason would have followed and the Irish Authorities passed an attainder depriving Lady Pamela and her children of Lord Edward's property. Charles made considerable efforts to prevent this and a petition was laid before the King though to no avail. Clearly however, there was sufficient wealth in the Fitzgerald and Lennox families to provide for Pamela and her children.

The Duke's sense of responsibility and kindness towards members of his family were not always easy to appreciate. His consideration for Lady Pamela was greatly welcomed by his sister Emily and the Fitzgeralds and served to remove earlier family rifts. On the other hand, the Duke had strongly disapproved of his sister Sarah's marriage to Sir Charles Bunbury and not only cut off her family money but also refused to buy her a wedding dress. This unsatisfactory marriage did not produce any children but Sarah had an affair with Lord William Gordon and had his child. She eloped with her lover and Bunbury decided to proceed with a parliamentary divorce. Needless to say the affair with Gordon did not last and, when he departed to Scotland, it was Charles who offered Sarah sympathy and seclusion at Goodwood, providing a house within the estate for her and her child. It was an act of kindness which impressed all his family.

The Duke retained strong views about army recruitment and his last appearance in Parliament was believed to be in 1804 when he briefly re-entered politics and spoke in favour of a committee on the state of defence. But poor health, declining powers of debate and the absence of any political influence meant that he could no longer hope to be given a role in government. In the following year, he was unable to go to Windsor where the King was to present the Horse Guards with a pair of silver kettle-drums. In 1795 he had been made Colonel of the Royal Regiment of Horse Guards, now the Blues and Royals, and though he had had a difficult relationship with the King ever since the Bedchamber resignation incident he wrote what was to be his last letter to his Sovereign expressing the pride of his declining life in having had command of the Horse Guards and his mortification at being unable to be present through illness. From then on his health deteriorated further and in his final illness he was cared for by Sarah Napier, his once troubled sister who by then had found happiness in a second marriage. He died on the 29th December, 1806 and was buried in the family vault in Chichester Cathedral. He was succeeded by his nephew, Charles Lennox son of Lord George.

The third Duke of Richmond was a respected soldier but an unpredictable man who could be arrogant, impulsive and over-bearing, yet highly imaginative, and in planning electoral reform he was one of the most far-sighted politicians of his time. Invested as Knight of the Garter in 1782, he was a man who should have achieved much more than his temperament would allow. His memorial is Goodwood where he and his wife made their home and where he created much that his descendants and the nation can value and enjoy today.

References:
D.N.B. Vol. XI p.923.
Olsen, Alison, *The Radical Duke* (Oxford 1961) pp.1n(2) & 3n(1).
Hillyard, Stella, *Aristocrats* (Vintage 1995).
Reese. *Goodwood Oak. The Life and Times of the 3rd Duke of Richmond* (Threshold 1987).

CHAPTER 25

Charles Lennox (b.1764 - d.1819) the 4th Duke of Richmond

C HARLES, THE ELDEST son of Lord George Henry Lennox and Louisa, is believed to have been born in a barn. His mother was apparently on a fishing trip in Scotland at the time and a nearby barn provided the only shelter and privacy available. It is surely ironic that it was into a barn and an adjoining farmhouse in Canada that that he was taken when his eventful life came to a premature end.

As a young man, he had followed the Richmond tradition by opting for military service and joining the Sussex Militia. He was only aged 14 when he was promoted to Lieutenant and he entered the army in 1785 when in his early twenties. By 1789 he had reached the rank of Captain and commanded a company in the Coldstream Foot Guards. He was described as a generally likeable and popular man yet he did not take criticism lightly and this aspect of his character was evidenced by his involvement in two duels, accounts of which were given in the *Gentleman's Magazine* and the *Sussex County Magazine* at that time.

Prince Frederick Augustus, the Duke of York and Albany, the Coldstream's Commanding Officer, became indignant about Charles Lennox's promotion to Captain which he believed was due to the Richmond influence with William Pitt the Prime Minster. He regarded Charles as a political enemy and in Daubigny's, a London Club frequented by army officers, he made disparaging remarks about the courage of the Lennox family. Not unnaturally, Charles took exception to this and he was so angry he challenged the Duke to a duel. His challenge was accepted by the Duke who responded with the words "I desire to derive no protection from my rank as a Prince or my station as Commanding Officer. When not on duty, I wear a brown coat, and I shall be ready as a private gentleman to give you satisfaction". The political character of the quarrel and the unusual if not unprecedented occurrence of a prince of the blood standing so near to the throne agreeing to risk his life in this way created intense excitement at the time.

It was announced that the "meeting with pistols" would take place on 26th August 1789 on Wimbledon Common, then a favourite resort for the settlement of affairs of honour. Agreement was reached that Richmond would be the first to fire but, after all the excitement, the sequel proved to be an anticlimax for the spectators. Charles Lennox shot but he merely grazed his adversary's wig whereas the Duke coolly responded by firing his own shot into the air, afterwards declaring that he held no animosity towards Charles Lennox and only came to give him satisfaction. The seconds concluded that both the principals had acted with the utmost coolness and intrepidity and, in an effort to gloss over the whole embarrassing affair, the officers of the Guards passed a resolution that Charles had behaved with courage in all the circumstances but not with judgement.

It is apparent that the Duke of York was far from popular at Court at that time whereas Charles Lennox, whose reputation appears to have been enhanced by the duel, was cordially received by the Queen, much to the Duke's displeasure. In the second of his two duels, Charles challenged a man named Theophilus Swift, a noted pamphleteer, who was believed to have maligned him in a publication of that time. The duel took place on a field at Uxbridge and, though Charles was unhurt, his shot hit Swift in the body without causing a fatal injury.

Though this later episode confirmed Charles Lennox's reputation as "an officer of courage and spirit" he decided that, because of his quarrel with the Duke of York, it would be prudent to depart the scene. He arranged to leave his regiment and make an exchange with Lord Strathavon who then commanded the 35th Foot stationed at Edinburgh Castle. When Charles travelled to Scotland to join his new regiment he must have been surprised by the warmth of his greeting and by the brilliant illumination of Edinburgh Castle in his honour. It was a welcome he acknowledged by entertaining his officers at a banquet and presenting his soldiers with ten guineas to drink his health. His stay in Edinburgh was a popular one; he was presented with the freedom of the City and made an honorary member and freeman of the Incorporation of Goldsmiths. He also gained popularity with the ordinary soldiers with whom he was quite prepared to play cricket. This was an unusual condescension in an officer of his rank though probably Charles' cricket-loving grandfather would have given his full approval.

It was in the same year 1789, when he went to Edinburgh, that Charles was married to Charlotte, daughter of Alexander, the 4th Duke of Gordon. The ceremony took place at Gordon Castle and it was an occasion which established an important link between the Richmonds and the Gordons though it was not until 1836, after her husband's death, that Charlotte became heir to the Gordon line. In the year following his marriage, Charles was elected M.P. for Chichester and he was re-elected in 1796, 1802 and 1806. He was an ardent supporter and personal friend of Pitt after whom he named his fourth son. It was a common thing for a serving officer of the army to undertake the duties of a Member of Parliament and it often encouraged promotion. Charles continued to hold his seat until the death of his father, when he succeeded to the Dukedom of Richmond.

There is no doubt that he was a keen sportsman, prominent in horse racing as well as being a good tennis player, but cricket was perhaps his greatest love and he was a capable batsman. In cricketing circles he is long remembered as being the prime mover in establishing the Marylebone Cricket Club. In the 1780's he was a member of the White Conduit Cricket Club and, when members became dissatisfied with their venue, Charles Lennox enlisted the support of George Finch, the ninth Earl of

Winchelsea, and they approached Thomas Lord, the lessee of the Allsop Arms in London to seek a more suitable site. Lord found a new ground on what is now Dorset Square. The MCC, as it became known, commenced playing there in May 1787 and the occasion was commemorated in a plaque which stands in the Square today. The lease on the ground in Dorset Fields ran out in 1810 and prior to this Thomas Lord rented land in St John's Wood. This did not prove popular and the Eyre family, who were the landlords of this second venue, offered another location which Lord took up and began preparing in readiness for the summer of 1814. It was the site which is now the Lord's Cricket Ground and its existence as the home of the MCC has much to do with the initiative of Charles Lennox, the fourth Duke of Richmond.

After his stay in Edinburgh, Charles was sent abroad and served with his regiment on an expedition to the Leeward Islands which resulted in the capture of Martinique. He was then sent with a battalion to take possession of some French posts on the Island of San Domingo. Soon after he arrived there in June 1794 a disastrous epidemic of yellow fever broke out and within two months he had lost forty officers and no less than six hundred other ranks. Charles Lennox seemed to escape infection and on his return to England he was given the rank of full Colonel and appointed aide-de-camp to the King. Two years later he became a Major General and then Colonel Commandant. By 1805 he was a Lieutenant General but in December of the following year came the death of his uncle the Third Duke and Charles succeeded to the Dukedom and Richmond titles.

The new Duke and his wife Charlotte by then had a large family and in all they had seven sons and seven daughters. This had the disadvantage of placing a heavy financial burden on his resources, leaving him with insufficient means to maintain the estates he had inherited, and to continue a building programme at Goodwood. Following the death of Pitt however, he was sworn in as a Privy Councillor and appointed Lord Lieutenant of Ireland. He could well have felt that this appointment would solve his financial problems but he was soon to find that Dublin Castle and Viceregal Lodge placed further burdens on his income. His first two years in Ireland were comparatively quiet but he then became worried about Catholic agitation and a possible change of policy in Irish affairs. When he broke up a meeting of Catholic followers without consulting London, he was rebuked but then entered into a lengthy correspondence about his position with Earl Bathurst, a member of the Government and husband of Charles' sister Georgina. He insisted that, though he was strenuously against the riotous Catholics, it was not on account of their religion but because of their revolutionary activities. Despite his view of the Catholics however, he remained in Ireland for six years and his lavish hospitality combined with his great interest in sport ensured for him a certain respect and popularity amongst the Irish people and particularly in Dublin.

During his stay in Ireland, he was joined by Colonel Arthur Wellesley, later to be Duke of Wellington, who had been returned as Member of Parliament for Rye and was given the office of Chief Secretary for Ireland. Though Wellesley was soon transferred to Copenhagen and then to Portugal for military duties, a close friendship built up between these two men and Charles Lennox's two eldest sons became members of Wellesley's personal staff.

Charles, Duke of Richmond, continued in the office of Lord Lieutenant of Ireland until 1813 and the Order of the Garter was conferred on him before he was relieved of his post by Earl Whitworth. It was evident that his lavish hospitality and the demands of his family had made him deeply in debt and, though he returned to Goodwood, his financial position was to be a continuing embarrassment. As a measure of economy and also perhaps to evade the annoyance of some important creditors he decided to move to Brussels. He and his wife had experienced family distress in that their eldest son had been badly wounded in Spain and their third son, Lord Henry Lennox, who was in the navy, was accidentally drowned in the Mediterranean at the early age of fifteen.

The arrival of Napoleon in France made new hostilities inevitable and Richmond had hopes of military employment. However, though he made application it did not succeed and he was condemned to be an idle spectator of the great Battle of

Waterloo which was to follow, though his two eldest sons were summoned to serve on Wellington's personal staff. It was difficult to find a suitable house in Brussels but he was able to rent a property in the market and tannery area of the Lower Town. It had belonged to Jean Simons, a well known coachbuilder and the entrance was past a lodge and stables from the Rue de la Blanchisserie. It was neither large nor grand and Wellington called it "The Wash House" yet it provided separate quarters for Lord March, the Duke's eldest son, and there was a long wing to the west which had been used to store carriages. For the younger children there was an annexe which was used as a schoolroom and a large garden in which they could play. It was this area rather than the main house that became the setting for the famous Waterloo Ball. When the Duke of Wellington was appointed British Ambassador to France, he visited the Richmonds in Brussels on his way to Paris and used the opportunity to assess the Belgian attitude towards France and also, with his military eye, he took notice of the useful defensive features of the land south of Waterloo. It was there, he predicted, that the battle with Napoleon would be fought.

Charlotte, Duchess of Richmond, was thought by those who knew her to have a greater love for power and publicity than her husband. Certainly she had a great gift for entertaining and was in the forefront of the social scene in Brussels. She had many friends and her numerous family of sons and daughters ensured that her house was a rendezvous for the younger set. Her greatest social achievement however was undoubtedly the memorable ball she arranged on the 15th June 1815, the eve of the great battle. It was an event recorded in history by Byron's famous verse "The Night before the Battle of Waterloo". The Duchess had done everything to make the ball the most brilliant of the season and even contrived to get some of the Highlanders to dance reels and strathspeys for the guests. Everyone felt that to cancel the ball was unthinkable yet throughout the afternoon and during the evening there was a great undercurrent of unease and anticipation as news of Napoleon's advance was awaited. The lines of Byron's poem most aptly describe the tension of that evening.

Did ye not hear it? No; 'twas but the wind,
Or the car rattling o'er the stony street;
On with the dance! let joy be unconfined;
No sleep till morn, when Youth and Pleasure meet
To chase the glowing Hours with flying feet -
But hark! - that heavy sound breaks in once more,
As if the clouds its echo would repeat;
And nearer, clearer, deadlier than before!
Arm! arm! it is - it is - the cannon's opening roar!

The Duke of Wellington and his party arrived soon after midnight when it became clear that war was inevitable and that all the regiments would be leaving early the next morning. Wellington and Richmond withdrew to a study when news reached the Ball that Napoleon was already advancing through Charleroi. Wellington asked for a map and for candles and he put his finger on Waterloo saying "I have arranged to meet him at Quatre Bras and, if I find myself not strong enough to stop him there, I shall fall back towards Blücher and fight him there".

The dancing and music continued despite the expectation of forthcoming battle and some officers stayed as if enjoying the ball despite what the morrow might bring. Wellington did not leave until well after midnight and it was after 2a.m. when he went to bed, yet he was up having breakfast of tea and toast at 5.30a.m. before leaving on horseback at 7a.m for the scene of the battle. Though he had implored the Duke of Richmond to remain in Brussels, Mercer's Waterloo Journal recorded everyone's surprise at seeing "a fine tall and upright old gentleman in plain clothes followed by two young men come galloping across the front from the Brussels road". It seems that Richmond wished to shake the hand of his friend and wish him well whilst ensuring that his two young sons, the Earl of March and Lord George Lennox were usefully employed, one as aide-de-camp to the Prince of Orange and the other as a member of the Commander in Chief's staff. They did indeed serve Wellington well in the midst of bitter conflict and death.

The complex and fluctuating battle began on the June 16th 1815, both at Ligny, where the large Prussian force was attacked by the French and suffered enormous casualties, and at Quatre Bras where Wellington with an army of Anglo-Dutch and Dutch-Belgian troops was attacked by the French Marshal Ney. Though the Prussians failed to hold their attackers, they were able to withdraw and re-form, helped by the French army's other involvement at Quatre Bras. Though the forces of Marshal Ney were superior in numbers, Wellington was able to withstand his attackers and, by astute generalship, eventually claimed a modest victory. The eventual and critical battle of Waterloo took place on the June 18th at Hougoumont where the French made a determined attack and may well have broken Wellington's lines had Napoleon released his reserve force, the Imperial Guard, but when Blücher with his remaining Prussians arrived to support Wellington, Napoleon was finally defeated. So ended one of the most important and fierce battles in European history; at the close, the death toll on the battlefield numbered as many as 44,000 men. It was a victory over Napoleon which was to prove of great importance to Britain and Europe, but gained at enormous cost and only achieved with the aid of Wellington's generalship and resourceful tactics.

After the battle, the Duke of Richmond continued to live in Brussels for another three years but, on 6th May, 1818, he received notice of his appointment as Governor in Chief of the British provinces in North America and Commander in Chief of the British troops stationed there. Whether or not he had sought such an appointment is uncertain but there is little doubt that his friendship with the Duke of Wellington had some influence. Certainly it was an appointment Richmond greatly welcomed if only because of his financial troubles but, with his extreme views, there were some who thought he was the last person who should have been chosen to fill that office. In fact, though he was entirely out of sympathy with the claims of French Canadians, his very personality was to gain him a lot of personal popularity.

He sailed from Spithead on the 18th June but did not reach Quebec until the end of July after what was, to say the least, a tedious voyage. With him were members of his family and Sir Peregrine Maitland, husband of his daughter Lady Sarah Lennox, who had been appointed Lieutenant Governor of Upper Canada. The Duke had instructions from London to improve the defences of British North America, expand internal navigation and encourage the settlement of disbanded soldiers and other immigrants. He soon made his presence felt and, after a series of visits to his garrisons and to Lake Erie he recommended the strengthening of the forts at Quebec, Ile aux Noix and Ile Sainte Helene in Lower Canada and at Kingston in Upper Canada. To improve the waterways he pressed for the opening for navigation of the Ottawa and Rideau Rivers and the construction of canals between Lake Ontario and Lake Erie.

Though he had also received instructions to continue the policy of his predecessors by being conciliatory towards Canadian political and religious leaders he clearly found it difficult to do so in important matters of government and provincial finance. Though he praised the Legislative Assembly, he did not conceal his discontent with the House of Assembly in which the Canadian Party dominated over their English Party rivals. Though he appreciated the difference between the settlers in Upper Canada and the French Canadians in Lower Canada, he agreed with the English Party's view that Canada should be one province and should not be divided. It was clear to him however that unification would not be easy and indeed, the aspirations of the French Canadians remain at the forefront today.

The Duke aroused Canadian Party criticism for breathing new life into the Royal Institution for the Advancement of Learning which was responsible for the colony's public schools and, as a means of popularising his administration, he placed great emphasis on all forms of sport. His family did much to promote the theatre, and balls and parties were more numerous than ever before. State parties as well as other hospitality at the Château, where the Duke's gold plate and racing cups were displayed, clearly impressed those Canadians who were invited.

He had succeeded Sir John Sherbrooke, who encouraged the development of a new settlement on the River Rideau, generally

The 4th Duke of Richmond.
REPRODUCED WITH PERMISSION OF THE NATIONAL ARCHIVES OF CANADA

204

recognised as an important means of communication should war develop with the United States, and in the early summer of 1818 four hundred men of the 99th and 100th Regiments accepted the offer of lands by the Rideau when they were disbanded in Quebec. They left the capital of Lower Canada in late July in a large fleet of Durham boats and bateaux and landed on a little peninsula which they called Richmond Landing where they camped below what were known as Chaudière Falls. Work then began on cutting a road inland to the township of Goulbourn on the Jock (or Jacques) River where a settlement was being developed to be known as Richmond. By the end of that summer considerable progress had been made, log houses were being built in the settlement and the road inland from Richmond Landing was well under way. In time, between four and five thousand people were to settle in the area.

It was in August, 1819 that the Duke set off on an extensive tour of both Canadian provinces. After entertaining his staff and the principal military officers and civil officials at a banquet he embarked on a Government steamboat for Montreal. His son and two of his daughters accompanied him and were to remain at Montreal to await his return from Upper Canada. The Duke's first visit was to Fort William Henry on the south bank of the Saint Lawrence River. There have been several conflicting accounts of events during this visit but all refer to an incident in which the Duke was apparently bitten by a pet fox owned by a soldier. It seems that the fox had been worried on board ship by an officer's bull terrier and, when the party landed at the Fort, the fox was in a highly excited state. The two animals may have begun to fight when on land and the Duke was bitten trying to separate them but, more likely, he stopped when mounting his horse and suffered the bite when attempting to pat and calm the fox. Perhaps, as his daughter Louise suggested later, he was only concerned to protect his own pet spaniel Blücher from becoming involved in any fight. What is certain is that the Duke received a bite or scratch from the fox, which was later destroyed, and the wound may have been the cause of his subsequent death from hydrophobia.

Nothing much was thought of this incident at the time and the Duke continued with his official engagements. The party moved on to York and Niagara and as far distant as Drummond Island before returning to Kingston where the Duke enjoyed himself playing cricket with the officers and men of the garrison. He then began a difficult journey across country to see the settlements on the Rideau and particularly to visit the township of Richmond named in his honour. It was a visit eagerly anticipated by the immigrants to the area yet it was destined to have a particularly tragic conclusion.

There were no roads in the area and and a distance of over 30 miles had to be covered mainly on horseback, on foot or by canoe. Detailed accounts of the journey to Richmond and its aftermath were given in a letter to Earl Bathurst written by a member of the party named Charles Cambridge and also in the Journal of one of the Duke's officers, Colonel Cockburn. The first destination of the party was Perth which they were able to reach by horseback and waggon on the 21st August. There the weather was very wet and Colonel Cockburn suggested that they should return rather than face what would be an exhausting journey to reach Richmond. However, the Duke elected to remain at Perth to see if the weather improved. By the 24th August the rain had cleared and the party were set to resume the next stage of the journey which was about fifteen miles. The Duke had eaten little breakfast and complained of a pain in his shoulder which kept him awake at night but he was determined to continue, though at their next stop he was obliged to rest and was clearly unwell. In the evening he was unable to enjoy his wine and was believed to say "I feel that if I was a dog I should be shot as a mad one". An assistant surgeon attached to the army was called and bled the Duke, after which he was said to feel better, but by the time he reached Richmond he was having difficulty in swallowing and was experiencing a convulsive effect that water produced on him.

At the tavern in the town his valet found the Duke could not look at a basin of water provided for washing and was able to use only a damp towel. At breakfast he had difficulty in drinking tea

The barn where the 4th Duke of Richmond died.

and his companions became only too aware of the the seriousness of his condition. They knew there was no cure for rabies, the main sympton of which was a terror of water. In the hope of returning to Richmond Landing, they left the tavern and, to avoid the river, they skirted a wood where there was some stagnant water. At the sight of it, the Duke hastily leaped over a fence and rushed into an adjoining barn where he collapsed. He was now suffering the usual paroxysms arising from hydrophobia and was clearly near the end of his life. His aides carried him from the barn into the adjoining house of a Mr Chapman. The Surgeon was called again and for a short time the Duke recovered sufficiently to to talk to his aides and address a letter to his daughter Lady Mary Lennox. In it, he requested burial in Quebec and, according to the Colonial Office Records, recalled an occasion five months earlier when he was bitten on the chin by a family dog which later became mad.

This recollection cast doubt on the theory that the infection came from the more recent fox bite. Towards the close of the day the Duke's condition deteriorated and about eight in the evening he died in the arms of his faithful valet.

Though she seemed to receive little mention in the aftermath of this tragedy, the figure of Maria Hill played no small part in attending to the Duke in his final hours. She was the landlady of the tavern locally known as "The Richmond Arms" which provided the honoured guest with comfort and care and with such food as he was able to enjoy. After his death, it was Maria who was asked to lay out the body of the Duke. A Lancashire lass, born Maria Glennan, she became the wife of an Irish Sergeant Major Andrew Hill and when he was sent to North America she served as a soldier assistant to the surgeons in the campaigns of 1812. No stranger to looking after the badly wounded and the sick she came to be regarded as the daughter of the 100th Regiment and there is no doubt that she suffered some extraordinary hardships during the Regiment's battles against the Yankees.

Maria Hill was clearly a woman of character. She could cook and she could sing and when her husband's army days were over, they decided to build a log cabin in Richmond which Maria felt was going to become an important township. She became a renowned hostess as well as a good business woman and the inn was soon the social centre of the area. The whole settlement was flattered by the visit of the Duke in those early days and "The Richmond Arms" was the only place thought good enough to provide him with the food and comfort he deserved. Yet apparently it was not until her 90th year that the full story came to be told of Maria Hill and the part she played in the tragic end of the 4th Duke of Richmond.

The Duke was buried below the pulpit in the Cathedral of the Holy Trinity in Quebec where there is a brass plate bearing his name and also a fine memorial tablet in the north gallery depicting a weeping female figure between crossed standards surmounted by a sword and wreath. There are several places in

The Memorials of the 4th Duke of Richmond.

IN MEMORY OF THE SERVICES, SELF-DEVOTION AND TRAGIC DEATH OF CHARLES LENNOX, FOURTH DUKE OF RICHMOND, A GALLANT SOLDIER AND GOVERNOR IN CHIEF OF CANADA, WHO DIED HERE, 28TH AUGUST, 1819.

HISTORIC SITES and MONUMENTS BOARD OF CANADA

Canada named after him, amongst the most notable being the Richmond where he died, and Richmond Hill in Ontario which the Duke visited in 1819, greatly impressing the local people. It was known then as the largest supplier of roses in Canada. One of the main thoroughfares in the City of Toronto was also named after the Duke as was the Richmond in New Hampshire. A township west of Ottawa was given the name March recognising that Charles Lennox was the Earl of March before he gained the Dukedom. Amongst the many places named Richmond outside Canada, and linked particularly with the 4th Duke, is a farm in South Africa which became the home of the Duke's daughter Sarah and her husband, Sir Peregrine Maitland, the first Governor of the Cape of Good Hope.

Apart from his sixteen years as M.P. for Chichester, Charles Lennox had given service in many ways including a period as High Steward of Chichester, Governor of Hull and of Plymouth and Lord Lieutenant of Sussex. He had also succeeded his uncle as Master General of the Ordnance. His widow died in 1842 at the age of 73 and was buried in Chichester Cathedral, the resting place of many members of the Richmond family. When the Duke went to Canada he gave power of attorney to his eldest son, Charles Gordon Lennox, Earl of March and, on his father's death, the young Earl succeeded to the Dukedom. The titles which passed to him included the Dukedom of Aubigny, a title which had been confirmed by Louis XVIII on the 18th of March, 1818, a year before his father's death.

References:
Bond, Courtney J., *City of Ottawa*, (Min. of Public Works 1961).
   Ottawa County, (Min. of Public Works 1968).
C.P.E. Vol.4 Nos.842/4.
Clarkson, C., *History of Richmond* (Bowman 1821) p.43.
Cockburn's Journal.
Colonial Office Records, Lower Canada 1819 Part 1 pp.112-118.
Country Life December 11th 1975.
The Cricketer August 1987 pp.26/27.

Goodwood published by Goodwood Estate Co.Ltd.

D.N.B. Vol. XI p.927 et seq.

Eggleston, Wilfred, *The Queen's Choice* (Min. of Public Works 1961).

Heyer, Georgette, *The Infamous Army* (Mandarin 1953).

Memoirs of the 4th Duke of Richmond (Chapman and Hill 1862).

Ontario Historical Society Papers and Records Vol. XXIV 1927, p.323 et seq.

Sussex County Magazine Vol .V and The Gentleman's Magazine May 1789 and May 1819.

Weller, Jac., *Wellington at Waterloo* (Napoleonic Library Greenhill 1992).

CHAPTER 26

Charles Gordon Lennox
(b.1791 - d.1860)
the 5th Duke of Richmond

IT COULD BE SAID that the young man who was destined to become the 5th Duke of Richmond was more dedicated to army service than his forebears. Yet his time as a soldier has probably been given extra emphasis in history because he was wounded in action in the Peninsular War and later served under Wellington at the great Battle of Waterloo. The story of his life begins at Westminster School where he not only received a good education but became a lover of cricket. He was an intelligent boy and his tutors were apparently agreed that if he had gone to university rather than the army, he would probably have become a distinguished scholar. But he was not diverted from his liking for army life and was gazetted as a Lieutenant in the 13th Regiment of the Dragoons and, rather surprisingly, became aide-de-camp to his father, then Lord Lieutenant of Ireland. His next move was to Portugal where, holding the courtesy title of Earl of March, he became aide-de-camp and assistant secretary to his father's friend Wellesley, the first Duke of Wellington. Active soldiering was soon to come his way and in 1814, when he was aged 23, he served in the Peninsular War as Captain in the 52nd Regiment. At the Battle of Orthez he was severely wounded in the chest and had to be sent home. At the time of the battle, a young surgeon named Dr Archibald Hair gave him prompt and decisive treatment which no doubt saved his life. The two were later to become

212

lifelong friends and Dr Hair became Charles' companion and private secretary.

Though his injury prevented him from riding and hunting, he recovered sufficiently to give further army service as aide-de-camp to the Prince of Orange in the campaign against the Netherlands and, after the Prince had been wounded at Waterloo, he joined Wellington's staff as an aide-de-camp. After Waterloo, he was decorated and gazetted as Lieutenant Colonel and, though he retired from active service, he continued to maintain an active interest in the Sussex Militia and in general military affairs. He never forgot the veterans of the Peninsular Campaign and, after a long fight, he gained public recognition for their services with

The 5th Duke of Richmond.
REPRODUCED BY PERMISSION OF THE NATIONAL PICTURE GALLERY

the result that medals were awarded to those who had been involved in the Campaign. The grateful soldiers subscribed to a huge silver table centre which is on display at Goodwood today.

At the age of 21, he was elected M.P. for Chichester and served his constituency for seven years. Agriculture was his particular concern and it continued to be his main political interest in later years. In Sussex, he was called upon to deal with riots by agricultural workers but, with the support of fifty of his tenant farmers, he harangued the disgruntled rioters and sent them home in good humour. He proved to be not only a liberal landlord but a knowledgeable farmer and an approved breeder of Southdown sheep. His interest in agriculture resulted in his election as President of the Smithfield Club which founded the Royal Agricultural Society in 1837 and he was later elected as President of that Society. After he succeeded to the Dukedom and took his seat in the Upper House he soon began raising questions on agricultural matters and it was on his initiative that an enquiry was set up into the wool trade.

His father died in 1819 and he succeeded to all the family titles, including the Dukedom of Aubigny in France, and although he then resigned from his parliamentary seat, he retained a strong influence on local affairs and was created Lord Lieutenant of Sussex in 1835, a position he held until his death. Two years before his father died, he had married Lady Caroline Paget, eldest daughter of the Marquess of Anglesey. It was a long and satisfactory marriage and, of their twelve children, the eldest son was Charles Henry Gordon Lennox who was destined to succeed to his father's titles.

Despite the freedoms resulting from Catholic emancipation late in the 18th century, Catholics were still debarred from sitting in Parliament and, in 1829, the Duke of Wellington decided that further reforms must be established including removal of the ban on Catholic parliamentary service. When the Catholic Emancipation Bill was presented to Parliament one of the most outspoken critics was the Duke of Richmond despite the family friendship with Wellington, but the Bill was passed, as was the

214

Catholic Relief Bill. Richmond continued to play an active role in political affairs and, in 1830, he proposed that a select committee should be set up to study the internal state of the country. He was particularly concerned about the working classes but, despite Whig support, his move was defeated. In November 1830, he joined Earl Grey's reforming ministry but, surprisingly, when he was offered the Ordnance Department, his appointment was opposed by the Army. After refusing the Mastership of the Horse, he ultimately accepted the office of Postmaster General and, during his period of office, the Irish Post Office was united with the Post Office of Great Britain and sweeping reforms were made in the postal service. Richmond's anti-Catholic views came to the fore again on the question of appropriations for the Irish Church and he and others resigned from the Government on the question. Thereafter, he sat on the cross benches.

He had already introduced a bill for the reform of the game laws and he was subsequently made a member of the prison discipline committee of 1835, and chairman of the committee of the House of Lords which suggested the abolition of the hulks, which were used as prisons. He was also one of the first commissioners appointed for the government of Pentonville prison. When Sir Robert Peel produced his free-trade measures, the Duke came forward as one of the leaders of the protectionist party and, in 1845, led the opposition to the Customs Bill in the upper house. In the same year, he became president of the Agricultural Protection Society which was founded to counteract the principles of the Anti-Corn Law League. In 1846, he moved the rejection of the Corn Bill in an uncompromising speech but his motion was nevertheless defeated. In 1852, he refused the offer of a position in Lord Derby's government.

In 1842 his mother, Lady Charlotte, had died leaving him heir to the Gordon estates and he then adopted the name of Gordon Lennox. The Gordon inheritance was particularly important in that it enabled him to complete additions to Goodwood House made by his great uncle, the 3rd Duke. The link with the Gordons having been established, he is known to have spent part of each

215

year in Scotland. The title of Duke of Gordon was to be revived in 1876 in favour of the succeeding 6th Duke of Richmond.

Charles Gordon Lennox, the 5th Duke of Richmond died of dropsy in 1860 but his wife Caroline outlived him and did not die until 1874. Though the Duke's ambitions in early life were confined to the army, his injury in the Peninsular War curtailed his active service and led him to concentrate on what proved to be an active political career. The King liked him for his intelligent work in the Cabinet but, as a right wing Tory, the Duke naturally had his critics, including the diarist Charles Greville who thought him prejudiced and narrow minded. Yet his interests were widely spread and included Vice Admiral of Sussex as well as a member of Sussex Militia, and Steward of the Jockey Club. In Scotland, he was Chancellor of Marischal College, Aberdeen and Hereditary Constable of Inverness Castle. Though his injury prevented him from riding, he always hosted the Goodwood races and the love of cricket which he seemed to inherit from his forebears led to his involvement in forming the Sussex County Cricket Club and, for a time, he was President of the M.C.C.

Like other Richmonds before him, the Duke was buried in Chichester Cathedral and perhaps the epitaph given to him sums up his character and the diverse nature of his achievements.

> His life was gentle and the elements
> so mixed in him, that nature might stand up
> and say to all the world "This was a man".

References:
Memoirs of C.G. Lennox, the 5th Duke. (Chapman & Hill, London 1862).
Kent, J., *Recorded Reminiscences of Goodwood and the Dukes of Richmond.* (Sampson Low 1896).
East Sussex Record Office - *Goodwood Estate Archives* Vol. III.
The Gentleman's Magazine 1860 Pt II p.669.
D.N.B. Vol.XI p.927

CHAPTER 27

The Gordons

THE HISTORY OF the Gordons, like that of the Lennox dynasty, can certainly be traced back in Scotland to the twelfth century, though their earlier roots are a little uncertain. The name of Gordon may have come from the manor of Gourdon in Normandy though other sources suggest it originates from the ancient British "gor-din", meaning a great hill fort. There seems little doubt however that the original Gordons were Anglo-Norman settlers in the borders of Scotland.

They are known to have held land in the twelfth century in Berwickshire as well as Huntly nearby and they were closely connected with their neighbours the Swintons, as well as with some of the other great border families. This was evidenced at the dawn of heraldry by their respective coats of arms which all included boars' heads, the tradition being that the King granted land to those who killed a wild boar which had seriously distressed the area. Sir Adam Gordon, an early chieftain, was a friend and supporter of the Lord of Badenoch who was fatally stabbed by Robert the Bruce. To avenge his friend, Sir Adam then gave his support to Edward I but, after Edward's death, the battle of Bannockburn and the harassment of Gordon lands by the English commander, he decided to transfer his support to Bruce. He was then rewarded with the Lordship of Strathbogie in Aberdeenshire, comprising an estate of 120 square miles, and this became the chief seat of the Gordon family. It was renamed "Huntly" after the family lands in Berwickshire. Robert the Bruce is also thought to have given Sir Adam the Cairngorm territory of the Earls of Fife which were certainly held by later Gordon chiefs. In 1320 Sir Adam was made the Scottish Ambassador to the Pope and brought to him the historic Declaration of Independence sealed at Arbroath. He died in 1333 and was succeeded by his son of the same name.

Despite their neighbourly connections, the Gordons were always feuding with the Swintons but they settled their differences in 1407 when Adam, Sir Adam's elder son, joined forces with Sir John Swinton to fight the English at Homildon Hill. Sir John knighted his fellow baron on the battlefield, but both were to die at the hands of the English forces. With Adam's death, the direct legitimate male line of the Gordons was brought to a close, though from the younger son William, sprang the Galloway, Irish and Virginian branches of the family. Sir Adam Gordon had a brother, Sir John Gordon, who had two natural sons named "Jock" and "Tam". From them were descended various Gordon chieftains in Buchan including the Earl of Aberdeen, Prime Minister during the Crimean War and the Marquess of Aberdeen who became Governor General of Canada.

Sir Adam had a daughter Elizabeth who married Sir Alexander Seton and inherited the barony of the Gordons and the lands in Huntly, Berwickshire and Aberdeenshire. From this marriage came the name of the Seton-Gordons and the son of the marriage, given the name Alexander, was created 1st Earl of Huntly and later Lord of Badenoch. He was succeeded by his son George who married the Princess Johanna daughter of James I and became the 2nd Earl of Huntly. From this marriage came Alexander, the 3rd Earl of Huntly, who was appointed Lieutenant of James IV, north of the Water of the Esk, and by the end of the 15th century, the Gordons were the principal power in north-east Scotland where they were the main instruments of government policy.

When George, the 4th Earl of Huntly, inherited the Earldom of Moray, he became the richest of all the Gordons and earned the title of "Cock of the North". Not only was he the wealthiest, he was probably the most powerful of Scottish landowners, so powerful indeed that he was led to contemplate establishing a

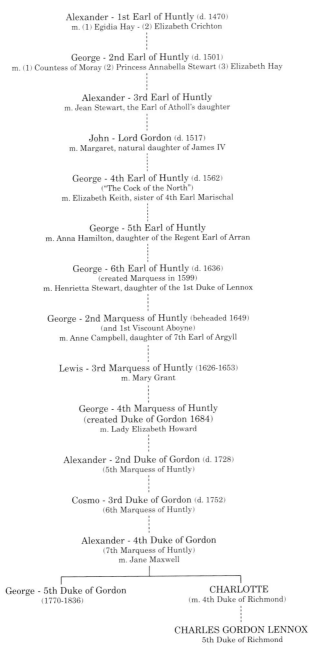

THE GORDONS AND THE RICHMONDS
Originating from Adam de Gordon

Alexander - 1st Earl of Huntly (d. 1470)
m. (1) Egidia Hay - (2) Elizabeth Crichton

George - 2nd Earl of Huntly (d. 1501)
m. (1) Countess of Moray (2) Princess Annabella Stewart (3) Elizabeth Hay

Alexander - 3rd Earl of Huntly
m. Jean Stewart, the Earl of Atholl's daughter

John - Lord Gordon (d. 1517)
m. Margaret, natural daughter of James IV

George - 4th Earl of Huntly (d. 1562)
("The Cock of the North")
m. Elizabeth Keith, sister of 4th Earl Marischal

George - 5th Earl of Huntly
m. Anna Hamilton, daughter of the Regent Earl of Arran

George - 6th Earl of Huntly (d. 1636)
(created Marquess in 1599)
m. Henrietta Stewart, daughter of the 1st Duke of Lennox

George - 2nd Marquess of Huntly (beheaded 1649)
(and 1st Viscount Aboyne)
m. Anne Campbell, daughter of 7th Earl of Argyll

Lewis - 3rd Marquess of Huntly (1626-1653)
m. Mary Grant

George - 4th Marquess of Huntly
(created Duke of Gordon 1684)
m. Lady Elizabeth Howard

Alexander - 2nd Duke of Gordon (d. 1728)
(5th Marquess of Huntly)

Cosmo - 3rd Duke of Gordon (d. 1752)
(6th Marquess of Huntly)

Alexander - 4th Duke of Gordon
(7th Marquess of Huntly)
m. Jane Maxwell

George - 5th Duke of Gordon
(1770-1836)

CHARLOTTE
(m. 4th Duke of Richmond)

CHARLES GORDON LENNOX
5th Duke of Richmond

219

state of near independence for his northern territories. This was to be his undoing for the King decided to act, depriving him of the earldom of Moray. This the Earl could not accept and rebelled against the decision but, in 1562, after the return and accession of Mary Queen of Scots, he was killed following an encounter at Corrichie. One version of his death suggests that he died of a stroke when brought into the presence of the Queen.

The next in line was his second son George, who married Anna Hamilton, daughter of the Regent Earl of Arran, herself a descendant of King James II. The succession then passed on to another George who became the 6th Earl of Huntly. In 1594, he was accused with the Earls of Angus and Errol of conspiring with the King of Spain for the restoration of the Roman Catholic religion in Scotland. After an early confrontation which ended in favour of Huntly and Errol, the King was forced by the Protestant nobles to lead an army to the north where they demolished Errol's castle of Slaines and Huntly's stronghold of Strathbogie, said to have been the finest house of the time in Scotland. Despite this affair, Huntly was able to regain the King's favour, perhaps because he married Lady Henrietta Stewart, eldest daughter of the King's favourite Esmé, Duke of Lennox and, in 1599, he was created Marquess of Huntly. His marriage to the Duke of Lennox's daughter established a new link between the Lennox and Gordon clans.

Their son was another George who became the 2nd Marquess and the 1st Earl of Aboyne. He was a staunch supporter of Charles I but his refusal to subscribe to the National Covenant resulted in his eventual capture after which he was beheaded. He had married Anne Campbell and the succession then passed to Lewis who became the 3rd Marquess during the short reign in Scotland of Charles II. His successor was another George, who became the 4th Marquess when he was no more than ten years old. He later married Lady Elizabeth Howard and, in 1684, he was created the 1st Duke of Gordon as well as Keeper of Edinburgh Castle, but because he came under suspicion of being a Jacobite sympathiser, he was forced to remain in Edinburgh.

The 2nd Duke of Gordon was Alexander and he created trouble by associating himself with the Old Pretender though he was

Gordon Castle.

pardoned on his surrender of Gordon Castle in 1716. Cosmo George, who became the 3rd Duke of Gordon was present during the critical part of the Jacobite rebellion of 1745. He had three sons, the eldest, given the family name of Alexander, became the 4th Duke and he gained popularity by writing a song "Cauld Kail in Aberdeen". He was made a peer of the United Kingdom and was a Knight of the Thistle and Lord Keeper of Scotland. He married Jane Maxwell and they had a son named George who became the 5th Duke of Gordon, though he proved to be the last of the line. They also had a daughter named Charlotte who was married at Gordon Castle in 1789 to the 4th Duke of Richmond. It was through this marriage that the links were created between the Gordons and the Richmonds.

The 5th Duke of Gordon had a distinguished military career and commanded the famous Gordon Highlanders, but he was severely wounded and, on his death in 1836, the Dukedom of Gordon became extinct and most of the estates, including Gordon Castle, passed to Charlotte. The Dukedom was recreated in 1876 and passed to the Charles the 6th Duke of Richmond, who then became the Duke of Richmond, Gordon and Lennox.

The Gordons remain one of the most widely recognised families in Scotland but there is little left of their Castle set on the banks of the Spey in north-east Moray, which played an important part in their history. It had begun as a "pillbox in a bog", a stronghold in a morass comprising a tower dating back to the 12th century which could only be approached by a causeway. It was for long known as the Bog o' Gight, the windy bog, and its successive lairds bore the title of the Gudemen o' the Bog but five centuries of fostering care converted it into a ducal palace without parallel in the North of Scotland.

It was George, the 2nd Earl of Huntly who had founded the Castle towards the end of the 15th century and he heightened the tower to six storeys but the 4th Duke of Gordon, who married Jane Maxwell, had ambitious plans for altering and extending the Castle. He consulted a famous Scottish architect, John Adam and also referred to plans presented by Abraham

Roumieu but in the end commissioned John Baxter of Edinburgh to replace all but the Old Tower with a huge new building with a frontage 170 metres long. When the new Gordon Castle was completed, it possessed great formal gardens and an islanded lake. There were magnificent interiors and the Castle was a fitting setting for the gay and brilliant Duchess who dazzled high society for a number of years. In 1773 when Boswell and Dr Johnson visited Elgin, where they saw the Gordon family vault, Boswell described Gordon Castle as having a "princely appearance".

The Castle passed with the other Gordon estates to the Commissioners of Crown lands in 1938 and the mansion itself was used by the army until 1948. By then, water damage had so affected the main block and west wing that they had to be demolished. Little but the historic old tower and the east wing remain, but the grounds were the scene in July 1976 of the first Gordon Highland Games to be held there for forty years, a reminder perhaps of the important part the Gordons continue to play in Scottish life. The present clan seat is at Aboyne.

References:
Moncrieffe, Sir Iain, *The Highland Clans* (Barrie & Jenkins 1967).
Bulletin of the Scottish Georgian Society 1973 Vol. 2.
Blundell, *Ancient Catholic Homes of Scotland* (Burns & Oates 1905).
Eyre-Todd, George, *The Highland Clans of Scotland* (1923).
Huntly, Marquess of, *The Cock of the North* (Thornton Butterworth 1935).
Salter, Mike, *The Castles of Grampian and Angus* (Folly Publications) (undt.).

CHAPTER 28

Charles Henry Gordon Lennox (b.1818 - d.1903) the 6th Duke of Richmond

CHARLES, THE 6TH DUKE of Richmond lived his years in the Victorian era, at a time when great statesmen like Benjamin Disraeli, Robert Peel, Lord Derby and Gladstone held the political stage. He was born at Richmond House in 1818 and, like other Richmonds before him, he was educated at Westminster School. Although some army service appealed to him, he first went to Christ Church, Oxford and graduated with a Bachelor of Arts degree in 1839. It was on the 27th of February in that year that he came of age and to celebrate the occasion, his father, the 5th Duke, put on the most magnificent entertainment ever known in West Sussex. After a stag hunt, some 300 gentlemen sat down to dinner in the tennis court area of Goodwood presided over by Charles' brother Lord George Lennox. In the evening there was a ball and supper attended by 700 guests and the celebrations concluded with a huge bonfire. It was indeed a day to remember and, on the Friday following, the Duke entertained 200 of his tenants and their friends to a dinner. The young Earl was presented with an elegant plate by his mother and it was a coincidence that the date of his 21st birthday was the anniversary of the Battle of Orthez when, in 1814, his father was badly wounded, surviving only because of the skill of his friend Dr Archibald Hair.

After University, the Earl was entered as a cornet in the Royal Regiment of Horse Guards and retired five years later with the rank of Captain. Though he did not see active service, he acted as aide-de-camp to Wellington, as had his father before him, and later to Wellington's successor, Viscount Hardinge. In 1841, he embarked on a political career and, having been elected as M.P. for West Sussex in the General Election of that year, he served his constituency for nearly twenty years. In 1859 he was made a Privy Councillor and his entry into the Upper House was not long delayed. His father died in 1860 and having succeeded to the Dukedom and the family titles, he was called to take his seat in the Lords where he soon made his presence felt.

In 1843, as the Earl of March, he had married Frances Harriet, daughter of Algernon Frederick Greville, Bath King-at-Arms who was Secretary to the Duke of Wellington for many years. March had been appointed aide-de-camp to Wellington the previous year. They had a family of six children, four of whom were boys, the eldest son being Charles Henry who became heir to the Richmond Dukedom. The eldest daughter was Caroline who became her father's constant companion. Though the Gordon estates had already passed to the Richmonds, the title of Duke of Gordon had expired and it was not until 1876 that it was revived in favour of the 6th Duke of Richmond. He then had an imposing array of titles. They were: Duke of Richmond, Earl of March - later passed to his eldest son - Baron of Settrington in the County of York, Duke of Lennox, Earl of Darnley, Baron Methuen of Torbolton (in the Peerage of Scotland), Duke of Gordon and Earl of Kinrara (in the peerage of the United Kingdom), Duke of Aubigny in France, and Hereditary Constable of Inverness Castle. He was also made a Knight of the Garter, an honour which had been bestowed on his predecessors.

After the death of his father, the new Duke chose to remain with his family in the Dower House of Molecomb allowing the main House at Goodwood to be closed and the interior refurbished. The Dukes of Richmond had gained a reputation for being leaders in agricultural matters and certainly the 6th Duke was no exception. His interest in farming and maintenance of the Goodwood estate were always paramount and he was concerned that the policy of tree-planting established by his forebears should be continued. A better water supply was needed at Goodwood and

The 6th Duke of Richmond.

he completed a new system which involved pumping the water from deep wells into a reservoir in the northern part of the estate. He had a particular concern for the well-being of his tenants and built 200 cottages for estate employees as well as planning a programme of reducing rents. Farming was always important to him and he inherited a flock of Southdown sheep which he did much to improve with such prize-winning success that the King decided to use the Goodwood Southdown strain for breeding at Sandringham.

North of the Border, ownership of Gordon Castle and the estates gave the Duke great influence as well as responsibilities in the Highlands. He gained respect for the help he gave to the crofters and small farmers on his estates and he is remembered with acclaim for building a new concrete harbour at Port Gordon. Amongst Scottish farming circles, he became well known as a breeder of quality Shorthorn cattle, and he served for a time as President of the Shorthorn Society. He was very fond of fishing and shooting and he spent three or four months each year at Gordon Castle enjoying salmon fishing on the Spey as well as grouse shooting and deer stalking further north at Glenfiddich Lodge.

Though the 6th Duke of Richmond's Goodwood estates were considerable, the Gordon estates were even more extensive. Figures given to a Royal Commission at the time gave the Goodwood estate figure as 19,716 acres of which 11,844 were arable and pasture with the rest either forestry or on the downs. There were thirty-two farms bringing in a total net income of £9,200. North of the border the estate comprised 269,220 acres in the counties of Inverness, Banff, Aberdeen, and Elgin, the length of the estate being about seventy miles. There were some 220,000 acres of mountain and rough pasture and the remainder was good arable land. Of the 882 tenants, 327 were known to be small farmers paying less than £10 a year. On an occasion reported in the Journal of the Royal Agricultural Society in 1903, the Duke responded to a presentation in Scotland in a manner indicative of his character.

"I look upon myself and the tenantry as members of one large, vast and I am happy to be able to add, united family. I am aware that I have a very large estate, that I have a large number of tenants of all classes, but I am further aware that I have inherited very great responsibilities. It is my duty - and I endeavour to carry it out - to look after the interests myself personally, individually, of the humblest crofter on this estate as well as of the wealthiest tenant".

The Duke had a life-long connection with the Smithfield Club and acted as its President on two occasions. His father had played an important part in forming the English Agricultural Society which was subsequently granted a Royal Charter. When Earl of March, the 6th Duke soon became a member of the Society and it was an association which lasted over sixty-five years. For two periods, he was President and, when the Society's Show was held in Cambridge, he received the honorary degree of LL.D from the University. His long service to farming was recognised by many, not least by the King, who, when Prince of Wales, made a speech celebrating the Society's fiftieth anniversary and when complimenting the Duke said that he had become recognised by everyone as "the farmers' friend". It was a description which certainly gave the Duke much pleasure.

Although he was elected a member of the Jockey Club in 1838 and became one of its most senior members, he never took such an active part on the turf as his father. He rarely attended meetings, the only exception being when the Club's summer general meeting was held at his home in Belgrave Square in London. He had succeeded to the Dukedom when the fortunes of Goodwood Racecourse were at their highest and when Ascot was the only comparable alternative. Though he saw to it that the Goodwood course was always well maintained, and even built a new grandstand, other courses began to offer more valuable prizes because of the "gate money" they received and Goodwood began to lose its racing supremacy. What it did not lose was its great social appeal and the Duke maintained the traditions of his predecessors by having a large party during its race week with a guest list which more often than not included the King and Queen and, on occasions, such notables as the Tsar of Russia and the German Emperor. The 4th Duke had given up the Goodwood pack of fox-hounds when the Charlton Hunt came to an end, but the 6th Duke re-established the pack making the Earl of March the Master of them. New kennels were built and the old ones converted into comfortable dwellings. However, the Goodwood hounds and hunt were discontinued at the close of the 1894-5 season.

In politics, the Duke was described in the press of the day as an old-fashioned Tory and, though he could not be regarded as a great orator, he was respected for the common sense of his outlook on a number of debatable subjects including the Irish problems and education. After several years in the Lords he was made President of the Board of Trade in the Derby-Disraeli cabinet of 1867 and, when Lord Derby died in 1870, he was selected to lead the Conservative party, then in opposition, in the House of Lords. The Party had needed someone with sound common sense as well as the ability to compromise and his selection was made despite the presence of other candidates like Lord Salisbury and Lord Cairns. The Duke did not always get on well with Disraeli, who nevertheless appointed him Lord President of the Council when forming his Government of 1874. It was in the following year that the Duke introduced the important Agricultural Holdings Bill which established freedom of contract between landlord and tenant and fully respected the position of the tenant. In 1876 however Disraeli was translated to the Upper House as Earl of Beaconsfield and he took the duties of leadership out of the Duke's hands.

A series of disastrous agricultural seasons culminated in 1879 and led to the appointment of a Royal Commission on Agriculture. The Duke was appointed Chairman and it was a role he filled with considerable success. It was largely due to his skill in bringing together a wide range of opinions that the Commission's Final Report was signed by all members without reservations and, in appreciation of his wise Chairmanship, his colleagues presented him with a silver inkstand and two silver candlesticks.

In 1880 Gladstone's Liberals came back into power, and Conservative leadership in the Upper House was taken over by

The Derby Cabinet of 1867 at which the expedition to Abyssinia was decided upon. The 6th Duke was a member of this Cabinet and is believed to be standing to the left of the fireplace.

Lord Salisbury. It was not until 1885 that the Duke came into Government again and, once more, he was appointed President of the Board of Trade by Lord Salisbury, followed by a newly established post of Secretary for Scotland. In the meantime however, he is known to have played an important role as mediator when serious difficulties arose between the Lords and the Commons over the County Franchise and Redistribution proposals of the Government. Considerable agitation had arisen in the country and there were meetings in Hyde Park and in several of the major cities to denounce the House of Lords, which had thrown out the Franchise Bill insisting that it must be submitted side by side with a Redistribution Bill. In the end a compromise was reached which provided the basis for our subsequent electoral system. There is little doubt that the negotiating skills of the Duke of Richmond played an important role in the ultimate agreement. It is known that Queen Victoria held him in high regard, and in September 1884 he was invited by the Queen to Balmoral. Lord Salisbury's Government was short-lived and the Duke retired from politics in 1886. The Duchess of Richmond died in the following year.

In his later years, the Duke spent much time in Scotland. He had arrived at Gordon Castle from Goodwood in July of 1903 apparently in fairly good health but he deteriorated and, surrounded by his family, he died on the 27th of September. Like his forebears, he was buried in Chichester Cathedral in the presence of a very large assembly of mourners including, as might be expected, a strong representation from the farming community for which he had done so much during his long life. A memorial window was installed in the Cathedral in his honour.

References:
Kent, J., *Records and Reminiscences of Goodwood and the Dukes of Richmond* (Sampson Low 1896).
D.N.B. (20th century edition) pp.129-131.
The Journal of the Agricultural Society Vol. 64 1903.
The Times September 28th 1903 page 5.

CHAPTER 29

Charles Henry Gordon Lennox (b.1845 - d.1928) the 7th Duke of Richmond

T HE LONG LIFE OF the 7th Duke of Richmond spanned 82 years in the reigns of no less than three monarchs, Queen Victoria, Edward VII and George V. He was a man of simple tastes who led an active life in widely different spheres but the high platforms of politics favoured by his father were not for him. True, he stood for some years as Member for Sussex constituencies and voiced his opinions particularly on moral and religious training in education and on the disestablishment of the Irish Church, which he considered to be an unwarranted attack on the Protestants. Though he held several positions of responsibility on Royal Commissions, service in the army seemed to appeal to him more than politics but, after his second wife died, he developed a great love of agriculture, taking a dedicated interest in the farms on his estates in England and Scotland. His knowledge of stockbreeding and his public work for agriculture became widely recognised and not only did he take over the role of "the farmers' friend" from his father, he was given the accolade of "the best landlord of the day". His estates in England and Scotland totalled nearly 300,000 acres but, unlike some great landed proprietors, he refused to put any estates on the market where they might be bought by men who would exploit the tenantry. Rents were low and, in consequence, there was a general spirit of prosperity and contentment.

Born in London during late December 1845, he was the first of the Richmond family to be educated at Eton. As Earl of March, he began his army career in 1865 when he joined the Grenadier Guards. Over the years he reached the rank of Captain and later became Colonel of a battalion of the Royal Sussex Regiment. He was well over fifty when the South African war broke out but he wanted to be part of it and in fact served with distinction at the front, being mentioned in despatches and made a C.B. His interest in the army continued in later life when he was made Honorary Commandant of the 4th V.B. The Gordon Highlanders and, prior to the Great War, he gave much support to the Territorial Army and to recruitment for the Gordon and Seaforth Highlanders. During the War, half of Gordon Castle was converted at his expense into a V.A.D. hospital.

For the last forty years of his life he was a widower and, in 1903, he was in his late fifties when his father died at Gordon Castle leaving him to succeed to the many family titles which included the Duke of Lennox, Earl of Darnley and Baron Methuen of Torbolton in Scotland. He also became Duke of Gordon and Earl of Kinrara in the peerage of the United Kingdom. Other positions held in Scotland were Hereditary Constable of Inverness Castle and Lord Lieutenant of Moray and Banff. These links with Scotland were very strong and the new Duke clearly felt at home when he went to Gordon Castle, where he mixed freely with his many tenants and visited the many farmsteads and crofts on his estates to discuss everyday farming problems. It was an indication of the respect in which he was held north of the border when, in 1917, he was elected Chancellor of Aberdeen University.

He was a sportsman, a keen stalker, a fine shot as well as an expert fly fisherman who insisted that his salmon tenants used only a rod and fly. When staying at Gordon Castle he was always to be seen wearing the Gordon kilt and a Balmoral cap, and it was his custom to sleep on a small pallet bed in a little narrow room overlooking the beautiful park of the Castle as well as the home farm on which there was a well known herd of Shorthorn cattle. Forestry was another of his interests and he transformed

The 7th Duke of Richmond.

the deer park at Fochabers, an area containing hundreds of acres, into a woodland where the Scots pines were said to be the finest in Scotland.

In England, the Duke took a great interest in the Goodwood estates and particularly in the Goodwood flock of Southdown sheep which had long been famous. The sheep historian M.L. Ryder has noted that the Southdowns kept on the chalk hills of Kent and Sussex since medieval times were probably typical of the original English shortwool sheep and that during the eighteenth century the wool sold at two shillings a pound, only Ryland wool fetching a higher price. From about 1780, John Ellman of Glynde began developing the Southdowns and from the early days of Goodwood the estate's flock of these sheep rose to a high standard of quality, improvements made by his father being continued by the 7th Duke. The fame of these Southdowns in farming circles had been shared for some decades with the herd of Aberdeen Angus cattle as well as probably the largest extant herd of Jersey stock, the breeding of which dated back to 1747.

The emphasis on high-quality livestock on the 7th Duke's estates at Goodwood and in Scotland was matched by his knowledge and success in tillage and general farming techniques. In 1916 he became President of the Royal Agricultural Society of England. In the middle of the Great War, it was a difficult year and one in which the future of the Society had to be decided but his wisdom, tact and skill did much to preserve the farming resources and stave off a national disaster.

In 1896, he had been made an Aide-de-Camp to Queen Victoria and he was continued in that office by her successors Edward VII and then George V, each of whom visited Gordon Castle for the stalking, fishing and shooting. During their reigns, they also visited Goodwood for what became a famous race meeting held in the park each year. In his early days, the Duke had ridden in a few races without much success, though he was reputed to be a fearless rider, and though he was never prominent as a racehorse owner he served with distinction as a member of the Jockey Club. He acted as Steward on two occasions and he served the Club during a difficult period of its history when rules were passed requiring jockeys to be licensed, preventing them from owning racehorses or indulging in any form of betting. As the owner of Goodwood Racecourse, the Duke carried out many improvements and he prompted a relaxation in the formal dress always associated with Ascot by appearing at one meeting wearing a pair of white flannels and a straw hat. He gave great house parties for the races and liked to travel to Gordon Castle with all his family as soon as the racing at Glorious Goodwood had ended.

The Duke had attended the Coronation of Edward VII and, following his family tradition, he carried the Sceptre and Dove at the Coronation of King George V. He married twice, the first being in 1868 to the beautiful and intelligent Amy, the daughter of Percy Ricardo. She died in 1879 and he married again three years later, this time to Isobel, daughter of William Craven but she was to die of typhoid after five years of their marriage. Though he was left a widower for the last forty years of his life he had the support of three sons from his marriage to Amy Ricardo and two daughters from his second marriage. His eldest son, given the family names of Charles Henry, succeeded him and one of his daughters, Isobel Sophie, became Duchess of Northumberland. The 7th Duke of Richmond died in January, 1928 and like his forebears, he was buried in the Cathedral of Chichester.

References:
Kent, J., *Records and Reminiscences of Goodwood and the Dukes of Richmond* (Sampson Low 1896).
The Times 19th and 23rd January 1928.
Goodwood Estate Archives (Vol III).

CHAPTER 30

Charles Henry Gordon Lennox (b.1870 - d.1935) the 8th Duke of Richmond

CHARLES HENRY, THE son of his father's first marriage, to Amy Ricardo, was born into an age of change. As a young man, he served in the South African War and later in the Great War, the aftermath of which brought problems to the Richmond family, made the worse because he became disabled and confined to a wheelchair.

His schooldays were spent at Eton as were those of his father and he then went to Christ Church, Oxford. For a time he served as Sussex County Commissioner for the Boy Scouts Association and his army career began as an officer in the Royal Sussex Regiment. With the Irish Guards, he served as aide-de-camp to Lord Roberts who was then Commander of. the forces in Ireland. In a similar role under Lord Roberts in South Africa he distinguished himself in operations in the Orange Free State where he earned the D.S.O. Back home, he reached the rank of Captain in the Irish Guards and was appointed under Sir Charles Douglas, Commander of the Home Forces. He retired with the rank of Major in 1912 only to be recalled at the onset of the Great War.

In 1903, his father succeeded to the Dukedom of Richmond and the young Charles Henry took the title of Earl of March. Like other Richmonds he was a lover of horses and frequently rode in point to point meetings. Hunting was one of his favourite pursuits and in 1901 he wrote a book on the old Charlton Hunt at

Goodwood, the story of which goes back to the time when the Mastership and hounds of the Hunt were passed to the 2nd Duke of Richmond by the Duke of Bolton. With an obvious interest in family history, he also edited a study of the life and letters of the 2nd Duke which was printed under the title of "A Duke and his Friends". In 1891-2, he travelled in Australia, New Zealand and Ceylon and kept a diary of his experiences. His visits to Scotland and Gordon Castle were always a joy to him and he liked nothing better than to fish on the Spey and in the little Fiddich burn, to stalk and to take part in the grouse shoot. Sadly for him these pleasures were to become a thing of the past with the beginning of the Great War when he was made Commandant of the Brigade of Guards.

Early in the War, when he was waiting to go with his Regiment to Gallipoli, he was seized with a high fever and an almost crippling paralysis, said to be the result of hardships endured in France and Belgium. It produced a wasting disease of the leg muscles, later diagnosed as poliomyelitis, and he had to resort to artificial supports and a wheel chair. To an active man with great ability and pride in his Regiment it was a tragic misfortune and his inability to go to Gallipoli with his men added to his physical suffering. In 1893 he had married Hilda Madeleine Brassey whose parents came from Preston Hall in Aylsford in Kent. During and after the War he and his wife kept in close touch with the Regiment and showed many kindnesses to the men who always regarded the Earl with great respect. Yet the War took its toll not only of many friends but also of his brother Esmé. After the death of their eldest son when only one month old, the Earl and his wife suffered perhaps their greatest loss when their second son, then Lord Settrington, who had been in France, volunteered for further service only to die from wounds received on the British Eastern Front in 1919 where he was supporting the White Russians against the Bolsheviks. It was indicative of the Earl's character that, for twenty years, he continued to bear these many misfortunes with great fortitude, courage and a complete absence of self-pity.

The 8th Duke of Richmond.

His father died in 1928. leaving him to succeed to all the family titles. As far as his health would allow, he continued his father's work at Goodwood but the aftermath of the War brought new burdens of taxation compelling him to take strong measures to preserve the homes of his ancestors. In Scotland, he had to sell his estate of Glenavon in Banffshire of about 45,000 acres but he sent letters to every tenant explaining that he was forced to sell the land to pay death duties. At Goodwood, he not only sold some land but also some beech trees and pedigree stock as well as books, pictures and even racing trophies. He decided to install a totalisator on the race course and registered a new company known as the Goodwood Estate Company. Despite the burdens of taxation, he managed to keep open the Goodwood and Gordon Houses and, though he was left unable to walk for the rest of his life, he travelled around the estate at great speed in his wheel chair, paths being cut through fields and crops especially to facilitate his progress. He and his devoted wife did all they could to care for others disabled as a result of the War. The Duke was aged 59 when he decided to buy some horses and have them trained at Goodwood. He won his first race in 1930 and in the same year he became a member of the Jockey Club.

As the two eldest sons of the Duke and his wife did not survive, their third son Frederick Charles, born in 1904, became Lord March and was destined to succeed to the titles. It was in 1935 that the Duke died at Goodwood at the age of 65 and, according to tradition, he was buried at Chichester Cathedral. He is remembered as a modest man whose strength of character enabled him to contend with war service, disablement, and family bereavements as well as the problems of maintaining his family's estates in the most difficult of times.

References:
Goodwood Estate Archives (Vol. 2).
The Times 8th May, 1935.

CHAPTER 31

Frederick Charles Gordon Lennox (b.1904 - d.1989) the 9th Duke of Richmond

FREDERICK CHARLES, WAS the third and only surviving son of Charles the 8th Duke and his wife Hilda, and he was only fifteen when the whole family was greatly saddened by the death of his elder brother, Lord Settrington, and Frederick Charles became heir to the Dukedom. By the time he succeeded to his father's titles however, he was over thirty years of age and his marriage to Elizabeth, daughter of the Reverend T.W. Hudson, had provided a son and heir, given the family names of Charles Henry. They also had a second son who became Lord Nicholas Gordon Lennox. During his early years as Lord Settrington and then Earl of March, Frederick Charles was in great demand as patron, president, chairman and director of many local and national organisations; he became Chancellor of Sussex University, a lay reader and an active chairman of the several Goodwood companies, yet he was probably the only Richmond descendant to possess an engineering bent, his greatest interest being in motor and aeronautical engineering. It was an interest which was to continue throughout his long life.

As a boy, he joined the Boxgrove troop of Boy Scouts and to his friends, he became known as Frederick Richmond. It was at Eton and particularly at Christ Church, Oxford that he developed his abiding interest in engineering. After University, he was apprenticed to Bentley Motors and he referred to his time there as being the best part of his education. By the age of twenty-five he had become a recognised motor racing driver and drove in the JCC High Speed Trial in which he gained a premier award. Following this, he became a member of the official Austin team and, at Brooklands, he gained his first major success when he won the 500 miles race with his partner Sammy Davis, a well-known competition driver. In 1931, he formed his own team of M.G. Midgets and proceeded to win the celebrated Brooklands Double Twelve race. He flew his own plane and by the beginning of the war in 1939 he had even designed and built an aircraft the subsequent production of which was prevented by the hostilities.

Having succeeded to the Dukedom in 1935, his motor racing gradually gave way to more involvement in the organisation of motor sport in which he played a variety of roles up to the out-break of the second world war. He also developed an interest in the motor trade and lent his name to several special-bodied cars. Despite his great enthusiasm for driving and aeronautics, the administration of Goodwood and the estates which he had inher-ited gave him much cause for concern. He was obliged to make an unenviable decision arising from the short period of seven years between the deaths of his father and grandfather. The impo-sition of a second set of death duties so soon after the first left him with little alternative but to dispose of the extensive family interests in Scotland, which included Gordon Castle, and to settle permanently on the Sussex estate of Goodwood.

When the war came, Goodwood House was taken over for use as a hospital and part of the estate was used as a base for fighter aircraft. With his aeronautical ability, it was natural for the Duke to serve in the Royal Air Force and he was stationed for a time in Washington D.C. where he worked on behalf of the Ministry of Aircraft Production. With the end of hostilities, he was faced with the task of rehabilitating Goodwood. His interest in the eques-trian scene was less intense than that of his ancestors and his love of motor racing took precedence in his future plans. He faced considerable opposition when he proposed to build a motor racing circuit on the estate, but when the circuit was completed, it quickly became established as a popular venue for meetings.

The 9th Duke of Richmond.

243

As its facilities and status developed, the circuit became the scene of increasingly important events including Formula 1 racing, the famous Tourist Trophy, the country's oldest motor race, and a series of nine-hour endurance races for sports cars. However, the year 1962 brought an incident which curtailed the use of the circuit on safety grounds. On Easter Monday that year Stirling Moss had his near fatal accident at Goodwood, effectively ending his professional driving career. The Duke was well aware of the increasing speeds which advances in racing car technology were making possible, and fearful of further accidents he reluctantly decided to close the circuit in 1966 except for minor club events. It was re-opened in 1998 on the 50th anniversary of its founding.

The Duke had been elected as President of the British Royal Automobile Racing Club which staged races on the circuit at Goodwood and he was well aware of its importance to competitors and spectators and their disappointment at its closure. The Duke's interest in motor racing resulted in his involvement not only in the Royal Automobile Club of which he became Vice President, but also the Guild of Motoring Writers of which he was founder and President for sixteen years. After the war, he developed an interest in photography and at the age of 50 began to paint with such success that he had three public exhibitions of his work.

The racecourse which was originally opened to the public in 1802 continued to prosper and, in 1980, the Queen opened the new £3 million grandstand. As the local press reported, such things as en suite bathrooms in the living quarters at Goodwood were not considered essential in those days, and even the Queen had to share. Lord March was reported by the local press as having breezed into a "communal" bathroom to find Prince Philip wallowing in a bath. Renovation work on Goodwood House had begun after the wartime hospital occupation and a major restoration of the Ballroom and other State apartments was completed by 1970. At that time however raising the £100,000 a year needed to maintain the House alone was a constant worry.

Since the time of William IV, the role of carrying the Sceptre and Dove at coronations has been undertaken by Dukes of Richmond and the 9th Duke performed this task at the coronations of both George VI and the present Queen. In his later years he handed over administration of Goodwood House and Estate to his son the Earl of March. The Duke died in November, 1989 at the age of 85 when he and his wife, formerly Elizabeth Hudson, had been married for 61 years. Though he is remembered particularly for his motor racing and aviation achievements, his life was devoted to a wide range of interests and he did much to maintain Goodwood during an exceptionally difficult period of its history.

References:
The Goodwood Estate Archives Vol. 2.
Chichester Observer 9.10.1986.
The Times 4.11.1989.
Country Life 24.7.1997 and 25.9.1997.

CHAPTER 32

Charles Henry Gordon Lennox the 10th Duke of Richmond. The Goodwood of Today

AFTER THREE HUNDRED years, Goodwood continues to be the stately home of the Richmonds, a place of treasured history with priceless furniture and a superb collection of paintings collected by generations of this remarkable family. It was in 1969 that the present Duke of Richmond, Charles Henry, then Earl of March, took over the administration of Goodwood and became Chairman of the Group of Companies responsible not only for the House but also the considerable estate of 12,000 acres and the great variety of activities which include the Racecourse, Motor Circuit, Aerodrome, Golf Club and Hotel. He did much to modernise and strengthen the management of the estate business and his particular interest in maintaining and improving Goodwood House was emphasised by the leading part he has played in both the Historic Houses Association and the Sussex Heritage Trust.

Born in 1929, he married Susan Grenville-Grey in 1951 and they have had five children, a son, who traditionally received the title of Earl of March, and four daughters. On the death of his father, the ninth Duke, in 1989, the Earl succeeded to the four Dukedoms and other titles, including the hereditary Constable of Inverness Castle. His abiding interest in the Church led him to become a member for the Diocese of Chichester of the General Synod and to give many years service as a Church Commissioner.

Goodwood House.

From 1968-75 he was a member of the Executive Committee of the World Council of Churches and his extensive ecclesiastical work has included being Chairman of the Chichester Cathedral Trust. For some three years he was Treasurer of Sussex University and became Chancellor in 1985.

Agriculture and horses have always played an important part in the lives of the Dukes of Richmond and their families and the 10th Duke has been President of both the South of England Agricultural Society and the British Horse Society. The Duchess has shared these interests with her husband and, being a great lover of animals, particularly horses, she was the first to organise dressage events at Goodwood. The Goodwood International Dressage Championships took place for twenty one years. From the time of the 2nd Duke, at the beginning of the 18th century, the Richmonds have always been involved in the game of cricket and this interest is reflected in the present Duke's Presidency of the Sussex County Cricket Club.

In 1994, like his father before him, the Duke handed over much of the management of Goodwood to his son, the Earl of March, and arranged to move into the nearby Dower House of Molecomb. The Earl then began an extensive three year refurbishment of the state rooms of the family home and, in time for the millennium, all the rooms of Goodwood have been restored to their original Georgian splendour. This historic House continues to be the focus of attention in an estate set in the Sussex Downs with extensive farmland and 1,900 acres of deciduous and coniferous forestry. There is a Home Farm of 2,800 acres and a Country Park of 180 acres which is available to the public. In June of each year, Goodwood Park is the scene of the annual Festival of Speed and the Goodwood Motor Circuit, founded by the 9th Duke in 1948, is used in late September to stage motor racing by historic cars. The Racecourse, which is nearly two hundred years old, provides twenty-one race days every year, the peak being the Glorious Goodwood meeting in July. The Aerodrome which was a fighter station in the last war, is now one of the busiest general aviation airfields in the south of England. A public house at the entrance to Goodwood Park named The Richmond Arms has now been converted into a modern hotel.

The Earl of March, has been much concerned with the refurbishment of the House, as well as with the varied activities provided by the modern Goodwood He has inherited a love of motor racing from his grandfather and is President of the British Automobile Racing Club. He was well known as a London advertising photographer and he is married to the Hon. Janet Astor, daughter of the late Viscount Astor and granddaughter of Nancy, Lady Astor, the first woman M.P. to take her seat in the House of Commons. The Earl now lives in the family home of Goodwood House with his wife and young family and the future of this historic stately home is well assured.

The name "Richmond" dates back over many centuries to the building of the Count Alan's Norman Castle at Richmond in England's North Yorkshire, the magnificent Keep and walls of which remain today and, though the lives of the early Counts and Earls of Richmond were closely bonded with the medieval conflicts of England and France, the Richmond family became stabilised with the acquisition of "Godinwood" and the successive Dukes of Richmond have played a most valuable part in the history of their country.

References:
Baird, Rosemary, *The official guidebook to Goodwood House* with
 a foreword by the Earl of March.
Who's Who 1998.

Index

251